Going Long

Training for Ironman-Distance Triathlons

Joe Friel
Gordon Byrn

THE ULTRAFIT
MULTISPORT
TRAINING SERIES

VELO press

Going Long: Training for Ironman-Distance Triathlons
Copyright © 2003 Joe Friel and Gordon Byrn

Before embarking on any strenuous exercise program, including the training described in this
book, everyone, particularly anyone with a known heart or blood-pressure problem, should be
examined by a physician.

Printed in the United States of America.

10 9 8 7

Distributed in the United States and Canada by Publishers Group West.

International Standard Book Number: 1-931382-24-7

Library of Congress Cataloging-in-Publication Data

Friel, Joe.
    Going long : training for ironman-distance triathlons / Joe Friel & Gordon Byrn.
       p. cm.
    Includes bibliographical references (p.) and index.
    ISBN 1-931382-24-7
       1. Ironman triathlons. 2. Triathlon—training. I. Byrn, Gordon. II. Title.

GV1060.73.F735 2003
796.42'57—dc21

                                                             2002044599

VELO VeloPress®
      1830 North 55th Street
      Boulder, Colorado 80301–2700 USA
      303/440-0601 • Fax 303/444-6788 • E-mail velopress@insideinc.com

To purchase additional copies of this book or other VeloPress® books, call 800/234-8356 or visit
us on the Web at velopress.com.

Cover and interior design by Ann W. Douden.
Cover photo by Delly Carr.
Illustrations by Wyanne Chase.

Contents

Foreword

I 've considered myself a good "student" of this sport for over twenty years. For me the first step to achieving excellence in triathlon has always been to seek out the best sources of information in order to make informed decisions about my training. I remember pouring over all of the old issues of *Runner's World, Track and Field News, VeloNews,* and *Swimming World* magazines in the library for months and months instead of studying for my exams in college.

There have been more than a few books written on the various aspects of triathlon since then, many of them very good. Most of the physiological principles of training we've learned from other sports have certainly stood the test of time. But triathlon is still a relatively new sport and there is still a lot of progress to be made. This is one of the things that keeps me interested in the sport along with the physical challenge of trying to get ready for events.

I respect Gordo and his opinions because he takes a similar, if not a more extreme approach to his triathlon education. He's humble enough to recognize his knowledge base, like his training base, can always be increased. To say he's consumed by this journey of finding out how to do this sport better would be quite an understatement. He lives triathlon 24/7, and this book is the end result of that affliction to date.

I met Gordo in 2000 when a mutual friend introduced us on a training ride. Over the last two years I've watched his development as a coach and an athlete. While there are a broad range of strategies that can be employed to achieve athletic success, this book will provide you with a safe and effective strategy for approaching the challenges of ironman-distance racing.

Whether you are training for your first or your fortieth ironman-distance race, I would encourage you to remember the following key points that I have learned from my years of racing.

"It ain't brain surgery." My long time confidant Kenny Souza used to say this to me regularly over the years to remind me to try to not over-analyze things too much. Don't stray to anything too exotic. You can think a lot, but there still has to be some regular, basic training done to improve your body.

"Little and often fills the purse." Training principles follow the basic laws of physics and human behavior. A regular dose of exercise every day isn't a new paradigm but it will get you there as sure as saving a bit in the bank every month.

"Train hard, eternal youth doesn't come cheap." Take a good look around at the average guy today. It's not a pretty sight is it? This sport is demanding and if you want to achieve it's going to take discipline and work.

In this book Gordo gives you a reference to come back to time and time again to keep you on track. He's done the research and put himself through every technique to put together a very concise guide to save you hundreds of hours pouring over hundreds of magazines and years of frustrating experiences. I'm sure reading this book will be a very valuable investment of your time.

Scott Molina
The TERMINATOR
Christchurch, New Zealand

In 1997, when I started racing triathlons professionally, I hired Joe Friel to coach me. My primary goal at that point was to make the Olympic team in 2000. My long-term goal was to succeed in Ironman-distance racing. Since then, I earned a spot on the U.S. Olympic team and competed in Sydney, switched my focus to long-course racing in 2001, and had immediate success under Joe's coaching. Having the wealth of information, training guidelines, and feedback from Joe has been pivotal to my success.

Going Long contains comprehensive data and instruction about long-course training, racing and schedules that Joe has made available to me in the past few years. It is presented in a manner that is easy to understand and apply to one's particular training and racing goals. It will educate, motivate, and inspire any athlete to perform at his or her fullest potential. Using periodization and the latest innovations based on extensive research, *Going Long* will help one tailor one's training to his or her specific physiology, goals, and time schedule.

Given the duration and intensity of long-course races, it is helpful to adhere to a regimented schedule. In my training with Joe, I have used periodization, which takes the athlete through several stages of training. It starts with preparation, which Joe refers to as "training to train." This is followed by the base training period during which the athlete focuses on longer workouts with lower intensity. Then the athlete moves on to the build period in which volume is decreased, but intensity is increased. Next, in the peak period, volume drops even more and race intensity is further emphasized. The culmination of these periods, leads to the race period, which is when the athlete is in prime condition to race and the focus is on maintaining sharpness. The last and not the least important, is the transition period when the athlete rests and recovers.

Ironman training is extremely time consuming. The typical Ironman athlete is faced with balancing not only long hours of swimming, biking, and running, but family, friends, work, and other interests. To add to it all, nutrition and rest are essential elements that cannot be forgotten. The principles that Joe has applied to my training are presented in *Going Long* to assist the athlete by providing a training timeline that allows him or her to effectively incorporate all essential elements of his or her lifestyle. This allows the athlete to maintain the very necessary balance between triathlon and life beyond triathlon.

Joe Friel is among the most respected coaches in the sport of triathlon. He has years of experience with racing and coaching in addition to an analytical and well-rounded approach that is influenced by his commitment to stay abreast of the latest research in the field. It is with his expertise and passion that *Going Long* is able to provide the reader with the finest long-course training resource available.

Work hard and keep it fun.

Ryan Bolton
Professional Triathlete

Preface

Gordo's Preface

When I bought my copy of *The Triathlete's Training Bible* in 1998, I knew very little about our sport, had never completed a triathlon, and couldn't swim more than a hundred meters without stopping. Through the application of Joe's principles I was able to dramatically increase my performance in a relatively short period of time. Who would have thought that a few years later I would be writing a book alongside one of the most respected coaches in our sport? I learn from Joe's experience on a daily basis and hope that you are able to benefit from what we have managed to learn so far.

This book is a summary of what we believe are the most effective training methods for long-course racing. Although there is a lot of detail inside, we encourage you to seek to understand the philosophy that underlies each chapter of the book. Take the spirit of each section and apply it to your own personal needs. Expose yourself to as many different coaches, athletes, sports scientists, and mentors as you can. Learn what you can from each of them, and then choose the path that you think is best.

We believe that this book is the first training manual to specifically address the needs and demands of the long-course athlete. Inside are the techniques that we apply to our own coaching and racing. There are many different ways to achieve athletic success. The training strategies presented inside have been proven to be both safe and effective for a wide range of athletes—from Ironman champions, such as Ryan Bolton, to fifteen-hour-plus Ironman finishers.

Joe's Preface

In 2000 Gordon Byrn flew in from Hong Kong and spent a weekend with me in Colorado. I was highly impressed not only with how well he understood the training principles I had described in *The Triathlete's Training Bible* but also with his enthusiasm for learning. He wanted to know everything there was to know about training for triathlon. I had never met anyone with such a thirst for knowledge. Unfortunately, I was not quite able to fully satisfy his thirst as I was then, and still am, only up to about 1 percent of all that must be known about the sport. Gordo is soon to pass me, I'm sure.

After running into him at races and sharing several e-mail conversations over the next few months, I realized that Gordo was not a fluke and that he was destined to be one of the most knowledgeable coaches in the sport. In self-defense I decided to ask him to join Ultrafit Associates, my personal coaching business. With his passion for people, solid head for business, love of all things triathlon, and gentle nature, he was immediately accepted by our coaches.

It soon became clear that Gordo and I thought alike on almost every matter. One day I suggested we write a book together on training for triathlon. As usual, he was already one step ahead of me and had put together a rough outline in his head while out for a long ride. And so the project began.

What you are about to read here is information-dense. I don't expect you'll be able to grasp it all with just one reading, although I'd suggest you give it a try. Once you have gotten through it the first time, this book will best serve as a reference as you buy equipment, set up a training program, confront your mental demons, peak for a race, make dietary choices, or consider any of the thousands of factors that go into successful long-distance triathlon racing. I'd suggest marking it up to personalize and better internalize the information. As you run into questions, to contact us through our website at www.Ultrafit.com. We look forward to hearing from you and promise to help however we can.

Acknowledgments

Gordo's Acknowledgments

I'd like to acknowledge my coauthor, Joe Friel. In 2000 Joe took a chance by hiring an athlete with little coaching experience (me). By believing that I would make a good coach he set in motion a chain of events that greatly improved my life.

This book would not have been possible without the selfless dedication of Wyanne Chase. Wy's editing, drawing, proofreading, and layout skills made this book happen.

I'd like to say thanks to my coaches over the years. For swimming—Ian Rayson in Hong Kong, Doug Huestis in San Francisco, and Roly Crichton in Christchurch. Mark Bouckoms for opening my mind (and hips) to the large benefits of dedicated yoga training. Mark Elliott for teaching me that there is more to strength training than maximizing my squat. John Hellemans for always calling it like he sees it. Scott Molina for helping me see what's possible.

Training long involves a fair amount of time on the road, and I'd like to acknowledge my training pals—Luke "Abs" Wimbush in Hong Kong, John "Johno" Newsom in New Zealand, Jonas "Big J" Colting and Clas "the Baron" Björling of Sweden, and Shanelle "Rainbow" Barrett. You've taught me more than you'll ever realize.

Thanks to Team Gordo: your questions, support, and dedication are a large part of what makes coaching fun.

Rob Docherty of XTri.Com started publishing my race reports back in 1999. In doing so, he launched my public writing career. Thanks, Mate.

Finally, I'd like to thank my brother, Chuck—whether I have been fit and fast or big and bloated, Chuck's always been there for me. Thanks, Amigo!

Joe's Acknowledgments

This book project turned out to be a great match between Gordo and me. Gordo wrote most of what you are about to read. My input was largely a matter of ensuring that we didn't stray too far from the principles I have been learning over the past thirty years. It was a match made in writer's heaven; I would not have thought it possible for two people to agree so often on so many matters over the course of six months. We seldom disagreed, and never on substantive issues. When we did find differences, Gordo typically bowed to my greater experience and let me have my way. Thanks, Gordo.

Chapter 1

The Iron Journey

> Unless you test yourself, you stagnate. Unless you try to go way beyond what you've been able to do before, you won't develop and grow. When you go for it 100%, when you don't have the fear of "what if I fail," that's when you learn. That's when you're really living.
> — Mark Allen,
> world champion triathlete

The spirit of Ironman® is much more than a race, more than a simple time goal. It is about the entire process of preparing yourself for one of the greatest endurance challenges you can face. Race day is but one aspect of your overall journey.

Can I Do It?

As coaches, we are asked this question about once a month: "to be or not to be . . . an Ironman®." Anyone can do the distance if they want it badly enough. There is no bigger challenge in triathlon than the ironman distance, and ultimately the decision is yours and yours alone. The right answer lies inside you. You will do the training, you will make the necessary commitments, and you will miss out on certain other aspects of your life. For many, the trade is worth it.

One is never "ready" for an ironman-distance race. The event is far too big for that. However, we firmly believe that anyone (and we mean anyone) can complete the distance so long as they have one ingredient: will. The will to train and, most important of all, the will to finish. You have to be doing this for yourself. You have to want to finish, badly. The reason is that there will be many moments in your training when you will want to quit. By not quitting you will learn a lot about yourself. You will get stronger; you will change. There aren't many things in life that give us the opportunity to test our inner strength. The ironman distance is one of those things.

We will be honest with you. These events are tough. That is what makes them so rewarding. To race to your true potential, you have to gamble. You have to believe in yourself. You have to go beyond what you think is possible. It is a true test of mental and physical strength. Your mind and body will beg you to slow down. Your spirit must push and overcome the test.

Many athletes wait until they have the confidence that they can race the full distance the way they want to before committing to a race. Others arrive at the start line with little experience and have a positive experience—regardless of their finishing time. There are even people who finish at the front of the pack and don't have a positive experience. Novices should remember that there is no rush to take on the ironman distance. The races aren't going anywhere and will be here for a long time. Like almost everything, there is no right answer, and you should go with what feels right to you. If you don't think you are ready, wait until you have greater confidence in your abilities.

Finally, we all race the full distance for ourselves. The race is so big that it is tough to do it for any other reason. If you are racing for yourself, only you can evaluate your result. It's like this for everything in life. If you do your best in preparation and execution, you should be satisfied with whatever result you get.

So how do you know you are ready to go long? You don't. You commit, train, and pray.

Success Traits

Go to any triathlon and watch the top athletes prepare. You may notice a common air about them. There are personality traits among successful athletes that give them that edge over the rest of the field. The following are eight personality traits common among successful athletes.

1. Confidence: There are two types of confidence: respect for yourself as a person and respect for your athletic abilities. The successful athlete scores high in both areas. Confidence in either area is easily lost, usually through our own initiative. Inside each of us is a small voice that likes to criticize. It often points out our shortcomings and limiters. Success comes in large part from merely learning to control that voice while providing constant positive feedback. You would be hard-pressed to find an athlete who would not benefit from increased self-confidence. Always act as if you are confident. It's amazing what that does for self-perception.

2. Focus: During times when an important outcome is on the line, such as a race or a hard workout, successful athletes have the ability to concentrate their mental and physical energy on the task at hand. Their mental wanderings from the immediacy of what they are doing are brief. During easy workouts they may take a mental siesta, but they don't daydream during the important sessions and tend to concentrate on the present, not the future or the past.

They repeatedly scan their energy reserves and movement patterns to make sure all is going well. Lacking this ability to focus, less successful athletes speed up and slow down repeatedly and later on can't understand why they were unable to maintain pace. Lesser athletes also dwell on the outcome of the race or workout and what others are doing rather than on their immediate situation. To improve, they must learn to do only what is required at the present moment and let the results take care of themselves.

3. Self-sufficiency: Successful athletes also take full responsibility for their actions during a race. They take calculated risks to try to win rather than trying not to lose. They are decisive and intuitively know that it's better to fully commit to a bad decision than to be uncommitted to the right decision. With the right mental state of mind it is sometimes possible to pull off what others may see as nearly impossible, but weak commitment is a sure loser.

4. Adaptability: Successful athletes have the ability in the heat of competition to analyze the situation, problem-solve, and adapt to a new set of circumstances. In time-oriented triathlon, there is a constant barrage of changing circumstances—wind, heat, humidity, fatigue, equipment, and competitors. Mother Nature can force midevent course changes, sometimes without any warning to competitors out on the course. Many athletes freak out and stop. Others adapt, keep their cool, and race on. How adaptable are you?

5. Emotional stability: Some athletes cannot maintain an even keel emotionally. In the course of a workout or race they experience fear, anger, frustration, disappointment, excitement, elation, and anticipation. All of this takes its toll on energy levels and focus and can often lead to lackluster race performances despite physical ability.

6. Quiet cockiness: Talented athletes know they have what it takes physically to succeed. The most successful ones never brag about this, at least not out loud. However, their assuredness is obvious to anyone who watches the way they behave and carry themselves. There is no doubt that they are cocky, but they don't talk about how good they are. The reason is that down deep they are afraid it would come back to haunt them. They also know that if they tried to dominate their peer group, then their fellow athletes' support would not be there when needed. Unabashedly cocky athletes usually wind up competing against everyone, including their teammates. Few are truly good enough to achieve all of their goals entirely alone.

7. Mental toughness: In their daily activities, the most successful athletes are concerned about the well-being of those closest to them, including their competitors, who are often close friends and training partners. However, in the heat of competition they really don't care about the feelings and emotions of their challengers, and they expect others to feel the same way about them. When the going gets hard, mentally tough athletes hang in there. This doesn't mean they never DNF (did not finish). There are circumstances when it is fully acceptable to decide this just isn't your day. However, this decision should never be made because the competition was greater than expected.

8. Appropriately psyched: There is an optimal level of arousal necessary for every sport and for different situations within a given sport. For example, going into an ironman-distance race with a high level of arousal is a sure way to blow up. Successful athletes know how much mental psyching is necessary and respond accordingly.

There is no athlete who is perfect in each of these areas. Each of us has one or more of these categories that need work. Some have more to work on than others. Just as with your physical limiters, you need to determine where your mental limiters lie and initiate strategies to improve them. These strategies are discussed in greater detail in Chapter 8.

Essential Attributes of a Coach

So, you have signed up for an ironman-distance race. You are excited and a little scared. You "know" that you have what it takes to finish but want to get the most out of the limited time you have to train. You have significant commitments in your nontriathlon life and would like to minimize the disruption for your family and work colleagues. You need some advice to get you through your iron journey and are thinking that a coach could be the way to go.

Having been on both sides of the athlete/coach relationship, we want to share some ideas on how to get the most out of your coach. Following are some key things to remember when considering a potential coaching relationship.

Trust: You will be trusting your entire season to another person. You should check the coach's credentials, experience, and background. Ask for references and speak to current clients. Review sample workout plans and discuss the coach's approach to building the season.

Goals: Communicate your key goals for the season. The best results are achieved by having a limited number of quantitative as well as qualitative goals. Set the goals early in the season and tailor the year toward achieving them.

Personality/style: There are a lot of coaches out there and just as many training philosophies. Different strategies work for different folks. You should make sure your coach's training style matches your needs. Particular things to watch for are the approach to intensity, volume, and recovery. This is where the variation can be greatest and will have the most significant impact on your performance (both positively and negatively).

The plan: Many coaches offer different levels of service and price points. Make sure you choose the plan that best fits your needs. If you are looking for frequent interaction, then make sure your coach will be happy with the level of assistance you require. Make your expectations known in advance and see what the coach recommends.

Share of mind: If you are paying for individual coaching, make sure you will get an adequate share of mind. Find out how many athletes are currently being coached. Discuss your coach's other commitments. Be sure you are confident that your plan will get the focus it deserves. Once again, make your expectations clear in advance.

Communication: You are buying your coach's advice, experience, and support. Ask a lot of questions. Understand what lies behind the yearly, monthly, and weekly planning. You will become a better athlete if you understand the reasons behind each session. It is also your job to make sure your coach understands how you are doing. Take advantage of every opportunity to update the coach regarding your progress. You need to be totally honest. If you were so tired you couldn't get out of bed, then make sure that message gets across. Be open and clear about what is happening. This is even more important in an online relationship because of the lack of visual feedback (tough to hide fatigue at the track but easy on the keyboard). Don't BS your coach! This honesty is essential when you are tired, injured, or not coping. Know when to back off. In our opinion, if your interaction is limited, then you are not being coached.

One plan: Once you have committed, paid your cash, built the season up . . . do the program. This sounds easy, but in fact, many people second-guess their coach and adjust the plan. There should be a reason behind every workout. If you have doubts, ask questions until you are satisfied. You are paying for expert advice, so use it.

Belief: Coaches should have the ability to create and enhance the belief of an athlete in their ability to achieve their goals. The power of belief is one of the strongest forces in life. The best coaches, friends, and training partners all share a unified belief in the ability of the athlete. People who do not serve this power of belief are best avoided. In our opinion, creating and enhancing the power of belief is the central role of the coach.

Structure: Because of their experience, coaches should have the ability to provide the athlete with a structured environment that will enable them to move safely and consistently toward their goals. Structure gives the athlete a feeling of control and confidence, thereby strengthening the power of belief and increasing the chances of success.

Clarity: There are two aspects of clarity: (1) coaches should be able to explain goals, sessions, technique, and strategies in a clear manner that the athlete can understand; and (2) coaches should strive to remain independent from an athlete's results so they can offer the athlete the benefit of an objective opinion.

Knowledge: Coaches should be constantly seeking new training techniques and expanding their knowledge about all aspects of training, nutrition, and recovery. The goal of every coach should be to become a mind-body master. Likewise, athletes who want to perform at the highest levels should make it a priority to understand the purpose of each session and to become mind-body masters in their own right.

Openness: Coaches should be open to (and with) their athletes. Athletes should know that they will not be judged by their coaches. Openness builds trust between coach and athlete, increasing the effectiveness of the relationship.

Responsibility: Coaches must take full responsibility for the programs they create. Likewise, athletes must take full responsibility for executing the coach's program to the best of their ability. When doubts arise, the coach and athlete should review the program together and agree on the overall strategy. This builds trust and strengthens the power of belief.

What Does It Take?
Hours

Smart training is the key to success in racing the ironman distance—quality over quantity. The focus of your training should be on your key workouts and recovering. Success is correlated to the duration and intensity of your key sessions, not your total volume.

For example, weekly key workouts for your first ironman-distance race would be something like one long swim of 75 to 100 minutes, one long ride of 4 to 5 hours (always run 15 to 30 minutes after you finish your long bike), and one long run of 90 to 135 minutes. Everything else should be oriented toward strength, aerobic maintenance, or skills.

Training

The most important things in long-distance training are naively elementary. It's surprisingly difficult, however, to convince athletes at all ability levels of the significance of these simple lessons. Those who accept and follow them always do better than the others.

Rest when you are tired. It's amazing how few self-coached athletes understand the significance of rest for improving performance. It must be the high work ethic so necessary for success in sport that causes them to disregard or trivialize feelings of fatigue. When athletes take rest seriously, quite often their workout quality and fitness improve. This leads to the next simple lesson.

Make the hard days hard and the easy days easys. Most highly focused athletes wind up doing just the opposite: They make their easy days too hard, and because of that, the hard days are too easy. All workouts gravitate toward the middle. By regularly including days off from training and extremely light workouts, the workouts meant to push the fitness envelope do just that. This lesson points toward another.

Set a few clear and simple goals for the year. More than three usually causes confusion. One is often enough to keep you on track. A good goal provides direction for training, but it needs to be posted someplace so it's seen every day. The cover of the training log is a good place. Don't get lost in just working out and racing.

Have a plan for achieving the goals. Goals without plans are wishes. A plan is like a road map—it points you in the right direction but may be changed along the way as some "roads" are found to be better than others. Take notes on a calendar when a few measurable benchmarks of steady progress are needed to reach the goal.

Every workout has a purpose. The purpose is either to do a workout that is one small step toward the benchmark or to rest so the next session can be that step. This brings us back to the first lesson.

The key things to remember are:

◆ Recovery is very important. Don't train when you are tired. You will need to increase your sleep when you increase your training.

◆ Gradually increase your training volume in each sport. For novices, forget about fast or really intense workouts. Focus on building skills, endurance, and strength.

◆ Buy a heart rate monitor and learn how to use it.

◆ If there is a local triathlon club, join it. There will be ironman-distance veterans and their information is very helpful.

◆ Take a rest week every third or fourth week. Drop the volume way down.

◆ Ride long on the weekends.

◆ Join a masters swim squad for technique tips. Work on form and general endurance in the water. When you are starting out there is no need to swim hard. Gradually extend one of your swims each week until you can swim a total distance of 4,000 meters (in a session, not in one go).

◆ Race at least two half ironman-distance races to learn. Once you have finished these two races you will have a small taste of what the full distance requires.

◆ Focus on time spent working out and ignore distance. Don't get caught up on "having" to run 25 miles a week, etc.

◆ Try to be consistent. It pays the biggest dividends.

◆ If you must take two days off per week, try not to have them be two days off in a row.

◆ Racing is high-intensity training.

◆ There are no shortcuts to fitness; it takes a long time to get good.

Weekends

Don't combine your longest run with your longest ride. Avoid the "death" weekends that many people recommend. Put your long run midweek and your long ride on the weekend (better for recovery). For example, ride long on Sunday, swim long on Friday, and run long on Wednesday. That gives plenty of recovery time.

Don't listen to people when they talk about their megaweeks. Train safely and within yourself. You should feel tired for only twelve to thirty-six hours after your key workouts. If you are tired for longer, back off. If you are stiff and it doesn't go away, back off.

It bears repeating: Smart training is the key to ironman-distance success.

Approaches to Training

Chapter 2

> It takes a long time
> to get good.
> —Scott Molina,
> world champion triathlete

The Importance of Consistency, Moderation, and Recovery

Many training breakdowns are due to illness, injury, burnout, and overtraining. Extended or frequent training breaks caused by such problems inevitably result in a loss of fitness. Consistency, moderation, and recovery are essential to achieve your potential.

Consistent training is the way to attain the highest possible fitness, so consistency must serve as the ultimate standard in all training decisions. Athletes achieve consistency by following a training philosophy, such as that discussed in this book, and by striving for moderation in training while resting at regular intervals.

Too many athletes do that one extra workout or push hard into that one last interval. Pushing the body past endurance, strength, and speed limits rapidly increases the chances of injury, illness, burnout, and overtraining. The intelligent athlete trains within the body's limits and infrequently stretches them just a little.

When a workout becomes very hard, your speed decreases noticeably, or your technique changes, it is time to call it a day. Athletes with a strong work ethic find calling a halt hard to do.

This is where a coach is beneficial because his or her objective and unemotional guidance will help to avoid breakdowns. For the self-coached athlete, there will be many times when you are unsure whether to continue or not. When unsure, always remember: If in doubt, leave it out.

Although challenging workouts are beneficial, they are beneficial only to the extent that they guide your overall fitness toward a peak and do not result in extended recovery periods. For this reason, most athletes schedule these workouts infrequently and, normally, only in the weeks immediately preceding a major race. Moderation in training leads to consistency in training. Consistency in training leads to continuous improvement.

Recovery is the most neglected aspect of training by highly motivated athletes. Few fully appreciate the physiological benefits that accrue during rest, especially during sleep. While asleep, the body releases growth hormone to repair damage from the day's training stresses and to shore up any physiological systems weakened by training. Without adequate sleep, fitness is lost regardless of how intense or long the workouts were.

A well-rested athlete looks forward to workouts, enjoys them, feels sharp and in control, and grows stronger after training. The quality of training with adequate recovery is far superior.

Training to Finish

The goal for many athletes who are contemplating their first attempt at the ironman distance is just to finish the race. Period. If they can also skip the medical tent and manage a smile, great. They are looking for advice on how to make their journey as satisfying (and pain free) as possible. If this profile sounds familiar, then you will find this section helpful.

These tips are taken from an article that Gordo wrote a few years ago, titled *The Golden Rules of Losing Your Iron Virginity*. We've updated the article and believe that these points apply to everyone. We have seen these mistakes repeated over and over by athletes preparing for their first ironman-distance race. We also discuss temptations that you will need to avoid throughout your athletic career.

Rule 1: You don't have to kill yourself in training. You know the race is grueling, so you think you will get tough by signing up for two marathons, half a dozen century rides, and a 3-mile, rough-water swim. Not recommended!

Successful endurance training is exactly like turning a Styrofoam cup inside out. So long as you take it slowly, you'll be able to do it. Try to rush things and—rip—you'll tear the cup. You are the cup.

Rule 2: Build technique and endurance in your first year. If you are making the jump from Olympic- or half-ironman-distance racing, more than likely your greatest limiter is base endurance. Most first-timers have averaged fewer than ten hours a week in training the season before their first ironman-distance race. Most of their previous training was done by feel: a little of this and a little of that.

Laying out a sketch of the year is essential. The core of your week is a long, slow distance session in each sport. Plan to build your swim up to 4,000 meters, your ride up to 5 hours, and your run up to 2.5 hours. Build up very slowly: three weeks forward, one week back, repeat. Never add more than 5 to 10 percent in terms of duration to any week or any long workout. You've got a lot of time, even if you are racing early in the season.

Everybody has his or her own idea of appropriate workout distances and durations; however, it is best to be a little conservative about the long stuff. This approach will enable you to recover quickly, maintain consistency, and avoid injury. The two most likely times for injury are during high-intensity training and when you run long after a long ride. Avoid these kinds of sessions.

A classic "Iron Weekend" is a 6-hour ride on Saturday followed by a 3-hour run on Sunday. These sessions are typically billed as "confidence builders." Experience, however, shows that such sessions are counterproductive. Lying on a couch with the ceiling gently spinning on a Sunday night can leave your confidence more shattered than built. Separate your key sessions by several days for best results.

In your second season of racing long, you should continue to focus on technique and endurance. At this stage, most athletes will also benefit from increasing (or adding) an appropriate strength-training program. Each year you should plan on returning to, and improving, the foundations of your sport (skills, endurance, and strength).

Rule 3: Focus on your key sessions, and make your key sessions focused. With your key sessions laid out, the rest of the week is easy to plan. Add other workouts so you get three sessions of each sport, including the key workouts. You have one goal each week: to hit your key sessions fresh and injury free. Everything else is maintenance. If you are whipped, take a rest day. If you are a little tired, use the session for skill and technique work. If you feel good, do some endurance work, but be sure to finish wanting more. Do what it takes to begin your key sessions feeling fresh.

This approach leads nicely to volume. Volume is an interesting topic. We all love to talk about our monster training weeks. For your first ironman-distance race, volume doesn't matter. Observation and science have shown that the most important predictor of success is the quality of your key sessions rather than the overall volume of your sessions. So if you are recovering well from your long sessions, don't sweat the volume.

A word on your key sessions: If you are following these guidelines, make sure your long workouts are high quality. Avoid long breaks, and make sure that the key sessions are true endurance workouts that build your base. Know your intensity zones, and stay within them. Long, slow distance always starts at an easy pace, but after 3 hours on the bike, you will be working no matter what the pace.

Rule 4: Sleep is more valuable than training. Do you drag yourself out of bed at all hours because your schedule said you had to ride X minutes at Y heart rate? By far the best thing you can do if you are exhausted is sleep. Better to miss a short workout on Thursday than a whole weekend because of an unexpected illness.

Of course, going to bed an extra hour early every night is a better option than missing training. Weekend naps are also great for the working athlete. Keep them under an hour and preferably before 2 P.M. for best results.

Rule 5: Forget about anaerobic endurance and high-intensity sessions. Be honest with yourself. Are you expecting to finish in the top 10 percent of your age group? Are you expecting to run the whole marathon? If the answer to either question is "no," then improving your anaerobic endurance is likely a waste of time. A track session can toast you for twelve to thirty-six hours. If you are going to fry yourself, do it in a manner that most benefits your race (e.g., a 4- to 5-hour ride).

Rule 6: Recovery is your friend. Make sure that you drop the volume way down every three to four weeks. Many excellent athletes give a blank stare when asked about their recovery strategy. Your recovery strategy is the most important part of your plan. Recovery is the time when you will make all your fitness gains.

Developing a clear recovery strategy will work wonders for your program. Appropriate nutrition, sleep, and hydration will help you get the most from your training.

You should end every recovery week feeling fresh and ready to get back to training. If you don't feel this way after a week, then your total volume is likely too high. Note that this week is for "recovery" rather than "rest." Try to stay active during your recovery. Maintain workout frequency, but drop the volume and intensity.

Rule 7: Check your ego at the door. Any time you are in a group situation, there will always be someone who wants to go faster than you, or a swim coach who thinks ten sets of 100-meter fly would be a great way to kick off the session. In these situations, swallow your pride and drop back. It is tough, but eventually you get used to it.

Know your session goals before you start, and do everything you can to stick to your goals. Group training workouts are the most dangerous for most athletes. The pace slowly creeps up, and before you know it . . . hammer time! For that reason, choose your training partners with care. Over the years, we have found that training with one or two friends is the best way to go. With the right group of people, there is someone to keep the pace in check and also someone to maintain workout momentum.

Rule 8: Keep your eyes on the prize. Remember your goals when you decided to start this journey, and keep the training fun. There is no point in putting all this time into the sport unless you are having a heck of a good time. When it all becomes a bit much (and it will), back off and reassess. The right answers will come to you.

Another issue athletes often struggle with is goal inflation. When you signed up for your first ironman-distance race, you might have been thinking that it would be nice just to finish. By the time the race comes around, you might start thinking that a time of 10:15 and a Kona slot are a very real possibility. Where did that idea come from? Until you are experienced at the distance and confident of your mental skills, keep your time goals to yourself. At 7 A.M. on race day, you'll have plenty of pressure. There is no need to make things tougher on yourself.

Training for a Personal Best

What are the key components to achieve a personal best? In reviewing numerous races with the athletes whom we coach, we have found certain recurring themes. Other parts of this book cover the specifics of how to address these points, but give some thought to these ideas, as they could contain the formula to take you to the next level.

The ability to focus is probably the single greatest limiter for most athletes. It is very difficult to stay oriented on a task for the eight to seventeen hours of an ironman-distance race. You can, and should, use shorter-duration races and your key workouts to strengthen the ability to focus. When athletes are able to focus, they are able to execute their race strategy and keep their "process" on target.

In any long race, this "process" tends to give out before an athlete's "performance" gives out. As athletes, each of us has our personal breaking point—the point in a training session, in a race, or in life at which each of us "cracks." We slow, quit, or break down. The art of training is to lean against our breaking points from time to time, thereby pushing our boundaries farther out. When we push too hard, we get injured, get depressed, and/or break down in some other way. All of these results are signs that we have gone too far. Elites (in life and sport) have the ability to push themselves, but, more importantly, they know when to back off. Racing well is very demanding. If you want to race well, then you must practice the ability to maintain mental strength when your body and mind start to doubt.

Train your mind slowly over time. Many people get down on themselves for not being able to maintain a fighting spirit for a whole race. The truth is, most people can't. That is why "slow" athletes can be relatively competitive at the ironman distance: They have trained their minds never to quit. All it takes is practice. Rest assured that when you are hurting, everyone else is feeling the same.

Nutrition is every bit as important as swimming, biking, and running for the long-course triathlete. If you want to race at your very best, then you have to fuel your body appropriately. The nutritional tips contained in this book will benefit your recovery, strength, body composition, and race performance.

Cycling muscular endurance is the heart of ironman-distance racing. The bike leg is the longest element of the race, so the reason is obvious. However, the benefits of superior bike fitness are not truly realized until the marathon.

Finally, ultimate success is not about being "fast." It is about being able to swim smart, ride strong, and run tough. We hope that the training philosophy outlined in this book will help you do exactly that.

Training to Qualify

Many triathletes have the desire to race the Hawaii Ironman® or to qualify to represent their country at a World Championship event. With the increasing number of athletes in our sport and increasing knowledge about effective training and racing techniques, qualification will continue to become more challenging. This section contains tips for increasing your odds of qualification at any event.

Identify your limiters and strengths: What are your limiters? Is your swim endurance below par? Are you constantly getting dropped on the second half of the bike? How about your run endurance? What about your strengths? Once you have done a personal analysis, it's time for the tough part: You need to build a program that works relentlessly on your limiters while doing the minimum to maintain your strengths. If you come from a single-sport background, you may be thinking, "But if I don't run, bike, or swim five times a week, then I will lose my edge." Rest assured that you will maintain your sport-specific strengths and become a better triathlete if you work on your limiters.

Build strength and endurance during winter: Weight training in the winter is essential. Your weight program should follow the formula in this book (see Chapter 16 for the program). As a direct result of getting stronger in the weight room, you can expect several breakthroughs in the pool and on the bike. Female, veteran, cycling-limited, and novice athletes have the most to gain from strength training.

With all that lifting, you are going to slow down in the pool and on the bike (running won't be affected as much). This slowdown can be a bit tough to take, but the program will pay off if you stick with it. If you are going into many of your sport-specific sessions a little tired, then focus on skills and endurance. Gradually bump up your long swim workouts to 5,000 meters, and also do several 3- to 4-hour small-chainring rides. Riding extended periods of time in the small chainring sounds easy, but do not doubt how tough it is. Two hours of spinning at 100 rpm or more is feasible, but by the three-hour mark you will be dying to use the big ring.

What about running? Keep your weekly long run between 90 and 120 minutes, and focus on bricks (three to five a week). If you are cycling indoors, bricks and duathlon-type workouts will help break up the monotony of indoor riding. Shake it up, do many different types of bricks, and really mix the time, speed, and order of the sports.

Racing: A duathlon or running race about once every two weeks will maintain your top-end aerobics. Avoid racing when you are in a period of high-intensity strength training.

Key race selection: If you can, choose three qualifying races, and have specific reasons for choosing each of them. Why three? You don't want to put all your eggs in one basket. You never know when you will hit one of those special days, or when you will hit one of those very painful days. You are likely to hit either one at any season.

Mental skills: We discuss this topic in detail in Chapter 8. We all have our mental weak spots. Experience shows that improved race performance comes from working on these areas. The best part is that your body can recover while your mind strengthens.

Consistency and commitment: Adopt a no-excuses policy with regard to workouts. Train in challenging conditions, and if your training buddies cancel on you, head out anyhow and be thankful for the opportunity to get stronger.

Recovery: Take a complete rest day once per week, or take plenty of active rest days and shorten the workout and/or lower the intensity when you are feeling tired. Make a commitment to get an extra hour of sleep every night and a forty-five-minute nap on Saturday and Sunday. The extra sleep will make a huge difference to both your state of mind and the quality of your training.

Muscular endurance: If you are weak on the bike, use the tips in Chapter 6 to improve your cycling. For most triathletes, cycling muscular endurance is the key to a solid long-course race. If you can get off the bike relatively fresh, then your race will be far easier. Obviously, superior cyclists need to tailor this advice to their own specific limiters.

Seek advice: Take every opportunity you can find to get additional information. Books, newsgroups, websites, e-mail lists, online coaching, race expos, professional athletes, videos—try them all. Not everything makes sense, but it is all useful information and forms a background against which you can tailor your program to your specific needs. There are a lot of experienced people out there who love to talk training.

Race smart: The final point is a little obvious but worth making. The longer the distance, the more important it is to show patience in the race. Many people (pros included) try to succeed by hammering the swim and the first half of the bike. This strategy nearly always results in underperformance. You are likely to set all your personal bests by focusing on superior execution of your race strategy. When you get in the zone, the time just seems to take care of itself.

Limits to Performance

A question that all athletes have from time to time is "How fast can I get?" or "How good can I be?"

If you are an age-group athlete, your potential is limited first and foremost by your commitment and desire to do what is needed. Basically, this means doing your very best to intelligently implement the tools that are contained in this book and other sources of knowledge. The path to athletic success can be difficult, and movement toward our goals can be slow, even nonexistent, at times. However, we each have the ability to achieve success beyond our wildest dreams.

As coaches and athletes, we firmly believe that every athlete's ultimate limiter is his or her commitment to train intelligently and do what is needed. This means a dedication to fundamentals—nutrition, skills, endurance, and flexibility. The lifestyle of a committed athlete is not for everyone. There must be a deep joy associated with this path and an understanding that hard work is what leads to a payoff. The notion of "hard work" is nearly always misunderstood in this context. The underlying philosophy of this book is that successful athletes are those who equate "hard work" with "focused play."

We can all become excellent athletes—but whether we become the best athlete (or person) that we can be is determined by whether it is fun for us to do what it takes.

Physiology of Fitness

What Are the Components of Fitness?

How can we measure physical fitness? Science has discovered three of its most basic components—aerobic capacity, lactate threshold, and economy. The top endurance athletes have excellent values for all three physiological traits.

Aerobic capacity: Aerobic capacity is a measure of the amount of oxygen the body can consume during all-out endurance exercise. It is also referred to as VO_2max—the volume of oxygen the body uses during maximal aerobic exercise. VO_2max can be measured in the lab during a "graded" test in which the athlete increases the intensity of exercise every few minutes until exhaustion while wearing a device that analyzes oxygen and carbon dioxide levels. VO_2max is expressed in terms of milliliters of oxygen used per kilogram of body weight per minute (ml/kg/min).

World-class male athletes usually produce numbers in the 70- and 80-ml/kg/min range. For comparison, normally active male college students typically test in the range of 40 to 50 ml/kg/min. On average, women's aerobic capacities are about 10 percent lower than men's.

Aerobic capacity is largely determined by genetics and is limited by such physiological factors as heart size, heart rate, heart stroke volume, blood hemoglobin content, aerobic enzyme concentrations, mitochondrial density, and muscle-fiber type. It can, however, be enhanced by training to a certain extent. An already well-trained athlete typically requires six to eight weeks of high-intensity training to achieve peak values.

As we get older, our aerobic capacity usually drops, as much as 1 percent per year after age 25 in sedentary people. For those who train seriously, especially by regularly including high-intensity workouts, the loss is far smaller and may not occur at all until the late thirties.

Lactate threshold: Aerobic capacity is not a good predictor of endurance performance. If all athletes in a race category were tested for aerobic capacity, the race finishing results would most likely not reflect their VO_2max test values because the athletes with the highest VO_2max values would not necessarily finish high in the category rankings. However, the highest percentage of VO_2max that one can maintain for an extended period of time is a good predictor of racing capacity. This sustainable percentage of aerobic capacity is a reflection of the lactate threshold.

Lactate threshold (LT), also sometimes called anaerobic threshold, is the level of exercise intensity above which lactate begins to rapidly accumulate in the blood as metabolism quickly shifts from dependence on the combustion of fat and oxygen in the production of energy to dependence on glycogen—the storage form of carbohydrate. The body is always creating lactate even when sleeping and resting. At such times, it may be in the range of about 1 millimole of lactate per liter of blood (mmol/L). As you start to exercise, more carbohydrate is used, so the lactate concentration of the blood rises. Lactate threshold typically occurs around 4 mmol/L. This is the level at which an Olympic-distance triathlon or a 40-km time trial is typically done. An ironman-distance race would be done at a substantially lower level. For comparison, an all-out, 800-meter run may put a runner at 20 mmol/L.

The higher this threshold is, as a percentage of VO_2max, the faster the athlete can ride for an extended period of time, as in a race. Once the lactate reaches a high enough level, beyond the threshold, there is no option but to slow down in order to clear it from the blood because lactate is one of the causes of muscular fatigue.

Knowing only lactate concentrations in the blood tells you absolutely nothing about readiness to race. Lactate levels in the blood must be compared with some measure of performance to have meaning. Usually this measure is pace (swimming and running) or power (cycling). Over the course of several weeks, if lactate concentrations go down for any given pace or power, or if pace or power rises for any given lactate level, then fitness is improving. Compared with aerobic capacity, lactate threshold is highly susceptible to enhancement by training.

Economy: Compared with recreational sports enthusiasts, elite athletes use less oxygen to hold a given, steady, submaximal velocity. The elite athletes are using less energy to produce the same power or pace.

Studies reveal that an endurance athlete's economy improves if he or she has a high percentage of slow-twitch muscle fibers (largely determined by genetics), low body mass (weight-height relationship), and low psychological stress; uses properly fitting, light, and aerodynamic equipment that limits body frontal area exposed to the wind at higher velocities; and eliminates useless and energy-wasting movements.

Fatigue negatively impacts economy as muscles that are not normally called on are recruited to carry the load. That's why it's critical to go into important races well rested. Near the end of a race, when economy deteriorates due to fatigue, you may sense that your swimming, pedaling, and running skills are getting sloppy. This deterioration will waste precious energy. The longer the race is, the more critical economy becomes in determining the outcome.

Like lactate threshold, economy can be materially improved by training. Not only does it improve by increasing all aspects of endurance but it also rises as you refine sport-specific skills. This is why drill work is critical in the base training phases as well as being a component of the year-round training regimen.

What Type of Fitness Is Required?

Generally speaking, two to five years in triathlon, or other endurance-type sports, is recommended before attempting an ironman-distance race. The purpose of this period is to build a solid technical, strength, and endurance base. However, many athletes are able to complete the distance, although not usually comfortably, on a lesser base.

At a minimum, athletes who are considering an ironman-distance race should be able to finish a half-ironman-distance race under 8 hours, swim 3,000 meters, ride 5 hours, and run 2 hours without requiring extended recovery time. (Please note that these are separate workouts!)

The Training Triad

Endurance: Ironman-distance racing is an endurance event. It doesn't matter how good any other aspect of fitness is—if endurance is poor, race fitness will also be poor. Endurance is the ability to finish the longest of races, to persevere regardless of pace, to merely continue for a long time.

Force: This element, which could also be called strength, is the ability to apply force to the pedal, to the ground, and to the water. Successful ironman-distance racing does not require significant maximal force but does require excellent muscular endurance (the product of force and endurance), particularly on the bike. Many athletes who ride a lot of hills find that their flat time trialing will suffer, specifically, the ability to push a solid gear in the flats—an essential skill for success in long-course racing.

A general recommendation is that force workouts should be different from high-end aerobic training. When seeking to build force, it is worth keeping the heart rate (and cadence) down. "Down" can mean different things for different people. A novice long-distance triathlete would stay down in, or below, heart-rate Zone 3, whereas an elite athlete would stay "down" at, or below, threshold.

With cycling, be very cautious about riding hills at cadences under 50 to 60 rpm. When training on hills at a low cadence, an athlete should aim for a moderate heart rate and not seek to drive it sky-high. Of course, this goal takes a certain level of cycling endurance. Most new cyclists will find their heart rates very high on any hill—for them, seated, gentle rollers can be a good way to safely increase cycling power.

Speed skills: The ability to make the movements of the sport efficiently at race pace or faster is very important. For endurance athletes, this means speed drills such as isolated leg drills or spin-up drills on the bike, strides and step counting on the run, and technique drills in the water to minimize drag. These skills are explained in Chapter 4.

How much can you improve your speed skills? Back in the 1970s, top American miler Steve Scott decided to go after the world record for the mile. That summer he improved his economy by 7 percent. A 7 percent improvement in economy (just another way of saying speed skills) is as good as a 7 percent improvement in VO_2max or lactate threshold. How much work would you have to do to accomplish these latter fitness elements? A lot.

Working on speed skills year-round, but with a great emphasis in the Base period, could pay huge dividends for your racing in the spring. This is the most neglected ability yet the one that holds the greatest potential for improvement among athletes at all levels.

It is worth pointing out that speed skills are not the same as "speed work." The approach that most athletes take to speed work is similar to anaerobic endurance. Anaerobic power (critical for sprinters) and anaerobic endurance (common for short endurance events) are rarely limiters for a long-course athlete. Because these workouts are difficult, painful, and generate high levels of lactate, many athletes believe they are the most beneficial. In fact, they are highly risky and counterproductive for many long-course athletes and nearly all novice athletes.

Muscular endurance: Muscular endurance (ME) is where force meets endurance. For the experienced long-course athlete, it is the critical component of fitness because it is the ability to apply a fairly large force for a fairly long time and is essential for cycling. Examples of ME workouts would be to ride (1) relatively long hills, taking 15 to 40 minutes to climb at a heart rate 10 to 15 beats per minute (bpm) below your lactate threshold; (2) a flat route in the big ring with efforts of the same duration; and (3) a rolling route with the same effort level.

This workout is similar to what is expected in a race for endurance athletes who need to maintain a high and steady pace for long periods. Muscular endurance is so crucial to race fitness and takes so long to fully realize that athletes should begin working on its most basic aspects in Base 2 (see Chapter 4 for explanation of different Base periods). In Base 3, the muscular endurance work starts, but efforts are shorter—for example, rolling hill rides mainly done in heart-rate Zones 1 and 2, while staying seated on the hills to build force.

Anaerobic endurance: Anaerobic endurance (AE) is the ability to generate superthreshold power and pace. Heart rates and power outputs are high—heart-rate Zone 5b and CP6 power zone—and therefore, the effort cannot be maintained for very long. High lactate levels are generated at these paces, and these workouts are painful.

Power: Power is the ability to apply maximum force quickly and economically. It is the combination of force and speed-skills abilities. This is the stuff that made sprinters like Mario Cipollini (cycling) and Carl Lewis (running) the great athletes that they were.

Power and anaerobic endurance, however, are seldom the things that determine success in long-distance triathlon events.

Limiters

Most athletes train the way they want to train. Athletes who are able to consistently improve season after season tend to train the way they need to train. It can be difficult for an athlete to focus on the areas that are holding him or her back because most of us developed our strengths in our favorite training areas. The intelligent athlete is one who is constantly addressing his or her limiters.

It is important to assess and understand your present fitness needs in order to make wise training decisions that will achieve your desired results while minimizing risk. It is essential that you are totally honest with yourself in assessing strengths and limiters.

Using a scale of 1 to 5, with 1 being the "worst" and 5 being the "best," rate your swim, bike, and run proficiencies. A score of 5 means that you are among the best, 3 indicates average for your category, and 1 places you at the bottom of the category.

Its important to know, first of all, which sport is holding you back. Second, you need to rate your endurance, force, and speed skills, using the same scale for each sport. When doing this, you must first decide what elements of fitness are necessary for success in the long-distance triathlon for which you are training. If the bike course, for example, has lots of hills and your cycling force is not very good, then bike force is a race-specific limiter for you. You may have found that your strength lies in shorter events, but you struggle just to finish an ironman-distance race. This problem would indicate that endurance is a limiter. If endurance is your key limiter, then your training plan should focus on endurance first and foremost before moving on to muscular endurance.

Also consider a focused strength-training program. Athletes who are new to cycling as well as female and veteran athletes have much to gain from a properly constructed strength program. Bike strength responds well to weights, followed by ME bike work. Seated hills are also a good way to build bike strength. Although cycling helps running, running does not appear to help cycling as much. In order to ride well, you need to ride quite a bit.

If the swim is your limiter, the abilities that you lack are more than likely endurance and speed skills, so you will need to focus on stroke mechanics, balance, and endurance. If you want to improve swim-specific strength, rubber stretch cords are quite useful and available at swim-supply and general sporting goods stores. It is essential to maintain excellent form at all times in the water. Working hard with poor form will very quickly lead you to a plateau, whereas working smart with excellent form is what leads to serious breakthroughs.

Some final tips to help guide you in determining your limiters. Please note that these are generalizations and should be interpreted in the context of your personal athletic history.

◆ Novices should assume that their key limiters are overall force, endurance, and speed skills.

◆ Athletes seeking to improve their swim times should assume that their sole limiter is speed skills until they are able to swim 1,000 meters in 19 minutes or less.

◆ Athletes seeking to improve their bike times should establish their endurance, then focus on muscular endurance.

◆ Athletes seeking to improve their run times should remember that long-course running requires very little raw speed (have a look at the results sheet for any ironman-distance race). What is required is the ability to swim and bike a long way at a solid aerobic pace without accumulating substantial fatigue. Overall endurance and bike muscular endurance are the key factors for being able to run well in an ironman-distance race.

◆ Whenever an athlete is unsure if his or her limiter is endurance or muscular endurance, then it is best to focus on endurance. Likewise, when unsure whether additional base training or build training is required, it is best to choose additional base training.

◆ Until your sport-specific performance is in the top quarter of your age group, you should continue to focus primarily on speed skills, overall body force, and endurance.

◆ Until your sport-specific performance is in the top 10 percent of your age group, there is little reason to perform AE-type workouts.

Patience and focused training will sort out any limiter over time.

Critical Success Factors

Highly motivated, intelligent endurance athletes are committed to doing what it takes to attain their goals. The role of a good coach (or book) is to help guide your enthusiasm to the areas where you will get the most return for your efforts. This role is even more important for the self-coached athlete because quite often these areas are the most difficult and challenging. However, when we make progress with our limiters, we realize greatly improved performance right away. It's just like the old saying: "A chain is only as strong as its weakest link." Once you determine your "weakest link" (greatest limiter), your performance will improve. If you continue to work only on your strengths, your "chain" (race performance) will never significantly improve.

For ironman-distance racing, critical success factors include the ability to focus, nutrition, the ability to ride strongly, and mental strength.

The ability to successfully execute a high-quality race requires an athlete to learn how to focus for long periods of time. This level of racing includes eating, drinking, going to the bathroom, racing smart, controlling pace, and staying strong. Typically, it is an athlete's process rather than his or her body that gives out during a race. Forgetting to eat, forgetting to drink, and riding faster than goal pace—these are examples of factors that can be controlled by an athlete who is able to maintain control over his or her race. You can practice your ability to focus during any workout—hard, easy, long, or short. It is a critical success factor for having a solid race. Athletes who have trouble focusing should start with shorter, easier workouts and progress toward harder, longer races.

Many athletes underestimate the role that nutrition plays in all aspects of physical performance. The path to elite nutrition is tough; however, if you want to race to your potential, then you have to fuel your body like an elite athlete. Remember the "Key Three":

1. Eliminate as many processed foods as possible.

2. Get the majority of your nutrition from lean protein, fresh veggies, and whole fruits.

3. Use starches and sugars in moderation, and only during and after training.

Do the preparation required to be able to push a strong gear in the flats. Build your strength and endurance first. Once you have established your endurance, you need to practice the ability to ride at a good pace for a long time in the flats. These are probably the most difficult sessions in which to maintain an even pace. They are also the best sessions for learning how to focus. These sessions can be done with other people, but you need to keep the momentum going for the duration of the ride. No talking, no long rests—these are not social sessions. These are ironman-distance-specific training sessions. If you want to race well, these sessions are what it takes. There isn't a much harder session to do perfectly than a 4- to 5-hour steady ride in the flats because that is a very long time to concentrate.

Maximize your mental strength. Every athlete has a breaking point—the point in a training session, a race, or in life where each of us "cracks." We slow down, quit, or break down. The art of life is to lean against our breaking points from time to time, slowly pushing our boundaries out. When we push too hard, we get injured and depressed and may even binge on food. All of these reactions are signs that we have gone too far. Elites (in life) have the ability to push themselves, but more importantly, they know when to back off. Racing well is very demanding. If you want to race well, you need to practice the ability to maintain mental strength when your body and mind start to doubt. How do you do this? Well, you "race"—racing is a skill that must be practiced. It is beneficial to race more because we all benefit from enhancing our ability to push.

These pushing skills are not needed at the start of a race. Anyone can push at the start of a race, and the smart athlete is the one who is able to show patience. The end of a race is when the smart athlete spends his or her mental strength, knowing that the most time is gained then. The hard fact is that if you slow at the end of the race, it is either your "process" (nutrition, hydration, and/or pacing) or your "mind" (mental strength) that has let you down.

More specific critical success factors for ironman-distance racing are cycling endurance, running endurance, and cycling muscular endurance.

Cycling endurance is the key to improvement. The ability to ride 112 miles and then run a full marathon requires a great deal of endurance. The better your cycling endurance, the more comfortable your ride will be and the more energy you will have for the run. Greater cycling endurance also helps to delay the onset and effects of fatigue.

Emphasize endurance training above all else in your first few years of training. Elite and experienced athletes must rebuild and maintain this ability each season. Time in the saddle; long, slow distance riding; and consistency are key to building cycling endurance.

Running endurance plays a major role in distance-racing success. However, owing to how hard running is on the body and its greater potential for injury, it is not recommended that you run long more than once per week, or for more than two and a half hours. Frequency and improved running economy are the keys to improving running, and your run will also enjoy endurance benefits from cycling volume.

Overall, ironman-distance racing is not about being fast. It is about being able to swim smart, ride strong, and run tough. So many athletes believe that they need to run hard and run a lot to perform well. Run training is important, but it is not the key to success. As coaches, we fully believe the keys to endurance racing success are outlined above.

Training Overview

The man who
competes with no one,
in all the world, has no
competitor.
— Lao Tzu, philosopher

Review of ATP Periods

There are a number of effective methods that can be used to successfully prepare for a long-course triathlon. This chapter outlines our view of the most effective method for the "typical" athlete to prepare for an ironman-distance race. In building your annual training plan (ATP), you should always interpret our advice in light of your experience and personal limiters. Remember that your ultimate success will be built on a platform of strength, endurance, and skill development. When in doubt, always refer back to the basics, for they are the foundation of performance and longevity in our sport.

Preparation Period

The period of training between the Transition (off season) and the early Base period is the Prep period. Most athletes will have a Prep period that lasts from four to twelve weeks. The exact length of the Prep period will depend on the timing of your first A-priority race and your experience in the sport. For ironman-distance racing, the training done in the Prep and early Base periods is highly valuable. In building your season, remember that only the strongest athletes are able to handle more than one Build period. By extending your Prep period, you can ensure that you arrive at your key races ready to go. A common planning error is for athletes to start race simulation workouts too far out from their race date. Many athletes, particularly those who are new to the distance, have experienced success without any Build periods.

The main purpose of the Prep period is to ease the body back into structured training, develop a training strategy for the upcoming season, prepare the body for the increasing requirements of the Base period, and improve fundamental and technical skills.

The general physiological adaptations that this period is intended to bring about are renewed cardiorespiratory (heart, blood, lungs) fitness through easy aerobic exercise, improved economy of movement through speed-skill development, and greater total body strength through weight lifting as well as rubber cords, isometrics, and other resistance exercises.

Athletes who use a shorter Prep period should maintain a training emphasis based on session frequency while keeping the duration and intensity of sessions low to moderate. This approach will enable the body to become reacquainted with structured training and ensure recovery from the previous season's efforts. Most athletes will find that their bodies take four to six weeks to adjust back to structured training. It is very important to remember that you are rebuilding fitness and to be patient with yourself. Most athletes will have memories of the levels of fitness achieved at the end of their previous season. In order to develop beyond previous highs, it is necessary to slow down and lay the foundations for continued development.

Athletes who use a Prep period of eight or more weeks may find that they are ready to start some longer endurance sessions after the four- to six-week initial adaptation period. Remember to keep these sessions reasonable in duration and to slowly stretch your endurance abilities.

Early in the Prep period, sessions should be relatively short and skills-oriented. It's also a good idea to include a considerable amount of cross-training activities, such as hiking, mountain biking, and cross-country skiing. These sessions should gradually stretch your endurance while keeping training intensity low and developing general fitness. Athletes who face climatic challenges (rain, cold, snow, and wind) should feel free to substitute alternative forms of indoor aerobic activity.

Weekly volume should be very comfortable, typically two to five hours lower than what you believe you can handle. Despite the lower volume, a recovery week is still recommended to maintain mental freshness and ensure continual physical adaptation. However, typically only one recovery week in the last week before the Base period begins is sufficient. This time can be used for testing.

Highly motivated athletes may be tempted to increase the intensity and duration of their key sessions. Particularly in the first Prep block of the year, be cautious with higher volume and intensity, as training at such levels during this period is counterproductive. It's not possible to maintain race fitness throughout the year. Attempting to do so will only lead to overtraining, burnout, or injury.

Early in the Prep period, testing should be aerobic in nature. Athletes looking to test lactate threshold values should wait until later in the Prep period or the early Base period. The end of the fourth week of Prep training is a good time to establish your baseline lactate threshold data because the results of these tests will allow you to gauge your progress in the months ahead.

Athletes with a longer Prep period should also consider slowly building their weekly volume to achieve a smooth transition to the Base 1 period.

Athletes targeting a late-season peak, novice athletes, and athletes living in climates with severe winters should consider an extended Prep period. The main benefits of this approach are a reduction in the risk of burnout and an increase in skill levels.

Base Period

Once you have completed the Prep period, you are ready for the Base period of training. The Base period is the most critical period for ironman-distance racing. After this base of fitness is laid down, the Build period begins, with workouts that increasingly mimic the demands of the event for which you are training.

Although many athletes believe that the key to race performance lies in the Build period, it is essential that you complete your Base period with the strength and endurance necessary to achieve your race goals. If your base fitness is not fully developed before the Build period begins, then your race fitness will never reach a very high peak. Coaches and athletes have used the analogy of a triangle—the broader the bottom of the triangle (Base), the higher the peak.

Why is base training so important? For one thing, if it's cut short for some reason, the athlete will not fully realize its three most important elements—endurance, force, and speed skills. Since the elements of training that are developed in the Build period grow from these qualities, their underdevelopment means that race-specific fitness suffers.

Build Period

When training for an ironman-distance race, the training in the late Base period and the Build period is essentially the same (other than volume). The purpose of the Build period is to prepare for the specific demands of the A-priority race. That means a lot of endurance and muscular endurance work plus force training under conditions that mimic the targeted race's course. By this time the training should be focused around race-simulation workouts that target your specific limiters. We recommend that athletes hold off on race-simulation workouts until after they are confident of their endurance.

For an experienced athlete, the key physiological limiter is nearly always cycling muscular endurance. See Appendix A for a summary of key workouts designed to enhance race performance.

When you are in Build period training, it is important to remember that your key focus should be preparing your body to race well over the distance and specific terrain of your A-priority race. You should schedule one or two race-simulation workouts each week. Typically, an athlete will do only four to seven of these key race-simulation workouts, so you should ensure that you are fully prepared for each session.

With the approach of your A-priority race, you will likely have the urge to increase your training volume above the levels recommended in this book. Remember that your race performance will be dictated by the duration and intensity of your key workouts, not your total weekly volume. In fact, if you are doing your race-simulation sessions properly, you will likely find that you need more recovery time in your Build period than during any other time of the training year.

Open-water swims are a useful addition to your Build period swim program. Do these with a partner and practice race tactics, including pacing and drafting.

Peak Period

The goal of the Peak period is to start the process of bringing you to a physiological peak for your ironman-distance race. The two most important elements of this period are intensity and recovery. The Peak period is discussed in detail in Chapter 9. Be sure to resist the urge to do "one last" megaworkout.

Race Period

There is one goal for all athletes during race week—to arrive at the start in the best condition possible. Race week is discussed in detail in Chapter 9.

Post-race Recovery

One of the most common mistakes an athlete will make after an A-priority race is to return too quickly to long sessions. Even at a very easy pace, the long sessions can leave you feeling spent.

It is common to start feeling quite strong ten to fourteen days after an ironman-distance race. You are likely experiencing the tail end of your peak. Don't let your mind trick you regarding the level of fatigue that accumulates in a long race. Even if you ended up "going easy" at the end of the race, the likely reason was that you were exhausted. The race leaves most athletes with a very deep fatigue. At the end of the season, many athletes will have small biomechanical problems from either their race or their training. Rest and flexibility work are the quickest path to a return to normal training.

Most athletes hit a second wave of fatigue the third week after an A-priority race, so there is nothing to be gained from rushing back to training. If you feel great, you could include some 30- to 60-minute sessions (total daily volume under one hour) of heart-rate Zone 1 swimming or cycling, or start with some easy weight lifting.

By giving your body a chance to heal, you will find that sometime in the two to four weeks after an ironman-distance race, it starts rebuilding itself. At that stage, you will realize just how tired you were. Your mind will try to convince you that you are different from everyone else, that you need less recovery. History has shown that almost everyone is best served by resting.

Rushing recovery is a false economy. When your body needs to rest, it will take the rest that it needs by any means necessary. Fatigue, illness, burnout, and injury are clues that additional rest is required.

Transition Period

After four to eight weeks of unstructured training, you will sense that you are ready to start back on your program. When coming back from a training break, emphasize frequency rather than duration or intensity. Simply put, frequency is your friend. Your aerobic systems will not be accustomed to structured training, and you will be many months away from your next key race. Therefore, your goals should be to stimulate your aerobic pathways, maintain your skill base, and start the process of rebuilding the strength that you will have lost over your break. Even if you are gearing up for another ironman-distance race, you should keep your focus on these three areas for your first block of structured training.

Weight: It is normal to gain some weight in the Transition period, often from a mixture of getting down to race weight and then slacking off on nutrition. The more control you are able to show in your nutrition, the less you will have to lose once you get back on your program. Some athletes gain as much as twenty pounds during this period. However, by following the "Key Three" (see Chapter 12), you can avoid the difficulties associated with trying to shed your off-season poundage. Athletes who are quick to gain (and slow to lose) pounds would be well advised to follow the "Key Three" at all times.

Speed: You will have lost aerobic fitness due to your transition break. This deterioration is normal, and you should expect to see material losses in strength when you come back. Stay calm—we bounce back pretty quickly, so the slowness and weakness should be temporary.

Consistency: Long breaks are costly in fitness terms. If you feel sickness or fatigue coming on, it is wise to immediately take off one or two days. There is a real fitness cost if you lose a week owing to illness. Consistent training is the easiest way to long-term improvement.

Fatigue: Many athletes will be coming off a lot of racing and more than likely pushed themselves very hard in their final A-priority race. It is easy to underestimate the accumulated fatigue in your system. Ironman-distance fatigue is unlike any other sort of fatigue you will ever have experienced (except maybe in ultramarathons). It is a very deep fatigue that takes a long time to shake. All athletes face this issue. The more motivated you are, the more you'll need to hold back.

The overall goal of the Transition period is mental and physical rejuvenation. This means . . . go with what you feel like. If you feel like doing nothing, then that is okay. Following are some specific guidelines to help you through your transition period.

Immediate Transition Guidelines

Immediately after your race, place your priorities in this order: Remove all heat stress, reestablish normal hydration levels, consume recovery foods, remove all heat from legs, and undertake a flexibility routine. A good tip for removing heat stress and leg heat is to stand in cold water up to your waist (i.e., return to the swim start).

If you feel faint, then elevating your legs, eating, and drinking will likely help you more than an IV. Take responsibility for your own recovery, race smart, and plan ahead.

Consider a sports massage in the two- to five-day period directly after the race. Although they may feel good, deep-tissue massages and hot tubs in the first twenty-four hours after the race are likely to cause further muscle trauma.

We highly recommend that there be no efforts above heart-rate Zone 1 for the first four days following a half-ironman-distance race and for ten days following an ironman-distance race. After this window, harder efforts should be done only in the pool (for the duration of your Transition period). If you have just completed your final race of the season, then there is no rush to get back to training and you should consider an extended period of little to no training.

Sleep as much as you want (and more than normal). Sleep is far more important than training during this time.

Eat high-quality foods. Your training volume will be low, so avoid sugars and high-glycemic-index carbohydrates and focus on nutrient-dense foods such as whole fruits, fresh vegetables, and lean protein. Note that lean protein does not mean fat-free processed meat. Whole cuts of "real" (ideally free-range) meat are superior.

Walk and stretch as much as you want. Easy spinning for 15 to 30 minutes prior to a stretching session is very useful because promoting circulation and mobility in sore muscle groups will speed recovery. Massage, yoga, and stretching are active-recovery activities that will also enhance your recovery.

Do no running for at least four days following a half-ironman-distance race and twelve days following an ironman-distance race. As an additional guideline, you should not start running until you feel that you are able to hold a steady pace on the bike. If you are unable to elevate your heart rate on the bike or feel breathless very quickly (in any session), then you need more recovery and total rest.

Somewhere in the four- to fourteen-day post-race window, you will likely start to feel better. At this stage, you can begin to test your recovery with steady aerobic efforts (heart-rate Zone 2) on the bike. Resist the urge to hammer yourself, and be very cautious in group situations. Such caution is especially essential if you had a DNF or a disappointing race because your mind will try to convince you to "redeem" yourself. Save your energy for preparing for next time rather than blowing your recovery period.Remember that, for a range of factors, race recovery for any distance can take up to four months. Keep resting until you feel ready to go. Rushing your race recovery is a false economy.

At all times, remember that if you feel like doing nothing, then doing nothing is okay. When you are tired, focus on low-impact active recovery. The deeper your base, the more likely you will benefit from active recovery. If you are completely nuked, then total rest is the best way to go.

Guidelines for Moving toward the Preparation Period

If you are deeply fatigued, then keep resting and focusing on low-impact active recovery. As a trained athlete, you will likely recover fastest with low-intensity work, and merely sitting still will normally not be the fastest way to bounce back. If you have a job where you sit a lot, then get up at least every ninety minutes to stretch. Walking, a few side bends, a few knee bends—it helps year-round but even more when you have post-race stiffness. After you have been feeling eager to train for at least five days, it is time to begin tapering back into training. Our tips assume that you are feeling ready to train again.

As swimming is the most skill-oriented of our sports, your first priority is to get back in the water. Frequent, moderate, and skill-oriented swims are best. Be very cautious with any muscular endurance work. Hard swimming on short rest intervals is the most risky form of training at this time.

Help preserve your aerobic pathways by getting back on your bike. Choose some favorite rides, and keep your pace and intensity low. On at least one ride, insert 15 to 30 minutes of steady riding at heart-rate Zone 2 to "test" your recovery. Your steady pace in this stage should be based on rating of perceived exertion (RPE)—don't drill yourself!

Your taper, the race, and the subsequent break mean that your strength will be close to a season low. Head back to the gym and ease back into strength training. It is very important that you do not try to add any strength. For at least the first three strength-training sessions, limit yourself to a single set of each exercise: twenty-five to thirty repetitions at an intensity that is "embarrassingly light."

If your swimming and cycling are going well, then it is time to add an easy run. Leave your heart-rate monitor at home, head out, and enjoy yourself. Again, choose a favorite route and stay flexible on duration. If you are feeling good, then a moderate run is okay—otherwise, keep it short.

Maintaining your skills inventory is a year-round priority, so always focus on form.

Watch your morning heart rate. It will give you a clue to your recovery. Continue to make sleep the number-one priority throughout this period.

You now have the benefit of a little distance from your race. Sit down and spend some time reviewing your race performance and write down the lessons you learned for the future. You should also consider your key limiters for achieving your future goals.

Finally, consider your goals: Do they represent what *you* want to do with *your* life? Are they appropriate and achievable? Are you committed to doing what it takes to achieve them? We race and train for ourselves. Be 100 percent honest with yourself. If your heart is not in long-distance racing, recognizing it will be the best choice for you.

Breakthrough Workouts

A breakthough (BT) workout is any workout or group of workouts that requires more than thirty-six hours to recover from. The nature of your BT workouts will vary throughout the year. Early in the season, or in your career, a four-hour easy ride could be considered a BT workout, but as your endurance increases, such a session could become an aerobic maintenance workout. Another example is strength training: After twelve weeks of base training, you may recover quickly from strength training, but at another time of the year strength training could require forty-eight hours of recovery.

BT workouts should be designed to focus on your A-priority race limiters. These are different for each athlete. Your role is to design appropriate BTs and allow enough recovery time. Most self-coached athletes tend to stack too many BTs into a block, and as a result, they do not get the recovery that they need in order to take their fitness to the next level. This is the primary cause of sport-specific and overall performance plateaus.

Generally, novice or older athletes should not schedule more than two BT workouts in a week. Experienced or elite athletes who recover quickly may schedule three BT workouts in a week. Stronger athletes may also be able to stack two or three workouts into a "BT day." However, you need to have a clear view of your goals and the key sessions within your days, weeks, and blocks.

Your easiest days should follow your toughest days. In other words, the best place for a rest day is after your toughest day of the week. However, this is a general rule, and there are situations in which it makes sense to vary it.

In the race season, BT quality is most important. Most athletes will find that they require additional recovery periods from their toughest sessions. It is far better to recover from a limited number of high-quality sessions than to push the volume up and do lots of "moderate" sessions. This becomes more important as your A-priority race approaches. Superior race performance results from *what* you do, not how *much* you do.

Breakthrough Workout Tips

Timing is an important consideration in scheduling your BT workouts. Most athletes will find that they have higher-quality BT sessions when they are able to complete their key sessions in the afternoon.

Some athletes will benefit from a cup of regular coffee taken 60 to 90 minutes prior to the start of a BT session. Athletes who elect to use caffeine should be cautious with its use, as it is most effective in low to moderate doses.

All longer BT sessions should begin with a low-intensity warm-up to allow your body to build into the session. This is particularly important for the longest BT sessions as well as those that incorporate high-intensity workloads.

BT sessions are an excellent opportunity to practice mental skills such as focus, pace, fatigue management, and cue words.

Pain, specifically during high-intensity sessions, should be carefully monitored. Build period BT sessions are difficult, and late in the workout athletes will be training through fatigue. The ability to train through fatigue is an important skill for you to learn. However, you should never train through pain. Knowing when to back off is important. All athletes should be very conservative during the Build period, when an injury can be costly in terms of race fitness. As a general rule, "If in doubt, leave it out."

Breakthrough Workout Recovery Tips

After a BT session, have a quick snack, shower, put on some comfortable clothes, and eat your main recovery meal. Once you have finished your meal, sit on the floor cross-legged with one or two pillows directly behind your back, and lean backward over the pillows. You will be doing a mild back bend and should feel your hip flexors and pelvis open. Relax into the stretch, then sit up slowly and reverse the upper and lower crossed legs. Lean backward over the pillows for the same length of time. This will ensure a balanced hip stretch.

Between this recovery exercise and the next one, walk around for four to eight minutes.

Now move your pillows against a wall, lie on your back with the pillows under your lower back, and place your legs up against the wall. The amount of support that you will need under your lower back will depend on your hamstring flexibility. Leave your legs against the wall for five minutes for each hour of your workout. When you have finished your wall time, roll gently onto one side. Stay on your side for a few minutes to ease the transition back to vertical.

The "legs up the wall" exercise helps get blood to your vital organs, allowing you to recover more quickly. If you are tired, then you may get sleepy. This exercise, combined with some deep breathing, is an excellent way to relax prior to a nap or bedtime.

Role of Volume, Intensity, and Frequency

There are as many different approaches to volume, intensity, and frequency as there are athletes. In general, novice athletes should focus on frequency over volume and intensity. The shorter the race distance, the more important intensity becomes. There are many different approaches to volume as well. There are no hard-and-fast rules, as there are examples of successful athletes using a wide range of methods.

Volume

Most competitors will compete in no more than one ironman-distance race per year, and it's normally timed for the end of their local race season. A few athletes will do two, but they are normally close together (the so-called double), which is effectively the same thing. Only a very small number of people actually do two or more ironman-distance races a year, distributed throughout the year, because these competitions usually involve significant travel and expense. Of that number, the majority are "social" competitors— in it more for the lifestyle than for serious competition. This leaves only a few hard-case "nuts" who actually race ironman distance every four to six months or so and are thus always building on a retained base.

For most people, doing one major long-course race a year allows them to start from scratch at the end of the off-season, compete in shorter events early in the season, work to pay the bills, etc. . . . Only at crunch time, having rebuilt the base needed to deal with the next step, do these athletes make the commitment to train for their impending race. The key commitment period is the final eleven weeks of training because the training in this period will have the greatest impact on your ultimate race performance. The more thorough your preparations leading up to this period, the higher the quality of your final preparations and, therefore, the greater the probability of superior race performance.

The volume that is appropriate for you depends upon your base, the time of year, your nontriathlon obligations, and your physiology. When you start your training each year, build the plan with a little less volume than you think you can handle. Once you have eight to twelve weeks of training behind you, take a second look at volume and adjust based on your recovery experience. When you are operating at the limits of your recovery abilities, even one or two extra training hours can push you over the edge.

Be particularly careful with your running volume. Many athletes run far too much for ironman-distance racing. Remember that the best place to build endurance and aerobic fitness is on your bike. Running beats you up, and the greatest challenge for most folks training for ironman-distance racing is how fast they can recover. There should be a specific purpose to each run session. Remember that there is no such thing as a "recovery run." Recovery sessions should be non–impact oriented.

When training at high volume, most athletes can handle only one high-intensity session a week. High intensity will vary for everyone according to their experience and fitness, but for most people it means threshold or above-threshold work. You will find that threshold and anaerobic exercise greatly increase your recovery needs. This type of training also increases the risks of burning out, illness, and injury. The deeper your base, the better your recovery, and the lower your nontraining stress, the higher your tolerance to intensity will become.

For your first ironman-distance race, you should target three key sessions each week (one for each sport): one long swim of 75 to 100 minutes, one long ride of 4 to 5 hours followed by a 20- to 30-minute transition run, and one long run of 90 to 150 minutes. Everything else is filler.

Training on a four-week cycle, your schedule may look something like this:

Week 1: Bike and swim week. Include one extra swim and one extra ride; for your running, the key workouts would be a transition run, a long run, and a Strides session.

Week 2: Run week. Include an extra run this week, and have the additional session focus on your greatest running limiter—for most athletes that would be a moderate-duration endurance session. As the season progresses, this session could include some muscular endurance training.

Week 3: Bike and swim week, as per week 1.

Week 4: Recovery week; maintain your workout frequency but at 50 percent of training-week volume, and schedule some testing toward the end of the week (see Table 4.1, Sample Testing Schedule).

Remember that your greatest time gains will come from focusing on your limiters. Your endurance target is to be able to swim 4,000 meters, bike 5 to 7 hours, and have the ability to run a marathon. Until you have the aerobic fitness for this task, "going hard" is likely a wasted opportunity for further endurance training.

You will find that you get the best results by separating your longest run from your longest ride. Avoid the monster weekends that many people recommend. Put your long run midweek and your long ride on the weekend for effective recovery. Scheduling a long ride on Sunday, a long swim on Friday, and a long run on Wednesday gives plenty of recovery time.

If in doubt, leave it out. Most first-timers spend the majority of their training year underrecovered. The focus should be on your key workouts and recovering. Success is correlated to the duration and intensity of your key sessions, not your total volume.

Table 4.1 Sample Testing Schedule

	Timeline	Swim	Bike	Run	Notes
Prep 1	October	1,000 meters	[LT]	LT	
Prep 2	November	500 meters	[LT]	Aerobic Function	500s: 4x500 on 12 minutes
Prep 3	December	Best Average	[Aerobic TT]	LT	Best Average: 12x100 on greater of 2 minutes' and 30 seconds' rest
Base 1	January	30-minute TT	[Aerobic TT]	Aerobic Function	
Base 2	February	1,000 meters	[LT]	VO$_2$max Pace /10K TT	Run: 10K TT on weekend; VO$_2$max Pace Test early in week
Base 3	March	Racing	Racing	Racing	Olympic Distance Race: check data against bike and run LTs
Build	April	1,000 meters	Race Simulation	Race Simulation	
Peak	May	Best Average	None	None	
Race	May	Racing	Racing	Racing	Half-Ironman Race
Base 2	May/June	Choice	Choice	Choice	Choice: No testing or confirmation testing
Base 3	June/July	Racing	Racing	Racing	Half-Ironman Race
Build	July/August	1,000 meters	[LT]	[LT]	
Peak	August	Best Average	None	None	
Race	August	Racing	Racing	Racing	Ironman Race

Intensity

High-intensity training is powerful medicine that should be used sparingly and treated respectfully. As coaches, our greatest concern with threshold work (close to, at, or above threshold) is that if an athlete is injured, sick, or tired, then he or she quickly loses the endurance gains that we have spent months building. Although high-intensity work is essential for elite athletes, 90 percent of the field in any race is average age groupers.

There can be too much emphasis on intensity in training, and newcomers can get the wrong impression when elite competitors start talking about their quality sessions. Consistency beats intensity in nearly all age-group situations.

The hardest workouts of the year should be limited to the Build and Peak periods because high-intensity workouts are the most potent stimuli for both improving and maintaining fitness. Your top-end fitness can be achieved in a relatively short period of time. Even during this time, workouts should be no more intense than slightly above the effort level at which you expect to race.

It is important to remember that training at the highest intensities year-round is ultimately detrimental to performance as you will eventually wind up sick, injured, burned out, or overtrained. Intensity levels during the bulk of your training should be devoted to building or maintaining endurance and strength.

Frequency

How often you work out is the most basic element of training for long-distance triathlon. Novice athletes typically work out five to six times per week, whereas an elite athlete may work out twelve to eighteen times in a week. The appropriate frequency varies for each level of athlete.

As your fitness improves, you will see increased benefits in active recovery instead of total rest days. Active-recovery workouts are just that—an easy spin on the bike, an easy technique swim, or some other form of nonimpact light aerobic exercise.

Frequency varies throughout the season. It should be increased early in the season to add training stresses on the body, and decreased prior to and during race season to allow more time for recovery. That said, consistent frequency throughout the year is the most effective way to maintain fitness.

VO_2max, or Anaerobic Endurance Training

The toughest part of VO_2max training is the initial time trial (TT). Most athletes will find that the training pace determined from the TT is actually a comfortable pace (for anaerobic work).

You must have an excellent endurance base before starting any high-intensity training. It is best to wait until you are seven to eleven weeks out from your A-priority races before starting these kinds of sessions.

Most new endurance athletes will benefit more from training endurance and muscular endurance than from VO_2max training. For example, in the first two years of cycling, your lactate threshold may rise 5 bpm per annum just from your muscles learning how to cycle. It may not be until your third season of focused bike training that high-intensity work is appropriate—even then it should likely be ME work, not VO_2max work.

We recommend that you train your skills and endurance, then muscular endurance, and finally anaerobic endurance. Not only is this the safest way to progress; it also mirrors the requirements of long-distance triathlon.

Anaerobic endurance sessions are biomechanically stressful as well as taking extra recovery time. Although many athletes believe that this kind of work is beneficial, research shows that greater results are achieved from endurance and ME work. The latter types of workout are also less risky and subject to quicker recovery.

Certain folks find VO$_2$max sessions fun, so small amounts of high intensity can be useful to maintain mental freshness. However, the heavy-duty VO$_2$max sessions should be attempted only by strong, experienced athletes who are biomechanically sound.

These sessions are risky. Don't blow your season trying to shave the last minute off your bike or run split.

Testing

The most critical data for you to memorize are your key training data, such as pace, power, and heart-rate zones. In order to get the most out of your training sessions, schedule frequent physiological tests. The second half of a recovery week is the preferred time to undertake sport-specific testing. Because of the important role played by the lactate threshold value, we recommend that you reconfirm your sport-specific lactate threshold every eight to twelve weeks.

Once reliable baseline data have been recorded, you may benefit from substituting races to reconfirm test data. When interpreting race data, consideration should be given to the terrain, temperature, effort, and duration of your effort. Races are most effectively used in the late Base and Build periods.

Remain conscious of the relationship between all training variables such as heart rate, pace, power output, and RPE. When heart-rate data appear to contradict other variables (most particularly RPE, pace, or power), then consider the possible causes. Don't limit yourself to what your heart-rate monitor is telling you.

Heart rate by itself tells you nothing about performance or well-being. It must be compared with something else to have meaning. For example, if heart rate and RPE are low while pace and power are normal to high, then fitness is likely high. If heart rate and RPE are high when pace and power are low, it could be a sign of inadequate recovery. You may be experiencing fatigue, lifestyle stress, or even overtraining. Depressed or elevated heart rate is often a leading indicator of fatigue or impending illness. There are other possibilities as well, so all we really know is that something is not right.

Novice athletes will need to test more frequently than experienced athletes. When new to a sport, threshold values can rise 5 to 15 bpm per annum for the first several years of focused training.

If you see a large change in threshold values between tests (10 bpm or more), you should consider the validity of the test results. If you believe the test to be valid, then gradually, over a series of weeks, adjust your training zones toward the new values. When adjusting training zones, increase the attention you pay to RPE indicators.

Refer back to Table 4.1, a sample testing program for an experienced age-group athlete. Note the mixture of aerobic, threshold, and anaerobic testing. The testing protocols in square brackets would be undertaken only if an athlete felt that reconfirmation was required. Most athletes would test no more than two sports in any one recovery week. If you have access to power-based testing, then you need to build critical power testing into your test schedule. Such sessions are stressful, so resist the urge to stack these workouts.

Remember that that there are no "right" answers for any test. Testing merely provides you with useful data, which you may then use to guide your training and track progress. Seasonal, climatic, and other external variables will influence your results.

Although laboratory testing is interesting from a sport-science perspective, our experience as coaches indicates that the standard forms of lab tests produce results of limited value. You will do your training in the field, so we recommend that you do your testing in the field as well.

Northern Hemisphere athletes who experience harsh winter conditions should perform indoor tests for correct winter training zones and outdoor tests to establish outdoor training zones. Nearly all athletes will have a variation in intensity zones between an indoor and an outdoor situation. This variation is most noticeable for cycling zones.

Occasionally, testing may indicate that you have lost fitness. When this disappointing result occurs, consideration should be given to the reasons behind it. The answers normally lie in the approach that has been taken with volume, intensity, and/or recovery. For most endurance athletes, a lack of recovery is the leading cause of reduced performance. Inability to control the many variables that affect a field test is also a consideration—weather, fatigue, diet, mental stress, tire pressure, course, running shoes, etc. Full details of the testing protocols can be found in Appendix B. Also see the "Testing Tips" sidebar.

Crash Cycles

Overcompensation is a standard training method—after a training stress is applied and the body is given ample recovery, fitness will begin to develop at a higher level. When these training stresses are closely spaced over an extended period followed by a long recovery phase, the level of overcompensation is enhanced. This supercompensation is called "crashing."

Crash cycles appeal to everyone and are appropriate for hardly anyone because they are highly risky. There are significant mental and physical benefits from this kind of training; however, it should only be attempted by the absolute strongest athletes who are

Testing Tips

Athletes should always undertake a thorough warm-up before any testing session. The warm-up should last between 20 and 75 minutes and include short efforts that build to target intensity and/or pace. For nonmaximal tests, experienced athletes will likely benefit from building these efforts to slightly beyond target intensity and/or pace. For all athletes, efforts of 15 to 90 seconds in duration are appropriate. As a rule, the higher the intensity of the test, the shorter the duration of the warm-up efforts. Typically, four to eight efforts are sufficient. Avoid the accumulation of high levels of lactate during your warm-up.

The **initial pacing** of any test effort should be slightly slower than what you believe is achievable for the test as a whole. It is far easier to recover from a start that is slightly slow than one that is slightly fast. This is critical in threshold and maximal testing, where high early lactate levels will distort test results. Build into all tests, and aim for a pace that will enable you to finish strong.

Although most athletes are able to perform best in the afternoon and early evening, we recommend that testing be done at the same time as the majority of your training sessions. For example, if you always swim or run in the morning, then it is best for these tests to be performed in the morning. Certain athletes will have material changes in their training zones through the day.

Do your best to ensure that tests are performed in as **consistent conditions** as possible. Although external factors such as temperature, humidity, and wind are impossible to control, you should note such conditions and consider them when interpreting data. For factors under your control, do your best to ensure consistency. The key variables that you can control are recovery, hydration, nutrition, session timing, and pacing.

completely biomechanically sound. It is important that you meet the following criteria before attempting a crash cycle:

- no recent injury history
- recover quickly from tough sessions—normally you only need four to five days in a recovery week
- are at the top of your age group (or elite) and want to take it to the next level
- are willing to accept injury in your life

An example of a crash week follows:

Monday	Swim endurance, bike endurance
Tuesday	Run endurance, bike active recovery
Wednesday	Swim endurance, bike endurance
Thursday	Off
Friday	Swim endurance, run speed skills, bike active recovery
Saturday	Bike endurance
Sunday	Swim endurance, bike endurance

An example of the following recovery week:

Monday	Off
Tuesday	Bike active recovery, swim active recovery
Wednesday	Run active recovery, bike active recovery
Thursday	Strength, swim active recovery
Friday	Run active recovery, bike active recovery
Saturday	Bike endurance, swim endurance
Sunday	Run endurance, swim active recovery

This is only one example of a way in which a crash cycle may be organized; however, it is preferable to crash only one sport at a time. Crashing running is too risky and should be avoided. Crashing swimming with good stroke mechanics is highly effective. For ironman-distance racing, crashing volume tends to yield superior results to crashing intensity.

Just as in your breakthrough sessions, it can be useful to probe your limits at times. World champion triathlete Mark Allen says, "Push your limits rarely; when you push them, push them hard." This can be an effective strategy for elite and experienced athletes.

If you think a crash cycle is for you, watch closely for the typical signs of overtraining because the risk rises dramatically during such buildup. Crash cycles shouldn't be attempted more than once for each racing peak and no closer than two weeks prior to your goal race.

Challenge Workouts

A safer way for you to push your limits is through challenge workouts. These workouts are different from breakthrough sessions in that they are tougher than what we would normally recommend and go a little beyond BT sessions. They are fun, keep training fresh, and provide athletes with motivating goals.

The early Base period is the best time for challenge workouts that have an endurance component. These are workouts that push your endurance—not your muscular endurance. Here are some examples:

- rim to rim on the Grand Canyon
- 3 miles easy open-water swimming
- double metric centuries, all on the small chain ring
- all-day hiking
- mountaineering
- riding to the next state, county, or city
- multiday hiking trips
- multiday bike tours
- mountain-bike tours

Allow plenty of time for recovery, and remember that the main goal of these sessions is to have fun while building endurance.

Time versus Distance

When scheduling your weekly workouts, think in terms of total training time, not distance traveled. To illustrate, an 8-mile run could be an aerobic maintenance session for an elite athlete, while the same distance would be a tough endurance session for a novice. Distance is even less relevant for cycling, where terrain, wind, and road surface all impact the nature of a ride. Refer to Tables 4.2 and 4.3 for suggested daily and weekly training hours. Do the time, and the miles will fall into place come race day.

Structuring Base and Build Weeks
Base Week Structuring

The primary goals of the Base period are to develop aerobic endurance, strength, and skills in each individual sport. The Base period is commonly split into three phases—Base 1, Base 2, and Base 3. Depending on your limiters, it may make sense to extend your base training right up until your goal race. You can have an excellent race experience by focusing your training on the fundamentals of endurance, strength, and skills.

The goal of Base 1 is to improve endurance and maximum strength. During this period, endurance workouts are longer, and the focus on technical skills increases. To balance the maximum-strength phase, frequent skills-oriented workouts are important to maintain your quickness.

For most athletes, we recommend reducing the duration of BT workouts; however, swim volume—but not intensity—can be increased.

For an experienced or elite athlete, a typical Base 1 week might be the following:

Monday	Masters' swimming, skills cycling, yoga
Tuesday	Endurance swim, skills cycling
Wednesday	BT ride with transition run, yoga
Thursday	Technique swim, skills running, strength training, easy spin
Friday	BT swim, skills cycling, massage
Saturday	BT run
Sunday	Strength training, aerobic ride

With the completion of the higher-intensity strength training, sport-specific ME work is introduced in Base 2. ME workouts should be done at moderate intensities in the initial stages to give you time to convert "gym strength" to sport-specific muscular endurance. Endurance workouts continue to increase in duration.

For most athletes, swimming will start to take a slight backseat as your focus moves toward bike, run, and brick sessions.

Base 2 is tricky because you will likely feel ready for some higher-intensity work. However, patience must be practiced to avoid peaking too soon. Therefore, we recommend that you continue to include plenty of endurance training to help channel your energy into a productive area of training. This approach will help you exercise the necessary control.

For an experienced or elite athlete, a Base 2 week might look something like this:

Monday	Masters' swimming, aerobic ride, yoga
Tuesday	Endurance swimming, bike BT (ME focus)
Wednesday	Endurance run (including skills work), yoga
Thursday	Masters' swimming, aerobic brick
Friday	Skills swimming, skills running, strength training, skills cycling
Saturday	Day off
Sunday	Endurance ride

Your weekly volume reaches a peak in Base 3. Intensity also rises slightly with the addition of more ME training. Athletes need to be very careful with intensity during their BT workouts, as individual tolerance for this kind of training varies tremendously. C-priority races can be used during this period as tempo or intensity sessions.

For an experienced or elite athlete, a Base 3 week may be structured like this:

Monday	Masters' swimming, aerobic ride, yoga
Tuesday	Endurance swimming, BT ride (ME focus)
Wednesday	Endurance run (including ME work), yoga
Thursday	Day off
Friday	BT swim (ME focus), skills running, strength training, skills cycling
Saturday	Masters' swimming, aerobic brick
Sunday	Endurance ride

Table 4.2 Daily Training Hours

Weekly Hours	Longest Ride	May be two-a-day workouts					
3:00	1:30	0:45	0:45	off	off	off	off
3:30	1:30	1:00	1:00	off	off	off	off
4:00	1:30	1:00	1:00	0:30	off	off	off
4:30	1:45	1:00	1:00	0:45	off	off	off
5:00	2:00	1:00	1:00	1:00	off	off	off
5:30	2:00	1:30	1:00	1:00	off	off	off
6:00	2:00	1:30	1:00	1:00	1:00	off	off
6:30	2:00	1:30	1:00	1:00	1:00	off	off
7:00	2:00	1:30	1:30	1:00	1:00	off	off
7:30	2:30	1:30	1:30	1:00	1:00	off	off
8:00	2:30	1:30	1:30	1:30	1:00	off	off
8:30	2:30	2:00	1:30	1:30	1:00	off	off
9:00	3:00	2:00	1:30	1:30	1:00	off	off
9:30	3:00	2:00	1:30	1:30	1:00	0:30	off
10:00	3:00	2:00	1:30	1:30	1:00	1:00	off
10:30	3:00	2:00	2:00	1:30	1:00	1:00	off
11:00	3:00	2:00	2:00	1:30	1:30	1:00	off
11:30	3:00	2:30	2:00	1:30	1:30	1:00	off
12:00	3:00	2:30	2:00	2:00	1:30	1:00	off

Table 4.2 continued

Weekly Hours	Longest Ride	May be two-a-day workouts					
12:30	3:30	2:30	2:00	2:00	1:30	1:00	off
13:00	3:30	3:00	2:00	2:00	1:30	1:00	off
13:30	3:30	3:00	2:30	2:00	1:30	1:00	off
14:00	4:00	3:00	2:30	2:00	1:30	1:00	off
14:30	4:00	3:00	2:30	2:30	1:30	1:00	off
15:00	4:00	3:00	3:00	2:30	1:30	1:00	off
15:30	4:00	3:00	3:00	2:30	2:00	1:00	off
16:00	4:00	3:30	3:00	2:30	2:00	1:00	off
16:30	4:00	3:30	3:00	3:00	2:00	1:00	off
17:00	4:00	3:30	3:00	3:00	2:00	1:30	off
17:30	4:00	4:00	3:00	3:00	2:00	1:30	off
18:00	4:00	4:00	3:00	3:00	2:30	1:30	off
18:30	4:30	4:00	3:00	3:00	2:30	1:30	off
19:00	4:30	4:30	3:00	3:00	2:30	1:30	off
19:30	4:30	4:30	3:30	3:00	2:30	1:30	off
20:00	4:30	4:30	3:30	3:00	2:30	2:00	off
20:30	4:30	4:30	3:30	3:30	2:30	2:00	off
21:00	5:00	4:30	3:30	3:30	2:30	2:00	off
21:30	5:00	4:30	4:00	3:30	2:30	2:00	off
22:00	5:00	4:30	4:00	3:30	3:00	2:00	off
22:30	5:00	4:30	4:00	3:30	3:00	2:30	off
23:00	5:00	5:00	4:00	3:30	3:00	2:30	off
23:30	5:30	5:00	4:00	3:30	3:00	2:30	off

Weekly Hours	Longest Ride	May be two-a-day workouts					
24:00	5:30	5:00	4:30	3:30	3:00	2:30	off
24:30	5:30	5:00	4:30	4:00	3:00	2:30	off
25:00	5:30	5:00	4:30	4:00	3:00	3:00	off
25:30	5:30	5:30	4:30	4:00	3:00	3:00	off
26:00	6:00	5:30	4:30	4:00	3:00	3:00	off
26:30	6:00	5:30	5:00	4:00	3:00	3:00	off
27:00	6:00	6:00	5:00	4:00	3:00	3:00	off
27:30	6:00	6:00	5:00	4:00	3:30	3:00	off
28:00	6:00	6:00	5:00	4:00	3:30	3:30	off
28:30	6:00	6:00	5:00	4:30	3:30	3:30	off
29:00	6:00	6:00	5:30	4:30	3:30	3:30	off
29:30	6:00	6:00	6:00	4:30	3:30	3:30	off
30:00	6:00	6:00	6:00	4:30	4:00	3:30	off
30:30	6:00	6:00	6:00	5:00	4:00	3:30	off
31:00	6:00	6:00	6:00	5:00	4:00	4:00	off
31:30	6:00	6:00	6:00	5:00	4:30	4:00	off
32:00	6:00	6:00	6:00	5:30	4:30	4:00	off
32:30	6:00	6:00	6:00	5:30	4:30	4:30	off
33:00	6:00	6:00	6:00	5:30	5:00	4:30	off
33:30	6:00	6:00	6:00	6:00	5:00	4:30	off
34:00	6:00	6:00	6:00	6:00	5:30	4:30	off
34:30	6:00	6:00	6:00	6:00	5:30	5:00	off
35:00	6:00	6:00	6:00	6:00	6:00	5:00	off

Table 4.3 Weekly Training Hours

		Annual Hours									
Period	Week	200	250	300	350	400	450	500	550	600	650
Prep	All	3.5	4.0	5.0	6.0	7.0	7.5	8.5	9.0	10.0	11.0
Base 1	1	4.0	5.0	6.0	7.0	8.0	9.0	10.0	11.0	12.0	12.5
	2	5.0	6.0	7.0	8.5	9.5	10.5	12.0	13.0	14.5	15.5
	3	5.5	6.5	8.0	9.5	10.5	12.0	13.5	14.5	16.0	17.5
	4	3.0	3.5	4.0	5.0	5.5	6.5	7.0	8.0	8.5	9.0
Base 2	1	4.0	5.5	6.5	7.5	8.5	9.5	10.5	12.5	12.5	13.0
	2	5.0	6.5	7.5	9.0	10.0	11.5	12.5	14.0	15.0	16.5
	3	5.5	7.0	8.5	10.0	11.0	12.5	14.0	15.5	17.0	18.0
	4	3.0	3.5	4.5	5.0	5.5	6.5	7.0	8.0	8.5	9.0
Base 3	1	4.5	5.5	7.0	8.0	9.0	10.0	11.0	12.5	13.5	14.5
	2	5.0	6.5	8.0	9.5	10.5	12.0	13.5	14.5	16.0	17.0
	3	6.0	7.5	9.0	10.5	11.5	13.0	15.0	16.5	18.0	19.0
	4	3.0	3.5	4.5	5.0	5.5	6.5	7.0	8.0	8.5	9.0
Build 1	1	5.0	6.5	8.0	9.0	10.0	11.5	12.5	14.0	15.5	16.0
	2	5.0	6.5	8.0	9.0	10.0	11.5	12.5	14.0	15.5	16.0
	3	5.0	6.5	8.0	9.0	10.0	11.5	12.5	14.0	15.5	16.0
	4	3.0	3.5	4.5	5.0	5.5	6.5	7.0	8.0	8.5	9.0
Build 2	1	5.0	6.0	7.0	8.5	9.5	10.5	12.0	13.0	14.5	15.5
	2	5.0	6.0	7.0	8.5	9.5	10.5	12.0	13.0	14.5	15.5
	3	5.0	6.0	7.0	8.5	9.5	10.5	12.0	13.0	14.5	15.5
	4	3.0	3.5	4.5	5.0	5.5	6.5	7.0	8.0	8.5	9.0
Peak	1	4.0	5.0	6.0	7.0	7.5	8.5	9.5	10.5	11.5	11.5
	2	3.5	4.0	5.0	5.5	6.0	7.0	7.5	8.5	9.0	10.0
Race	All	3.0	3.5	4.0	4.5	5.0	5.5	6.0	7.0	7.0	8.0
Tran	All	3.0	3.5	4.5	5.0	5.5	6.5	7.0	8.0	8.5	9.0

Annual Hours

Period	Week	700	750	800	850	900	950	1000	1050	1100	1150	1200
Prep	All	12.0	12.5	13.5	14.5	15.0	16.0	17.0	17.5	18.5	19.5	20.0
Base 1	1	14.0	14.5	15.5	16.5	17.5	18.5	19.5	20.5	21.5	22.5	23.5
	2	16.5	18.0	19.1	20.0	21.5	22.5	24.0	25.0	26.0	27.5	28.5
	3	18.5	20.0	21.5	22.5	24.0	25.5	26.5	28.0	29.5	30.5	32.0
	4	10.0	10.5	11.0	12.0	12.5	13.5	14.0	14.5	15.5	16.0	17.0
Base 2	1	14.5	16.0	17.0	18.0	19.0	20.0	21.0	22.0	23.0	24.0	25.0
	2	17.5	19.0	20.0	21.5	22.5	24.0	25.0	26.6	27.5	28.8	30.0
	3	19.5	21.0	22.5	24.0	25.0	26.5	28.0	29.5	31.0	32.0	33.5
	4	10.0	10.5	11.5	12.0	12.5	13.5	14.0	15.0	15.5	16.0	17.0
Base 3	1	15.5	17.0	18.0	19.0	20.0	21.0	22.5	23.5	25.0	25.5	27.0
	2	18.5	20.0	21.5	23.0	24.0	25.0	26.5	28.0	29.5	30.5	32.0
	3	20.5	22.0	23.5	25.0	26.5	28.0	29.5	31.0	32.5	33.5	35.0
	4	10.0	10.5	11.5	12.0	12.5	13.5	14.0	15.0	15.5	16.0	17.0
Build 1	1	17.5	19.0	20.5	21.5	22.5	24.0	25.0	26.5	28.0	29.0	30.0
	2	17.5	19.0	20.5	21.5	22.5	24.0	25.0	26.5	28.0	29.0	30.0
	3	17.5	19.0	20.5	21.5	22.5	24.0	25.0	26.5	28.0	29.0	30.0
	4	10.0	10.5	11.5	12.0	12.5	13.5	14.0	15.0	15.5	16.0	17.0
Build 2	1	16.5	18.0	19.0	20.5	21.5	22.5	24.0	25.0	26.5	27.0	28.5
	2	16.5	18.0	19.0	20.5	21.5	22.5	24.0	25.0	26.5	27.0	28.5
	3	16.5	18.0	19.0	20.5	21.5	22.5	24.0	25.0	26.5	27.0	28.5
	4	10.0	10.5	11.5	12.0	12.5	13.5	14.0	15.0	15.5	16.0	17.0
Peak	1	13.0	14.5	15.0	16.5	17.0	18.0	19.0	20.0	21.0	21.5	22.5
	2	10.5	11.5	12.0	13.0	13.5	14.5	15.0	16.0	16.5	17.0	18.0
Race	All	8.5	9.0	9.5	10.5	11.0	11.5	12.0	13.0	13.0	13.5	14.5
Tran	All	10.0	10.5	11.5	12.0	12.5	3.5	14.0	15.0	15.5	16.0	17.0

Build Week Structuring

Designing a week of training in the Base period is fairly simple when compared with the Build period. Before describing how to plan your training for these more complex Build weeks, we'll first explain what the Build period is about. This will help you understand why the week is designed as it is.

In classic periodization, there are two periods of training that precede the first A-priority events of the season: the Base and Build periods. The most significant difference between these two is how racelike the workouts are in each. In the Base period, the workouts are not necessarily similar to the stresses that will be encountered in the race. The exception is that for ultra-endurance events, such as an ironman-distance triathlon, endurance workouts are similar to what is expected in the race because long, slow distances and hill strength are common to these types of races and to Base training.

In the Build period, the workouts become increasingly similar to racing, culminating in the Peak period, when the workouts are essentially miniraces at levels of intensity greater than those reached on race day. Often, actual races of lower priority may be substituted for workouts in the Build and Peak periods to better prepare for A-priority events.

To properly schedule workouts for the Build period, it's important to know two things: what the demands of your key races are and how your athletic strengths compare with these demands. Build training must focus on areas where there are gaps. In other words, concentrate your training on your key race limiters (see Chapter 3).

Build period planning is not recommended until your limiters have been identified and you have the skills, endurance, and strength to complete your race distance. Many athletes fail to consider their limiters and train blindly. Such pointless training is common and prevents even the very talented from achieving their potential.

Once your limiters have been established, it's a good idea to focus training on them once or twice each week. Assuming you are doing three BT workouts weekly, that means you will have at least one other weekly session dedicated to maintaining your strengths. If your scheduling or recovery considerations mean that you can complete only two key sessions a week, then you should maintain your strengths within one of your BT sessions.

When planning a Build week, it is also necessary to know how quickly you recover from BT workouts of various types. If your recovery is good (diet, rest, low stress, massage, active-recovery sessions, etc.), then it is possible to schedule multiple BT workouts in a week. If recovery is slow, which is often the case with veteran athletes and novices, it may be possible to complete only one or two such sessions in a week of training. Remember that the quality of the BT workouts is far more important than the quantity.

Separate your BT workouts by at least thirty-six hours. For most, forty-eight to sixty hours set aside for recovery is optimal. If your BT session quality suffers, you should extend your recovery time. The majority of each BT session should be done at an intensity that mimics ironman-distance race pace. For most athletes, it is not usually necessary, and may be counterproductive, to train at intensities that are greater than 110 percent of goal-race intensity. In other words, one of the purposes of training in the Build period is to prepare for the exact stresses expected in the race. The closer you get to the race, the more critical this pacing becomes.

With all of this in mind, a typical Build period week of training may look something like this:

Monday	Rest, active recovery or weights
Tuesday	Key-limiter BT
Wednesday	Active recovery, speed skills, and/or rest
Thursday	BT to maintain key strength
Friday	Active recovery, speed skills, and/or rest
Saturday	Key-limiter BT
Sunday	Aerobic maintenance (endurance, force, speed skills)

As the Build period progresses, it is a good idea to combine limiters and strengths into single workouts. After all, a race is not composed of just one element, such as muscular endurance. There are typically many physical abilities challenged within a race. Combining several elements into one session makes training even more racelike.

Elite and experienced athletes may schedule multiple sessions on a given day, but such planning should never compromise recovery. Some athletes may be able to handle two or even three workouts on a recovery day so long as the intensity and duration are low relative to their training load. If training performance is substandard, question your recovery strategy. The all-too-often-chosen solution is to make the easy days a little harder in a poorly thought-out attempt to raise the average training intensity of the week. This approach almost always has just the opposite effect.

The last consideration for this period is the nature of the recovery week that completes each two- to three-week period of race-specific training. The first few days of each of these recovery weeks should be dedicated to rest by including downtime and fewer, shorter, and easier workouts than usual. Near the end of the week, after you are positive that your body is rejuvenating, is a good time to test progress with a time trial or a race. It's a good idea to get in two or more races before the first A-priority events of the season. Not only will these serve as tests of progress, but they will also allow you to practice the strategy and tactics you are considering for the A-priority races.

If all goes well in the Build period, you should come into the Peak period feeling significantly more fit and confident than you did at the end of the Base period.

Key Training Indicators
Heart Rate

Heart-rate monitors for training by heart rate have become a standard tool since the 1980s. In spite of the value a heart-rate monitor lends to training, athletes should avoid relying on it solely, as it is not the only measure that should be monitored.

Heart rate by itself does not tell you how well you're performing in a workout or a race, yet many athletes try to draw conclusions from one number. For example, many athletes believe that if they can't get their heart rate up, they should stop the workout. A low heart rate could be bad, but then again, it might be good. One of the physiological side effects of improving aerobic fitness is an increased heart-stroke volume—more blood is pumped per beat. Simply put, you need to work harder to get your heart rate up owing to your increased fitness. So a low heart rate in a workout or race may be telling you that your fitness is high and to keep going—not that you should stop.

Another misuse of the heart-rate-monitor number is drawing incorrect conclusions about one's state of well-being. Many athletes believe they are overtrained if their resting heart rate is high. It is not possible, however, to reach an accurate conclusion by looking at resting or exercising heart rates because heart rate by itself tells you nothing about performance or well-being. To have meaning, it must be compared with other measures such as RPE, power, and pace (as discussed below).

Heart-rate training zones are best tied to the standard of lactate threshold. Often maximum heart rate is used to determine zones; however, exercising at such intensity may not be safe for some athletes. LT is a better indicator of what the body is experiencing, as percentages of maximum heart rate are not as precise as basing zones on LT. Using the testing protocols discussed in Appendix B, you can establish your heart-rate training zones.

Table 4.4 Cycling Heart Rate Zones

Find your LT pulse (bold) in the Zone 5a column. Read across, left and right, for training zones.

Zone 1	Zone 2	Zone 3	Zone 4	Zone 5a	Zone 5b	Zone 5c
Active Recovery	Extensive Endurance	Intensive Endurance	Threshold Training	Threshold Training	VO$_2$max Intervals	Anaerobic Repetitions
<109	109–122	123–128	129–136	**137–140**	141–145	146+
<110	110–123	124–129	130–137	**138–141**	142–146	147+
<110	110–124	125–130	131–138	**139–142**	143–147	148+
<111	111–125	126–130	131–139	**140–143**	144–147	148+
<112	112–125	126–131	132–140	**141–144**	145–148	149+
<113	113–126	127–132	133–141	**142–145**	146–149	150+

Zone 1	Zone 2	Zone 3	Zone 4	Zone 5a	Zone 5b	Zone 5c
Active Recovery	Extensive Endurance	Intensive Endurance	Threshold Training	Threshold Training	VO$_2$max Intervals	Anaerobic Repetitions
<113	113–127	128–133	134–142	**143**–145	146–150	151+
<114	114–128	129–134	135–143	**144**–147	148–151	152+
<115	115–129	130–135	136–144	**145**–148	149–152	153+
<116	116–130	131–136	137–145	**146**–149	150–154	155+
<117	117–131	132–137	138–146	**147**–150	151–155	156+
<118	118–132	133–138	139–147	**148**–151	152–156	157+
<119	119–133	134–139	140–148	**149**–152	153–157	158+
<120	120–134	135–140	141–149	**150**–153	154–158	159+
<121	121–134	135–141	142–150	**151**–154	155–159	160+
<122	122–135	136–142	143–151	**152**–155	156–160	161+
<123	123–136	137–142	143–152	**153**–156	157–161	162+
<124	124–137	138–143	144–153	**154**–157	158–162	163+
<125	125–138	139–144	145–154	**155**–158	159–163	164+
<126	126–138	139–145	146–155	**156**–159	160–164	165+
<127	127–140	141–146	147–156	**157**–160	161–165	166+
<128	128–141	142–147	148–157	**158**–161	162–167	168+
<129	129–142	143–148	149–158	**159**–162	163–168	169
<130	130–143	144–148	149–159	**160**–163	164–169	170+
<130	130–143	144–150	151–160	**161**–164	165–170	171+
<131	131–144	145–151	152–161	**162**–165	166–171	172+
<132	132–145	146–152	153–162	**163**–166	167–172	173+
<133	133–146	147–153	154–163	**164**–167	168–173	174+
<134	134–147	148–154	155–164	**165**–168	169–174	175+
<135	135–148	149–154	155–165	**166**–169	170–175	176+
<136	136–149	150–155	156–166	**167**–170	171–176	177+
<137	137–150	151–156	157–167	**168**–171	172–177	178+
<138	138–151	152–157	158–168	**169**–172	173–178	179+

Table 4.4 continued

Zone 1	Zone 2	Zone 3	Zone 4	Zone 5a	Zone 5b	Zone 5c
Active Recovery	Extensive Endurance	Intensive Endurance	Threshold Training	Threshold Training	VO_2max Intervals	Anaerobic Repetitions
<139	139–151	152–158	159–169	**170**–173	174–179	180+
<140	140–152	153–160	161–170	**171**–174	175–180	181+
<141	141–153	154–160	161–171	**172**–175	176–181	182+
<142	142–154	155–161	162–172	**173**–176	177–182	183+
<143	143–155	156–162	163–173	**174**–177	178–183	184+
<144	144–156	157–163	164–174	**175**–178	179–184	185+
<145	145–157	158–164	165–175	**176**–179	180–185	186+
<146	146–158	159–165	166–176	**177**–180	181–186	187+
<147	147–159	160–166	167–177	**178**–181	182–187	188+
<148	148–160	161–166	167–178	**179**–182	183–188	189+
<149	149–160	161–167	168–179	**180**–183	184–190	191+
<150	150–161	162–168	169–180	**181**–184	185–191	192+
<151	151–162	163–170	171–181	**182**–185	186–192	193+
<152	152–163	164–171	172–182	**183**–186	187–193	194+
<153	153–164	165–172	173–183	**184**–187	188–194	195+
<154	154–165	166–172	173–184	**185**–188	186–195	196+
<155	155–166	167–173	174–185	**186**–189	190–196	197+
<156	156–167	168–174	175–186	**187**–190	191–197	198+
<157	157–168	169–175	176–187	**188**–191	192–198	199+
<158	158–169	170–176	177–188	**189**–192	193–199	200+
<159	159–170	171–177	178–189	**190**–193	194–200	201+
<160	160–170	171–178	179–190	**191**–194	195–201	202+
<161	161–171	172–178	179–191	**192**–195	196–202	203+
<162	162–172	173–179	180–192	**193**–196	197–203	204+
<163	163–173	174–180	181–193	**194**–197	198–204	205+
<164	164–174	175–181	182–194	**195**–198	199–205	206+

Table 4.5 Running Heart Rates Zones

Find your LT pulse (bold) in the Zone 5a column. Read across, left and right, for training zones.

Zone 1 Active Recovery	Zone 2 Extensive Endurance	Zone 3 Intensive Endurance	Zone 4 Threshold Training	Zone 5a Threshold Training	Zone 5b VO$_2$max Intervals	Zone 5c Anaerobic Repetition
<120	120–126	127–133	134–139	**140**–143	144–149	150+
<120	120–127	128–134	135–140	**141**–144	145–150	151+
<121	121–129	130–135	136–141	**142**–145	146–151	152+
<122	122–130	131–136	137–142	**143**–146	147–152	153+
<123	123–131	132–137	138–143	**144**–147	148–153	154+
<124	124–132	133–138	139–144	**145**–148	149–154	155+
<125	125–133	134–139	140–145	**146**–149	150–155	156+
<125	125–134	135–140	141–146	**147**–150	151–156	157+
<126	126–135	136–141	142–147	**148**–151	152–157	158+
<127	127–135	136–142	143–148	**149**–152	153–158	159+
<128	128–136	137–143	144–149	**150**–153	154–158	159+
<129	129–137	138–144	145–150	**151**–154	155–159	160+
<130	130–138	139–145	146–151	**152**–155	156–160	161+
<131	131–139	140–146	147–152	**153**–156	157–161	162+
<132	132–140	141–147	148–153	**154**–157	158–162	163+
<132	132–141	142–148	149–154	**155**–158	159–164	165+
<133	133–142	143–149	150–155	**156**–159	160–165	166+
<134	134–143	144–150	151–156	**157**–160	161–166	167+
<135	135–143	144–151	152–157	**158**–161	162–167	168+
<136	136–144	145–152	153–158	**159**–162	163–168	169+
<137	137–145	146–153	154–159	**160**–163	164–169	170+
<137	137–146	147–154	155–160	**161**–164	165–170	171+
<138	138–147	148–155	156–161	**162**–165	166–171	172+
<139	139–148	149–155	156–162	**163**–166	167–172	173+
<140	140–149	150–156	157–163	**164**–167	168–174	175+

Table 4.5 continued

Zone 1	Zone 2	Zone 3	Zone 4	Zone 5a	Zone 5b	Zone 5c
Active Recovery	Extensive Endurance	Intensive Endurance	Threshold Training	Threshold Training	VO$_2$max Intervals	Anaerobic Repetition
<141	141–150	151–157	158–164	**165**–168	169–175	176+
<142	142–151	152–158	159–165	**166**–169	170–176	177+
<142	142–152	153–159	160–166	**167**–170	171–177	178+
<143	143–153	154–160	161–167	**168**–171	172–178	179+
<144	144–154	155–161	162–168	**169**–172	173–179	180+
<145	145–155	156–162	163–169	**170**–173	174–179	180+
<146	146–156	157–163	164–170	**171**–174	175–180	181+
<146	146–156	157–164	165–171	**172**–175	176–182	183+
<147	147–157	158–165	166–172	**173**–176	177–183	184+
<148	148–157	158–166	167–173	**174**–177	178–184	185+
<149	149–158	159–167	168–174	**175**–178	179–185	186+
<150	150–159	160–168	169–175	**176**–179	180–186	187+
<151	151–160	161–169	170–176	**177**–180	181–187	188+
<152	152–161	162–170	171–177	**178**–181	182–188	189+
<153	153–162	163–171	172–178	**179**–182	183–189	190+
<154	154–163	164–172	173–179	**180**–183	184–190	191+
<155	155–164	165–173	174–180	**181**–184	185–192	193+
<155	155–165	166–174	175–181	**182**–185	186–193	194+
<156	156–166	167–175	176–182	**183**–186	187–194	195+
<157	157–167	168–176	177–183	**184**–187	188–195	196+
<158	158–168	169–177	178–184	**185**–188	189–196	197+
<159	159–169	170–178	179–185	**186**–189	190–197	198+
<160	160–170	171–179	180–186	**187**–190	191–198	199+
<160	160–170	171–179	180–187	**188**–191	192–199	200+
<161	161–171	172–180	181–188	**189**–192	193–200	201+
<162	162–172	173–181	182–189	**190**–193	194–201	202+

Zone 1	Zone 2	Zone 3	Zone 4	Zone 5a	Zone 5b	Zone 5c
Active Recovery	Extensive Endurance	Intensive Endurance	Threshold Training	Threshold Training	VO$_2$max Intervals	Anaerobic Repetition
<163	163–173	174–182	183–190	**191–194**	195–201	202+
<164	164–174	175–183	184–191	**192–195**	196–202	203+
<165	165–175	176–184	185–192	**193–196**	197–203	204+
<166	166–176	177–185	186–193	**194–197**	198–204	205+
<166	166–177	178–186	187–194	**195–198**	199–205	206+
<167	167–178	179–187	188–195	**196–199**	200–206	207+
<168	168–178	179–188	189–196	**197–198**	199–207	208+
<169	169–179	180–189	190–197	**198–201**	202–208	209+
<170	170–180	181–190	191–198	**199–202**	203–209	210+
<171	171–181	182–191	192–199	**200–203**	204–210	211+

Rating of Perceived Exertion (RPE)

Perceived exertion is one of the best measures of intensity, particularly for experienced athletes. One of the most important skills for a novice athlete to acquire is the ability to link RPE to the other indicators of training intensity. As you increase or decrease pace, your RPE will also change, reflecting greater or lesser stress. RPE used in conjunction with other intensity indicators helps an athlete decide whether or not he or she needs to push harder or back off. For example, a low heart rate and high RPE are a sign that fitness and well-being are probably good. A high heart rate and low RPE suggest that something isn't right. Think your way through the various possibilities.

An example of when to ignore heart rate and rely on RPE involves an athlete who lives at an elevation of 5,000 feet climbing to 14,225 feet. The athlete would use heart rate early in the event but would change to RPE as he progressed higher. Had this athlete stuck exclusively with heart rate, then he might have unnecessarily slowed because altitude and reduced oxygen cause the heart to work harder to get the same amount of oxygen. In other words, a higher heart rate relative to RPE is normal at high altitudes. Another example would be an athlete under increased heat stress. In hot and humid conditions, heart rate can be 5 to 10 bpm above normal. In these situations, the use of RPE is critical for success. The Borg Scale of Perceived Exertion (Table 4.6) is applicable to any sport and is used by sports scientists to determine at what level a subject is working.

Table 4.6 Borg Scale of Perceived Exertion

Zone		RPE	Description
1	Recovery	6	
1	Recovery	7	Very, very light
1	Recovery	8	
2	Extensive Endurance	9	Very light
2	Extensive Endurance	10	
2	Extensive Endurance	11	Fairly light
3	Intensive Endurance	12	
3	Intensive Endurance	13	Somewhat hard
3	Intensive Endurance	14	
4	Subthreshold	15	Hard
5a	Threshold	16	
5b	Anaerobic Endurance	17	Very hard
5b	Anaerobic Endurance	18	
5c	Power	19	Very, very hard
5c	Power	20	Kaboom!

Power

In the same way that heart-rate monitors revolutionized training methods in the early 1980s, powermeters will change the way athletes train. When it comes to cycling performance, comparing heart rate with power (e.g., on a CompuTrainer or with a Power-Tap) is an excellent way to measure changes in fitness. If heart rate is low and power is normal to high when compared with previous performances, then fitness is high. If heart rate is high and power is high, you are probably still building aerobic fitness. If heart rate is low and power is also low, you may be experiencing fatigue, lifestyle stress, or even overtraining.

When doing interval work, even though heart rate and RPE will be higher, the actual work done—power output—will likely decline as you become fatigued. With power, the heart-rate profile will be less steep, but the work done will be steadier. When doing intervals based on heart rate, athletes are, in reality, working much harder than heart rate alone would appear to indicate. Table 4.7 gives an example of intensity relative to the average power produced in a best-effort thirty-minute time trial (CP30). Training by power is discussed further in Chapter 6.

Table 4.7 Power Training Zones

Description	Percentage of CP30
Threshold	100
Cruise intervals	90–100
Sprint triathlon	90–93
Olympic distance	87–90
Half-ironman	80–87
Intensive endurance	73–80
Endurance	67–73
Easy	< 67

Pace

Prior to 1980, training intensity was based primarily on pace. Today, swim and run pace on established courses may be used in conjunction with heart rate, just as power is used on the bike. For example, after running or swimming a given distance at a given heart rate, the resulting time may be compared with previous such tests to gauge progress.

For the experienced athlete, pace is the best gauge for swimming intensity; however, it is less of a consideration for running and least beneficial for cycling owing to changes caused by such variables as wind and hills.

As with the five heart-rate training zones, there are five levels of pace. The steady pace usually forms the bulk of your training program. This is the pace at which you train your oxygen-processing mechanisms, relevant for health and fitness as well as performance.

The following is a five-zone pace scale designed by Dr. John Hellemans of the New Zealand Multisport Training Centre.

1. *Easy*—Easy pace is mainly used for a warm-up or as a main part of a longer session. The pace is very comfortable. Heart rate corresponds to Zone 1 intensity.

2. *Steady*—Steady pace is one gear up whereby the heart rate corresponds to Zone 2 intensity. This is a pace where you can still have a conversation but you are slightly out of breath.

3. *Moderately hard*—This pace requires concentration to maintain the intensity, although when you are fit you can keep this up for a longer period of time. Heart rate corresponds to heart-rate Zone 3 or Zone 4 intensities. The oxygen supply still keeps up with the oxygen demand and therefore your metabolism is still efficient as all the lactate produced is being cleared.

4. *Hard*—At this pace your muscles will accumulate lactate, which causes a heavy sensation and rapid depletion of your energy stores. Heart-rate intensity is threshold.

5. *Very hard*—This is close to maximum pace, also called sustained speed or VO$_2$max pace. Most athletes can sustain this pace for approximately six minutes.

Table 4.8 Estimated Running Zones by Mile Pace

Use your time for a 5km or 10km running race (not triathlon split) to estimate your running zones.

5km	10km	Zone 1	Zone 2	Zone 3	Zone 4	Zone 5a	Zone 5b	Zone 5c
14:15	30:00	6:38+	5:52–6:37	5:27–5:51	5:09–5:26	4:59–5:08	4:37–4:58	4:36–max
14:45	31:00	6:50+	6:02–6:49	5:37–6:01	5:18–5:36	5:07–5:17	4:45–5:06	4:44–max
15:15	32:00	7:02+	6:13–7:01	5:47–6:12	5:27–5:46	5:16–5:26	4:53–5:15	4:52–max
15:45	33:00	7:13+	6:23–7:12	5:56–6:22	5:36–5:55	5:25–5:35	5:01–5:24	5:00–max
16:10	34:00	7:25+	6:33–7:24	6:06–6:32	5:45–6:05	5:34–5:44	5:10–5:33	5:09–max
16:45	35:00	7:36+	6:43–7:35	6:15–6:42	5:54–6:14	5:42–5:53	5:18–5:41	5:17–max
17:07	36:00	7:48+	6:54–7:47	6:25–6:53	6:03–6:24	5:51–6:02	5:26–5:50	5:25–max
17:35	37:00	8:00+	7:04–7:59	6:34–7:03	6:12–6:33	6:00–6:11	5:34–5:59	5:33–max
18:05	38:00	8:11+	7:14–8:10	6:44–7:13	6:21–6:43	6:09–6:20	5:42–6:08	5:41–max
18:30	39:00	8:23+	7:24–8:22	6:53–7:23	6:30–6:52	6:17–6:29	5:50–6:16	5:49–max
19:00	40:00	8:34+	7:35–8:33	7:03–7:34	6:39–7:02	6:26–6:38	5:58–6:25	5:57–max
19:30	41:00	8:46+	7:45–8:45	7:12–7:44	6:48–7:11	6:35–6:47	6:06–6:34	6:05–max
19:55	42:00	8:58+	7:55–8:57	7:22–7:54	6:57–7:21	6:44–6:56	6:14–6:43	6:13–max
20:25	43:00	9:09+	8:05–9:08	7:31–8:04	7:06–7:30	6:52–7:05	6:22–6:51	6:21–max
20:50	44:00	9:21+	8:16–9:20	7:41–8:15	7:15–7:40	7:01–7:14	6:31–7:00	6:30–max
21:20	45:00	9:32+	8:26–9:31	7:51–8:25	7:24–7:50	7:10–7:23	6:39–7:09	6:38–max
21:50	46:00	9:44+	8:36–9:43	8:00–8:35	7:33–7:59	7:18–7:32	6:47–7:17	6:46–max
22:15	47:00	9:56+	8:47–9:55	8:10–8:46	7:42–8:09	7:27–7:41	6:55–7:26	6:54–max
22:42	48:00	10:07+	8:57–10:06	8:19–8:56	7:51–8:18	7:36–7:50	7:03–7:35	7:02–max
23:10	49:00	10:19+	9:07–10:18	8:29–9:06	8:00–8:28	7:45–7:59	7:11–7:44	7:10–max

5km	10km	Zone 1	Zone 2	Zone 3	Zone 4	Zone 5a	Zone 5b	Zone 5c
23:38	50:00	10:31+	9:17–10:30	8:38–9:16	8:09–8:37	7:53–8:08	7:19–7:52	7:18–max
24:05	51:00	10:42+	9:28–10:41	8:48–9:27	8:18–8:47	8:02–8:17	7:27–8:01	7:26–max
24:35	52:00	10:54+	9:38–10:53	8:57–9:37	8:27–8:56	8:11–8:26	7:35–8:10	7:34–max
25:00	53:00	11:05+	9:48–11:04	9:07–9:47	8:36–9:06	8:20–8:35	7:43–8:19	7:42–max
25:25	54:00	11:17+	9:58–11:16	9:16–9:57	8:45–9:15	8:28–8:44	7:52–8:27	7:51–max
25:55	55:00	11:29+	10:09–11:28	9:26–10:08	8:54–9:25	8:37–8:53	8:00–8:36	7:59–max
26:30	56:00	11:40+	10:19–11:39	9:36–10:18	9:03–9:35	8:46–9:02	8:08–8:45	8:07–max
26:50	57:00	11:52+	10:29–11:51	9:45–10:28	9:12–9:44	8:54–9:11	8:16–8:53	8:15–max
27:20	58:00	12:03+	10:39–12:02	9:55–10:38	9:21–9:54	9:03–9:20	8:24–9:02	8:23–max
27:45	59:00	12:15+	10:50–12:14	10:04–10:49	9:30–10:03	9:12–9:29	8:32–9:11	8:31–max
28:15	60:00	12:27+	11:00–12:26	10:14–10:59	9:39–10:13	9:21–9:38	8:40–9:20	8:39–max

Table 4.9 Estimated Swimming Zones by 100-meter or 100-yard Pace

Use your average split time for a 1,000-meter or 1,000-yard time trial.

1,000 m/yd	Zone 1	Zone 2	Zone 3	Zone 4	Zone 5a	Zone 5b	Zone 5c
9:35–9:45	1:13+	1:09–1:12	1:04–1:08	1:01–1:03	0:58–1:00	0:54–0:57	0:53–max
9:46–9:55	1:15+	1:11–1:14	1:06–1:10	1:02–1:05	0:59–1:01	0:55–0:58	0:54–max
9:56–10:06	1:16+	1:12–1:15	1:07–1:11	1:03–1:06	1:00–1:02	0:56–0:59	0:55–max
10:18–10:28	1:18+	1:14–1:17	1:09–1:13	1:05–1:08	1:02–1:04	0:58–1:01	0:57–max
10:29–10:40	1:20+	1:15–1:19	1:10–1:14	1:06–1:09	1:03–1:05	0:58–1:02	0:57–max
10:41–10:53	1:22+	1:17–1:21	1:12–1:16	1:08–1:11	1:05–1:07	1:00–1:04	0:59–max
10:54–11:06	1:23+	1:19–1:22	1:13–1:18	1:09–1:12	1:06–1:08	1:01–1:05	1:00–max
11:07–11:18	1:24+	1:20–1:23	1:14–1:19	1:10–1:13	1:07–1:09	1:02–1:06	1:01–max
11:19–11:32	1:26+	1:21–1:25	1:15–1:20	1:11–1:14	1:08–1:10	1:03–1:07	1:02–max
11:33–11:47	1:28+	1:23–1:27	1:17–1:22	1:13–1:16	1:10–1:12	1:05–1:09	1:04–max
11:48–12:03	1:29+	1:24–1:28	1:18–1:23	1:14–1:17	1:11–1:13	1:06–1:10	1:05–max
12:04–12:17	1:32+	1:26–1:31	1:20–1:25	1:16–1:19	1:13–1:15	1:07–1:12	1:06–max

Table 4.9 continued

1,000 m/yd	Zone 1	Zone 2	Zone 3	Zone 4	Zone 5a	Zone 5b	Zone 5c
12:18–12:30	1:33+	1:28–1:32	1:22–1:27	1:17–1:21	1:14–1:16	1:08–1:13	1:07–max
12:31–12:52	1:35+	1:30–1:34	1:24–1:29	1:19–1:23	1:16–1:18	1:10–1:15	1:09–max
12:53–13:02	1:38+	1:32–1:37	1:26–1:31	1:21–1:25	1:18–1:20	1:12–1:17	1:11–max
13:03–13:28	1:40+	1:34–1:39	1:28–1:33	1:23–1:27	1:20–1:22	1:14–1:19	1:13–max
13:29–13:47	1:41+	1:36–1:40	1:29–1:35	1:24–1:28	1:21–1:23	1:15–1:20	1:14–max
13:48–14:08	1:45+	1:39–1:44	1:32–1:38	1:27–1:31	1:23–1:26	1:17–1:22	1:16–max
14:09–14:30	1:46+	1:40–1:45	1:33–1:39	1:28–1:32	1:24–1:27	1:18–1:23	1:17–max
14:31–14:51	1:50+	1:44–1:49	1:36–1:35	1:31–1:35	1:27–1:30	1:21–1:26	1:20–max
14:52–15:13	1:52+	1:46–1:51	1:39–1:45	1:33–1:38	1:29–1:32	1:23–1:28	1:22–max
15:14–15:52	1:56+	1:49–1:55	1:42–1:48	1:36–1:41	1:32–1:35	1:25–1:31	1:24–max
15:43–16:08	1:58+	1:52–1:57	1:44–1:51	1:38–1:43	1:34–1:37	1:27–1:33	1:26–max
16:09–16:38	2:02+	1:55–2:01	1:47–1:54	1:41–1:46	1:37–1:40	1:30–1:36	1:29–max
16:39–17:06	2:04+	1:57–2:03	1:49–1:56	1:43–1:48	1:39–1:42	1:32–1:38	1:31–max
17:07–17:38	2:09+	2:02–2:08	1:53–2:01	1:47–1:52	1:43–1:46	1:35–1:42	1:34–max
17:39–18:12	2:13+	2:05–2:12	1:57–2:04	1:50–1:56	1:46–1:49	1:38–1:45	1:37–max
18:13–18:48	2:18+	2:10–2:17	2:01–2:09	1:54–2:00	1:50–1:53	1:42–1:49	1:41–max
18:49–19:26	2:21+	2:13–2:20	2:04–2:12	1:57–2:03	1:53–1:56	1:44–1:52	1:43–max
19:27–20:06	2:26+	2:18–2:25	2:08–2:17	2:01–2:07	1:56–2:00	1:48–1:55	1:47–max
20:07–20:50	2:31+	2:22–2:30	2:12–2:21	2:05–2:11	2:00–2:04	1:52–1:59	1:51–max
20:51–21:37	2:37+	2:28–2:36	2:18–2:27	2:10–2:17	2:05–2:09	1:56–2:04	1:55–max
21:38–22:27	2:42+	2:33–2:41	2:22–2:32	2:14–2:21	2:09–2:13	2:00–2:08	1:59–max
22:38–23:22	2:48+	2:38–2:47	2:27–2:37	2:19–2:26	2:14–2:18	2:04–2:13	2:03–max
23:23–24:31	2:55+	2:45–2:54	2:34–2:44	2:25–2:33	2:20–2:24	2:10–2:19	2:09–max
24:32–25:21	3:02+	2:52–3:01	2:40–2:51	2:31–2:39	2:25–2:30	2:15–2:24	2:14–max

Cardiac Drift

Cardiac drift is a condition in which the heart rate increases as the workout progresses despite no increase in pace or power. A lot of factors can cause this effect. Fatigue and hydration status are probably the most common contributors. Heat stress will elevate heart rate, but probably more from the beginning of a workout than over time. However, heat stress speeds the onset of fatigue, thereby contributing to drift.

Most people talk about cardiac drift in terms of a rising heart rate. In endurance events, you may also see a declining heart rate over time. Once you move beyond your endurance base, you start to lose the ability to elevate your heart rate. In other words, your level of muscular fatigue inhibits your ability to place a demand on your cardiovascular system. This effect is seen in nearly all athletes at the latter stages of an ironman-distance race.

Skills

Among endurance athletes, perhaps the most overlooked aspect of performance is skills. Most know the intricacies of interval sessions, hill repeats, tempo workouts, and the like, but many leave movement proficiency to chance.

This is an important point because improving economy of movement means less energy is wasted, allowing faster times and greater duration in training and races. In fact, scientists have demonstrated that three physiological variables are key to endurance performance—aerobic capacity (VO_2max), lactate threshold, and economy. Of these three, the one with the most room for improvement in experienced athletes is usually economy.

The intelligent athlete is constantly thinking about form; however, a particularly good time to work on skills is easy training days. There may be three or four such sessions a week, with each devoted to one or more skills in which you have a personal limiter.

It's possible for an already fit and experienced athlete to improve economy, and therefore performance, by 5 percent or more in a year by working on skills a little bit every week. This level of economy enhancement has been accomplished even with world-class athletes. For the rest of us, there is tremendous room for improvement.

Fundamental Skills

Fundamental skills provide the building blocks upon which proper sport-specific technique rests. Many long-course athletes come to triathlon from a nonathletic background, so building and strengthening fundamental skills is one way to increase economy and reduce susceptibility to injury.

With respect to triathlon, the key fundamental skills can be broken down into two subcategories—movement and awareness skills.

Movement skills such as walking, running, skipping, jumping, hopping, leaping, and bounding assist in the ability to move the body from one place to another. Nonmovement skills, also known as stability skills, consist of balancing, turning, and twisting.

Awareness skills relate to movement of the body within the athletic arena. These skills include spatial awareness, depth perception, proprioception, and rhythm as well as the abilities required to process visual, tactile, and auditory feedback. As children, it is likely that we developed these skills through play—games such as tag, dodge ball, soccer, and baseball all develop a range of fundamental skills. Hence, the triathlete who supplements his or her Prep and early Base periods with cross-training activities gains an added benefit.

Athletes can benefit from incorporating a range of fundamental skills into their training programs. What follows are drills that target fundamental skills. The first two drills are best performed without shoes.

Alphabets: Stand on your right leg and trace large letters of the alphabet with your left foot. Change your support leg and repeat. Close your eyes to increase difficulty.

Leaning tower: Start with two legs as support. Lean forward, backward, and sideways. As skill level increases, move your feet closer together, then try with a single support leg. Once that is mastered, try with your eyes closed.

Single-leg squat touches: Perform a single-leg squat and touch the ground. Touches should be to the front, side, and rear. Use either hand for touching. Touches that involve crossing over the body increase difficulty. When squatting, bend at the ankle, knee, and hip. Movement should be slow and controlled. Once mastered, close your eyes for increased challenge.

Lines: On a bicycle, ride a straight line—edges of roads and parking lots are a good place to find these lines. Drill difficulty can be increased by looking down, looking over one shoulder, or reaching for a water bottle. As skill level increases, try to stay on one edge of the line. This drill should never be attempted in traffic.

In addition to specific drills, activities such as yoga, jazz dance, scrambling, trail running, mountain biking, cross-country skiing, body surfing, and rock climbing as well as team sports such as softball, basketball, and soccer all contribute to increasing your inventory of fundamental skills.

Give consideration to your inventory of fundamental skills. If a particular skill is lacking, then the early season is the perfect time to close this gap. When learning any new skill, we recommend following this progression:

- ◆ Learn the proper movement pattern for the skill.
- ◆ Learn to perform the skill at speed.
- ◆ Increase the load under which the skill is performed.

◆ Increase the situational stress under which the skill is performed (i.e., do it in front of a crowd).

Flexibility—The Benefits of Yoga

When you combine a strong aerobic engine with good position, you get speed. If you want to be an elite athlete, a commitment to a structured flexibility program such as yoga is essential. The fastest elite athletes in our sport have outstanding bike positions. To achieve this takes only time—not genetics, not hard miles, not volume. It is relatively free speed. As well, there are clear benefits to recovery, strength, and economy.

If possible, try to find an instructor who is familiar with multisport or endurance athletes. Discuss what you are trying to achieve and have him or her develop a personal program for you involving a fusion of various styles. When you are tired, stick to mainly floor work. As you learn and become more flexible, begin adding more traditional poses; however, be sure that you are ready for the progression. A few exercises in isolation might not be best for most people.

One to two hours per week is the minimum time that you need to devote to get any results. As for other aspects of your training, the results are related to dedication and consistency.

For working athletes, we recommend a flexibility program rather than a full-on yoga regimen. One session a week is okay, but you should supplement with at least two solo sessions of a minimum of 20 minutes. These sessions should focus on employing the stretching techniques that cover the parts of your body where you hold tension. See Appendix E for a simple flexibility progression.

Your yoga should focus on restorative poses. Avoid strenuous poses. Standing poses can be quite tiring for many people and interfere with recovery. Do a lot of floor work, and keep it mellow.

Many athletes tend to drop yoga sessions unless they schedule them. The first thing they drop is stretching. However, experience has shown that this is a big, big mistake. Stretching has one of the largest rates of return (per hour invested) of all your training activities for an athlete with pretty reasonable flexibility. An inflexible athlete would have an even greater rate of return.

Tips for getting started:

◆ Start slowly.
◆ Learn the fundamentals.
◆ Take your time.
◆ Focus on the seated postures first.
◆ Never force a pose.
◆ Focus on frequency—this is very important.

Running Technique

There is not an athlete in triathlon who doesn't want to figure out how to run faster. One of the most common statements we hear from highly motivated athletes is "I have to run faster."

Too many athletes believe that the quickest way to run faster is to run more and run harder. In fact, most athletes are already running close to, or more than, the run volume required for success. The purpose of this section is to give you some ideas on how to run smarter and how to get the most speed out of a given level of aerobic fitness.

What is good running form? In our experience, it is

Smooth: The athlete looks comfortable; the head, shoulders, and hips are stable and travel in a consistent horizontal plane. In other words, there is very little vertical movement of the head, hips, and shoulders.

Balanced: The athlete's legs, hips, and arms all contribute to forward (as opposed to lateral) movement. Viewed from behind, the athlete has no lateral movement and the pelvis remains stable.

Relaxed: The athlete's shoulders, jaw, and arms are relaxed. The only tension in the body is specific muscle tension required for running. All nonrunning muscles are relaxed. Breathing is rhythmic and calm.

Many athletes who are seeking to improve their running form start with a focus on their feet, in particular their foot strike. Although heel striking is a sign of poor economy, it is a symptom rather than a cause of poor form.

An athlete can easily eliminate a heel strike by pointing his or her toes at the moment of impact. The heel strike will disappear, but the overall stride will be no more economical. In fact, this modification can lead to a wide range of overuse injuries, as the muscles and tendons of the lower leg must decelerate the runner with each impact.

So where to start? The most effective approach is to seek a combination of correct body alignment and cadence. These two factors account for the majority of economy gains that you can attain.

It is worth emphasizing that running speed comes from the correct manipulation of body alignment and cadence. Stride length is the result, not the source, of speed.

Body Alignment

Body alignment is often referred to as an athlete's "pose" or "stance." The proper configuration is for the shoulder, hip, and ankle joints to all be aligned (see Figure 4.1). For ease of explanation, let's call this alignment the "Stance Line."

Once a correct stance is achieved, forward motion is generated by moving the top of the Stance Line forward of the center of balance so that the athlete is, effectively, falling. Cadence is then used to efficiently transform gravity's downward pull into forward motion. Watch any child run and you will quickly see this principle in action. You will also see what happens when the child's cadence is unable to keep up with the body's inclination. They fall down!

Athletes unaccustomed to this stance will find that the position feels very "vertical"; this is a good cue for proper alignment. A technique for maintaining good body alignment is to focus on running tall, with an open chest and pelvis. With experimentation you will find that you need very little tilt of the Stance Line. In fact, at all speeds up to a seven-minute-per-mile pace, the correct stance is very close to vertical.

When making the transition from cycling to running, many athletes find that their hip flexors tighten. Here are three things to watch for when running off the bike:

Figure 4.1

Excessive trunk lean: Athletes with this issue often have good leg turnover but, in order to achieve the required lean, bend at the waist and put their hips behind their Stance Line (see Figure 4.2). An athlete can correct this problem by focusing on: (1) shoulders back, (2) head up, and/or (3) open pelvis.

Tight shoulders: This problem is common when athletes seek to increase their speed. Tension enters the body, and the athlete finds that he or she is shrugging (see Figure 4.3). Focusing on relaxed shoulders is more economical and also increases lung capacity.

Figure 4.2

Head imbalance: Allowing the chin to drop toward the chest or to be excessively elevated will also cause the athlete to be out of balance (see Figures 4.4 and 4.5). Viewed from the side, a runner with efficient form will have his or her neck in alignment with the spine, with no excessive curvature either forward or backward.

Cadence

Watch any good runner within a group of novices, and you will quickly note that he or she almost always has faster leg turnover. Leg turnover in itself is not necessarily economical because it is important for foot strike to occur at the base of the Stance Line. Foot strike in front of the base of the Stance

Figure 4.3

Figure 4.4

Figure 4.5

Line requires the athlete to support the body as it moves over and beyond the point of impact.

When most novice runners seek to increase their cadence, they find that their heart rate increases materially. If this happens to you, shorten your stride until you are able to run at the desired intensity. You will likely feel that you are running with "baby steps," and that is probably the best sign that you have it right. Indeed, in Gordo's running at up to a 5:20-per-mile pace, he continues to feel as if he is running with short strides.

As a general rule, most runners should seek a minimum cadence of 85 cycles per minute for their long slow distance pace and 90 cycles per minute for 10K race pace and faster. If you are currently running with a cadence significantly lower (i.e., more than 5 cycles per minute) than these targets, you should seek to gradually lift your cadence over a series of months. Rapid changes in cadence place undue stress on the body and are not necessary. Your goal should be to move toward these targets over six to eighteen months.

Strides

Though there are many different running drills available, many drills are inappropriate because they reinforce undesirable movement patterns. It is essential that you understand the objective of each drill as it relates to your personal technical limiters. Simply doing drills will not improve running economy. The most effective approach is to use specific drills to teach specific movement patterns and enhance an overall technical awareness.

Strides are our preferred drill for improving run economy. Put simply, Strides are short bursts of fast running with perfect form. Strides are an excellent way to improve running technique and should be incorporated year-round. Tips for Strides:

Protocol: Do Strides at least once a week. A single set per session is sufficient, with six to eight intervals per set.

Recovery: Recover by walking back to the starting point. Remember that this is a skills session, not an aerobic training session. Therefore, the recovery interval is intentionally long to ensure that you maintain perfect form throughout the session.

Timing: Novice athletes should undertake Strides at the start of a run session or as a stand-alone workout. In the early season, athletes may find it time effective to include Strides in advance of a cycling skills session, also known as a skills reverse brick (see "Skills Reverse Brick" sidebar for a session example). Athletes with strong running technique may wish to do Strides at the end of a run workout. All athletes will benefit from using Strides as part of their race and run-test warm-ups.

Pacing: Strides should be done at between 800-meter and 1-mile race pace, about 90 percent of maximum speed. Strides should not be done "all out." Many athletes find it beneficial to start easy and increase speed through each interval as well as across a set of Strides. Quite often, you will find that tired legs will come alive during a set of Strides that starts easy and builds through the set.

Distance: Each stride should last for thirty left-foot strikes, a total of sixty foot strikes. You will find it easiest to count the foot strikes on one side.

Cadence: Aim to complete each stride in about 19 seconds; this implies an overall cadence of 95 cycles per minute. Athletes can enhance leg speed by doing downhill Strides as well as running downwind.

Equipment: Strides are best done barefoot on grass. When weather or safety conditions do not permit bare feet, a very light shoe can be used. Barefoot Strides increase the natural feedback that occurs when an athlete is heel striking. Much of this valuable feedback is lost with a highly cushioned shoe. Check the area first to make sure it is free of glass, thorns, or anything else that may cut. Don't run barefoot if there are breaks in the skin on your feet.

Other Drills

In addition to strides, the following sequence is recommended to help guide you through the correct movement pattern for your legs. When most of us were "taught" to run (something we already knew how to do as children), we were instructed to raise our knees high. The trouble with running with high knees is that athletes tend to draw the heel forward when lifting the knee, which results in a foot strike in front of the Stance Line.

What to do? Rather than focusing on knee lift, focus on heel lift. Heel lift occurs when the heel is drawn up along the Stance Line. But wait! The elite runners that you have seen always have their trailing heel well behind their Stance Line. However, this is a result of their forward velocity, and the correct firing pattern is to draw the heel up the Stance Line.

Mirror Drill: The easiest way to start learning this firing pattern is to use the Mirror Drill. Stand sideways to a full-length mirror and draw your right heel up your left inseam, allowing your toes to hang down (see Figure 4.6). You may find that your heel tends to pull forward or backward. You want your heel to track straight up your inseam (note that your inseam is along your Stance Line when you are standing still). When

Figure 4.6

Figure 4.7

Figure 4.8

learning the Mirror Drill, start with a slow movement, one leg at a time. Keep your foot relaxed as you lift your heel. Once you have mastered the movement pattern, hold your upper body in your running stance. Continue with this drill until you are able to perform rapid heel lifts with perfect tracking and form.

Marching Drill: The next progression is the Marching Drill. With a full-length mirror at your side for feedback, alternate heel lifts. Start slowly and gradually speed your transitions from leg to leg. When you feel comfortable with your form, take this drill outside and slowly move forward while combining perfect heel lift with slow forward motion and proper arm carriage. Remember that the goal of this drill is to teach your legs the correct movement pattern. The speed of forward motion does not matter. Indeed, many athletes will find that they make very little forward progress at all.

Toe Drill: When you feel that you have mastered the Marching Drill, you can progress to the Toe Drill. In the Toe Drill, you complete each heel lift by moving onto the toe of the supporting leg (see Figures 4.7 and 4.8). This drill enhances your proprioceptive skills and increases pelvic stability. The Toe Drill should be done with slow to moderate pacing, as its benefits are balance and strength related.

Skip Drill: The final step in the drill progression is to add a skip into the Toe Drill. This drill is called the Skip Drill. As you move onto your toe, insert a slight forward skip. The Skip Drill enables you to increase your cadence and train the rapid firing of the muscles required to generate heel lift. When done correctly, the head, shoulders, and hips are stable with minimal vertical lift.

The Toe and Skip Drills are complementary and can be included in your warm-up or inserted into the middle of the walk-back recovery used during Strides.

Adaptation

When you are making changes to your running form, your average pace may decrease. Endure the adaptation phase, as improved running economy is one of the easiest ways to improve your run speed. Genetics will set the upper limit on your aerobic gains; dedication and attention to detail set the limits on your running form. Superior technical form can enable an athlete to race beyond his or her inbuilt aerobic limitations.

We'll leave you with a quotation from one of Gordo's New Zealand–based running coaches. When asked to define running form, he replied, "It's what you're left with when you're buggered." For long-distance triathlon, the athletes who can hold form the longest have a clear advantage over their rivals.

Running Drills

These drills can be used as part of a warm-up for a sustained speed session and as part of a running-strength/core-conditioning session. Some of these drills require a fair degree of coordination. If you are doing the drills only one to two times per week, give your muscles plenty of time to "learn" correct technique. Some of the drills will be a little awkward at first. This is normal.

With economy training, it's best to do short workouts frequently rather than long ones infrequently. Once the nervous system begins to tire or you experience difficulty maintaining focus on technique, no further improvements will take place. For the same reason, these workouts are best early in a session. Don't do them when fatigued.

Though these drills can be done anywhere, doing them on a soft surface is highly recommended. Note that the explosive drills are stressful on the body. Start slowly with a small number of repetitions. Typically, we recommend a selection of drills four to six times for 20 to 80 meters. In between the drills, jog easily or walk. Because these drills are either technique or strength oriented, there is no need for concern about average heart rates.

Downhill Strides: After a warm-up, run down a very slight grade for 20 seconds at about the pace you would run a 400-meter race. In other words, the pace is well short of a sprint but is fairly quick. Run six to eight of these Strides, relaxing during each. Walk

Skills Reverse Brick

Doing a traditional brick means that you would be fatigued for the Strides. For those of you who want to improve your running form and economy, it is essential that you be fresh and relaxed when doing Strides.

Run 10 to 15 minutes at an easy pace to warm up, then do six to eight Strides with walk-backs; focus on cadence and run easy to steady for the rest of the workout.

Transition

Bike 10 to 15 minutes easy: low-cadence riders focus on a slightly higher cadence, then begin speed drills—dominant leg, single leg (if on trainer), and/or spin-ups. Continue to focus on cadence and ride easy to steady pace for the rest of the workout.

Tips for Running Strides

1. Relax, particularly your shoulders, upper back, and jaw.
2. Concentrate; know what aspects of your form you are trying to improve.
3. Remember that the walk-back is essential. Take your time with the recovery. This is a skills session. The rest of your week is for adding endurance.
4. Do your Strides with bare feet wherever safe to do so.

back after each Stride, taking about 90 seconds to do so. Walking is important for the success of this workout—don't run the recoveries.

Uphill Strides: Hills and stairs can also be used to enhance heel lift. Athletes can use short-duration stair and hill repeats (on long recoveries) to help increase proper heel lift. When using hills and stairs for technical improvement, interval duration should be short and recovery periods long. The best stairs for this kind of work are the "half stairs" found in most stadium bleachers. Remember that the goal is to train your ability to rapidly lift your heel up your Stance Line. Run six to eight Strides, as before, and walk back after each.

Plyometrics: In a weekly session, spend 10 to 20 minutes working on power with plyometric exercises. Just as with uphill running, this type of exercise has been shown to improve economy in runners. This form of training is best done during the Base period. Be careful with plyometrics because the risk of injury with certain types of exercises is great.

Sideways Running: No crossover, almost like a skip. Traveling in one direction, bring your back foot and leg up to your lead foot and leg without passing it. Move your lead foot away and forward and then bring your rear foot up again. You are almost bouncing forward but going sideways and not crossing the legs.

Sideways Crossovers: The same as sideways running, only this time you cross over and rotate your hips and shoulders as the left leg moves in front of and then behind the right leg. Think fast feet on this one. It's best to start slow and then build up the speed.

Backward Running: Hold normal running form and jog easily backward. Speed can be increased over time. You can also do quick accelerations to forward running from the backward running.

Hands-on-Head Running: Alternate between normal running and hands-on-head running. If you have any lateral movement in your normal running gait, then it will become more pronounced. This is a good drill for promoting running stability.

Front Bench Drill: Face a bench and place your left leg on the bench. Draw the right heel quickly up toward your butt (see Figure 4.9). The goal is a quick movement up and a minimization of ground contact time. Hold arms in regular running position. Start with ten repetitions with each leg and build gradually toward thirty. Once you hit thirty repetitions, drop back down to twenty and add another set. The purpose of this drill is to train the ability of the leg to fire quickly and lift the heel up the Stance Line. This is an explosive drill and should be done only by strong and experienced athletes.

Rear Bench Drill: Facing away from the bench, place your left leg up on the bench behind you (knee bent, toe resting on the bench), draw your right heel up toward your butt, and hold your arms in normal running position (see Figure 4.10). You may find that you need to do a little jump with your right leg to get it off the ground. The resting leg does not contribute anything to this drill (aside from balance). Aim for a quick action with minimal ground contact time. Start with ten repetitions with each leg and build gradually toward thirty. Once you hit thirty repetitions, drop back down to twenty and add another set. Like the Front Bench Drill, this is an explosive drill that should be done only by strong and experienced athletes.

Figure 4.9

Knee Lift: Come up onto the ball of your left foot while raising your right knee. Grab your right knee and lift up while maintaining proud form. If you have trouble with balance, keep your supporting foot flat on the ground. Speed is not important on this one.

Quick Feet: For this quickness drill, take baby steps and work on a very, very fast leg action. Arms and feet move very quickly. There should be little in the way of knee action; movement is on and off the balls of the feet. Forward speed is not important, as the goal is to quickly fire the legs so that the heel travels up the Stance Line.

Figure 4.10

Bounding: Running tall, extend the push-off phase and bound. Relax the shoulders and use your arms as part of the drive phase (see Figure 4.11). This is a plyometric drill designed to build run-specific strength; it can be incorporated into warm-ups, hill repeats, and endurance running sessions.

Loping Run: From a crouched position, bound forward with a side-to-side component. Your feet should strike the ground about 5 feet apart. Rather than driving forward, the body is driven side to side. In the previous drill, you push straight ahead; in this drill, your arms swing from side to side.

Two-Legged Jumps: This is a great drill to load the legs before doing an interval, or just as a drill on its own. Swing the arms forward when jumping. Start from a low position. Absorb the impact by bending the knees quickly on

Figure 4.11

landing. The legs act like springs, coiling down on impact and springing forward when jumping. It is important that the legs absorb the impact, rather than the knees and hips.

Low Walking: Get into a crouch with your thighs parallel to the ground and arms folded across your chest. Walk around in this position, or stay still and (ever so slightly) oscillate up and down. Maintain until the quads start to burn, then maintain some more.

Cycling Skills

Bike-handling skills are perhaps the most neglected single aspect of cycling. Triathletes with superior bike-handling skills will complete their bike legs faster, more comfortably, and with lower energy consumption. This leaves them with more energy for the run. Those who have difficulty cornering, descending, and handling the bike in the wind should address those specific areas over the off-season and early Base period. Here are a few basic cycling skills and how to go about developing them.

Pedaling

Pedaling a bike seems simple, but few triathletes are really good at it. When you ride with someone who pedals efficiently, there is an obvious difference, but it is difficult to describe. To improve your pedaling skills, it's important to smooth out the leg's directional changes at the top and bottom of the stroke.

The best place to practice pedaling skills is on an indoor trainer, as there will be no distractions such as traffic, dogs, or other riders to break your concentration. The sound of the indoor trainer can also be a valuable feedback device for an athlete seeking to smooth his or her pedaling stroke. Here are a few pedaling drills.

Horizontal Pedaling: Don't think about the pedal stroke as being up and down or even circular. Think of it as horizontal; at the top and bottom of the stroke your legs are transitioning to go the other direction—either forward and down or back and up. An increase in energy output here decreases the need for a very high effort at 3 o'clock.

There are several elements of the stroke you can focus on to develop this horizontal-pedaling skill. The best mental focus for most riders involves driving the toes toward the ends of their shoes at the top of each stroke. Another mental cue that works for some is scraping mud off at the bottom. Yet a third focus involves throwing the knees over the handlebars. Concentrate on only one of these at a time.

Isolated Leg Training (ILT): While riding on an indoor trainer, place a chair on either side of the bike. Place one foot on a chair and pedal with the other for 30 seconds, focusing on your critical-stroke mental cue from above. Then switch legs and pedal for 30 seconds with the other, still focusing on your technique. Keep your cadence at around 90 rpm throughout. After working both legs, pedal normally for another minute with both legs, sustaining the same sensation of proper technique. Repeat several times.

Dominant Leg: It's not safe to do ILT on the road, but a drill that can be done anywhere you ride is the Dominant Leg drill. While pedaling with both feet clipped into the pedals, use one leg to do almost all of the work for 30 seconds while the other leg is "lazy." Otherwise, this drill is just like the ILT drill. Pay attention to the road—don't watch your feet.

Heel above Pedal: Don't allow your heel to drop below the level of the pedal on the downstroke—keep the heels slightly elevated. This effectively "rotates" the crankset forward and sets you up for horizontal pedaling. It will take some getting used to, and you'll probably find that your legs become fatigued sooner for the first few days after you adopt this technique if you've been an "ankler" in the past.

Increased Cadence: Mashing is not economical. Continually working on raising your cadence improves your economy. Each of us has a comfortable cadence range. Any time we get outside it, we feel sloppy. By discovering your range and staying near the top end of it several times each week, you can shift your comfortable range upward. One way to do this is to buy a handlebar computer with a cadence monitor and check it during your rides.

Spin-ups: This drill helps you become more economical at higher cadences. Either on the road or on an indoor trainer, while riding in a low gear, gradually increase your cadence over a 30-second period until you begin to bounce on the saddle. Then slow the cadence until you are no longer bouncing and hold it for a few more seconds. The key to this drill is relaxation. Relax your toes, your grip on the bars, and your face. Try to be as smooth and relaxed as possible. Make it seem almost effortless. Do several of these within a ride, separating them with a few minutes of "normal" cadence.

Pedal Recovery: What you do with the leg that is on the recovery side of the stroke is critical to your economy. If this leg rests on the pedal, the other leg will have to work harder to lift it. Be careful not to pull up with the recovery leg (except when climbing or sprinting) because it will cause a tremendous waste of energy. Instead, try to simply "unweight" the recovery pedal. In other words, if you weren't clipped in, the weight of that leg would be taken off the pedal as it came back up. In reality, this won't happen because of the centrifugal force of pedaling, but we can move closer to this ideal.

Balance

You probably learned to balance a bike as a child, and how to do it never crosses your mind while riding now. It's pretty simple. However, situations may arise during a race or ride that challenge your balancing skills. For example, you might need to avoid a crash that happens unexpectedly right in front of you, or a dog may run onto the road and hit your wheel. These situations require more balance skill than simply riding a straight, unobstructed line down the road.

Some drills can help you become more adept at balancing the bike. Always do them away from traffic and obstructions that may cause an accident. Seldom-used parking lots are often a good choice. Here are a few examples.

Bottle Pickup: Place your water bottle on the pavement while riding slowly. Then turn around and come back to pick it up. To make these moves, you will need to stop pedaling and keep your foot low on the side you lean to while ensuring that the front wheel stays straight with the frame. Go slowly at first, and as you get the hang of it, gradually go faster. A tall bottle will help you get started, but then progress to a shorter bottle. When this starts to feel easy, try placing the bottle on its side so that you have to reach lower to pick it up.

Slalom Ride: Set up four or five water bottles about 8 feet apart in a straight line. Practice riding a slalom course through the bottles by leaning the bike—not your body—to the inside of each turn. Take one or three pedal strokes between bottles so that the inside pedal is always up. It should feel like a rhythmic dance when done smoothly. As you get better, try riding faster.

Bottle Jump: Lay an empty plastic water bottle on its side on the pavement. Ride at it fast several times and attempt to jump the bottle without touching it. Try it in both the upright and crouched positions.

Aero Position

When it comes to riding a bike on a flat, level course, aerodynamic drag is the greatest challenge. At speeds greater than about 12 mph (20 kph), more than half of the total mechanical work done by the rider is spent overcoming air resistance. Air resistance increases exponentially relative to velocity rather than linearly as you might expect. In other words, as you speed up, air resistance increases at an ever-increasing rate. At 25 mph (40 kph), penetrating the air makes up 82 percent of the total resistance that must be overcome. When riding into a headwind, the rider's resulting velocity is essentially increased by the speed of the wind, requiring even greater effort to overcome drag. On cold days, the air's resistance is greater yet because cold air is denser.

Most of this air resistance is a result of the frontal area presented to the wind by the rider's body. The greater the frontal area, the greater the air resistance. Compared with sitting upright on the bike with the hands on the tops of the handlebars, a standard aero position reduces frontal area by more than 21 percent on average.

Though aerodynamics is an important consideration for long-distance triathlon, the criteria of safety, comfort, and power production tend to dominate the position. Athletes should remember that the most aerodynamic position is seldom the optimal position for long-course racing.

Braking

To control speed, the rear brake is used more often than the front. This brake is often "feathered," meaning that pressure is applied gradually and in small amounts to reduce speed, as when preparing for a corner. In an emergency situation where an immediate stop is needed, both brakes are applied, with the front brake given the most force. In such a situation you should also slide back on the saddle to weight the rear wheel to prevent it from skidding and losing control. This position also helps to prevent an "end-o," as in end over end.

When descending a hill, you must be careful when using the front brake. Pulling it aggressively can easily result in a crash. Apply the rear brake primarily on a fast descent, feathering the front brake only if more slowing power is needed. It is most stable to do the majority of braking before heading into a turn; braking in the middle of a turn can unbalance a bike and result in a crash.

Cornering

One of the most dangerous times in a ride, especially a fast one, comes when negotiating corners. The first rule of cornering is not to brake in the corner. If the turn is free of gravel and water, you should be able to take it at full speed by leaning. If it's necessary to slow down, brake before you get into the turn. Then let go of the brake levers as the turn begins.

The most important time in taking a corner is the early part. If the critical speed and line you have selected are right, then you will have no problems. Practice approaching corners repeatedly at various speeds. Make it second nature to judge how fast to take them. The line you select depends on your speed. A fast speed requires a more gradual and sweeping turn than does slow cornering.

Sit in the middle of your saddle, not on the nose or back end of it. This position will help you better maintain balance. As the turn starts, stop pedaling so that the inside knee is high, put most of your weight on the outside pedal, and lean to the inside. The lean of the bike should be greater than the lean of your upper body. To accomplish this, keep your head upright so that the line of the eyes is parallel to the surface of the road. Never lean your head into a corner.

When the bike becomes more upright as you come out of the corner, begin to pedal again. It is common to stand up out of a corner and accelerate.

Many athletes are afraid to corner. Given that confidence is essential for good cornering, these athletes will benefit from pre-race reconnaissance in which the technical aspects of the bike leg are reviewed, ridden, and practiced. Large time savings can be easily achieved from a detailed review of technical sections. These time savings require no additional fitness, merely an investment of time. Race week is an excellent time for undertaking these activities, particularly when a friend is willing to offer car support.

Climbing

Body mass has a lot to do not only with how well you climb but also with how you climb. Smaller riders (less than 2 pounds of body weight for every inch of height) usually climb best when out of the saddle, whereas bigger riders (more than about 2.3 pounds per inch) climb more effectively seated. Top riders between these extremes often alternate between sitting and standing when climbing but spend more time seated. The standing position is less economical on a moderate grade, but on a steep hill standing reduces the feeling of effort.

When starting a long, steady climb, select a lower gear so that the cadence is relatively high. As you progress up the hill, shift to higher gears. This helps to prevent fatiguing muscles early in the climb, allowing you to finish strongly. Doing it the other way around—going from a high to a lower gear—is associated with slowing down. In a high gear, your cadence may be as low as 60 rpm. The lower your cadence, the greater the strain on your knees and muscles. Even if you spin at 100 rpm on the flats, you'll likely find that a slower cadence is more effective when climbing.

If alternating between sitting and standing positions during the climb, shift to a higher gear while standing and back to a lower gear for sitting down, especially near the bottom of the climb, when your gear is somewhat lower. You can't spin as fast when standing, so a higher gear is necessary then. Near the top of the climb, you may not need to shift up because the gear will already be high.

When standing, allow the bike to sway gently from side to side without weaving off line. Do not exaggerate this movement. It should happen naturally as the pedal goes down and the hand on the same side pulls to counterbalance the leg force.

When seated, scoot back on the saddle and place your hands on the brake hoods or bar tops rather than on the drops. This position will keep your head up so you can better see what's ahead and open up your chest to allow for easier breathing. Upon standing, grip the brake hoods to better balance the bike. Keep the grip light. Squeezing the bar does nothing to improve climbing and only wastes energy. Bernard Hinault, one of France's greatest riders, used to say that when climbing he kept his fingers as loose as if he was playing a piano.

If the front wheel veers off line with every stroke due to using too high a gear, locking the elbows, or choking the handlebar, the rolling resistance increases by up to 30 percent. Don't make climbing any harder than it already is. Pay close attention to maintaining a straight line.

Descending

Coming back down a hill at high speed requires concentration and trust. You must concentrate on the road ahead, potential dangers on the side of the road (pedestrians, dogs, deer, cars), and other riders and traffic around you. You must also trust your bike and your handling skills. If these are questionable, slow down. It's better to lose a few seconds in a descent than to make a trip to the emergency room.

Most riders have a fear threshold—a speed above which they feel out of control. As you become more experienced at descending, your threshold will rise, but it will never go away. When the threshold approaches, the tendency is to grab the brakes and hang on for dear life. This could make matters worse as the heat buildup from the friction of brake pad against rim may cause the brakes to begin to fail.

Slowing down on a descent is an art form based on using your body as a sail to control speed, evenly distributing your weight between the front and rear wheels, and briefly and repeatedly applying the brakes, using the rear brake primarily. This system allows the brake pads and rim to cool between applications.

If speed is your goal on a descent, the tucked position with the hands on the aerobars, the back flat with head close to the hands, knees in, and the cranks parallel with the road surface will let you fly. If your skills are solid and you have confidence in them, you can descend on the aerobars provided there are no side streets, blind corners, traffic, or other potential dangers.

Drafting

Although draft-legal racing is changing the way elite athletes are training, drafting applies only to short-course triathlon. However, solid drafting skills are beneficial even for long-course triathletes when riding in large groups and for overall bike-handling skills. In addition, drafting the wheel of a stronger rider can increase the quality of specific goal workouts. Drafting can also save your workout if your energy begins to run low because the power requirement when drafting can be reduced by as much as 39 percent, depending on how many riders are ahead of you.

When drafting, follow the other rider's wheel, staying 6 to 24 inches behind and a couple of inches to the side so you can see ahead. The side you're on should be slightly downwind. Don't look at the other rider but rather at the hub of your lead rider's wheel or his or her hip. Sighting on the hip keeps your eyes up a little higher so you can see down the road and also be aware of the lead rider's slowing cadence. Use your peripheral vision to see what he or she is doing. Never overlap the leading wheel.

An effective way to learn to draft is to ride with road racers on their weekly club rides. Be sure to leave your aerobars at home.

If you are a tentative rider, then you need to realize that you must face your fears to overcome them. The fastest way to improve is to build your skills and confidence gradually. Practice your personal technical limiters in safe, comfortable environments at low speed. As your confidence improves, increase drill difficulty and riding speed. Always remember to breathe when feeling nervous; this reduces the tension in your body and will enable smoother movement patterns. All of the above skills are areas in which a skilled rider can pick up "free speed" in an ironman-distance race (with the exception of drafting, of course!).

Recommended Reading

Crouch, Jean. *The Runner's Yoga Book*. Berkeley, CA: Rodmell Press, 1990.

Evans, Mark. *Endurance Athlete's Edge*. Champaign, IL: Human Kinetics, 1997.

Hellemans, Dr. John. *The Training Intensity Handbook*. Napier, New Zealand: KinEli Publishing, 1998.

Progressions for Athlete and Coach Development. Developed by Human Kinetics for U.S.A. Swimming, 1999.

Romanov, Dr. Nicholas. *The Pose Method of Running* (video). Romanov Academy of Sports Science, 1997.

Scott, Dave. *Dave Scott's Triathlon Training*. New York: Fireside, 1986.

Sources

Personal conversations with coaches Dr. John Hellemans and Mark Elliott, New Zealand Multisport Training Centre run sessions.

Chapter 5

Training for the Swim

Technique is a choice.
—Todd Kemmerling, coach

Because the swim is the shortest of the three events in an ironman-distance triathlon, many athletes are tempted to do the bare minimum in their swim preparation. Although this strategy can make sense for strong swimmers as well as severely time-constrained athletes, swim training provides a range of benefits to the endurance athlete.

In addition to becoming a better swimmer, the benefits associated with swim training are:

◆ **Nonimpact aerobic work:** Swimming provides additional aerobic training in a low-impact environment. This combination enables most athletes to achieve a greater volume of aerobic work without compromising their recovery from their other training.

◆ **Recovery:** Because it promotes overall circulation, swimming can be used for active-recovery sessions. In addition, many athletes find water to be a calming influence that reduces their overall stress levels.

◆ **Improved race efficiency:** For slower swimmers especially, the reduction in time spent in the water means that in a race situation, they are able to start replenishing themselves sooner. Although there are often greater time savings to be found in focused bike and run training, decreasing the time spent in the water can have clear nutritional advantages for an ironman-distance athlete.

Technique

As water is far denser than air, effective swimming starts with becoming comfortable moving through this alien environment. Humans spend the majority of their time upright and out of the water, so there are strong built-in urges that need to be overcome for successful triathlon swimming.

Essentially, there are two ways to swim faster. The first is to decrease drag by streamlining body position, and the second is to increase propulsion by improving aerobic and anaerobic fitness. Of these two, scientific studies have found that reducing drag has the potential to produce the greatest gains. Drag is the retarding force created by turbulence around the body as it moves through the water. The more streamlined the body is, the lower the resulting drag force.

If there were only two things you could do to improve your swimming, they would have to be increasing workout frequency (not high yardage) and a focus on technical improvement. Technique and the ability to maintain stroke mechanics over time are the most important aspects of swimming for all athletes. Only after these aspects are established should you focus on increasing your endurance and, ultimately, adding ME sessions.

Given that swimming is a very technique-intensive sport, workout frequency plays an important role. Specifically, it is difficult to achieve a material improvement without a minimum of three 60-minute swims per week.

There is a natural progression for most swimmers:

1. Develop an efficient body position by focusing on balance, relaxation, and smoothness through all aspects of the swimming cycle.
2. Increase the effectiveness of each stroke by improving your catch and pull mechanics.
3. Using superior balance and stroke mechanics, increase stroke rate while maintaining technical excellence and distance per stroke.

Focusing on bilateral breathing can greatly increase swim economy and help you learn to relax in the water. However, you need to be willing to endure the transition period, where you may slow as your body adjusts to the new movement patterns. By having patience, you will become a more efficient swimmer. In triathlons, efficiency may not always translate to improved swim times; however, reduced energy expenditure in the water will translate to more energy for your bike and run.

Triathletes who come from a nonswimming background have to remember that they have the experience of the average 9- to 12-year-old! In order to reach your swimming potential, you must build your fundamentals. This means a commitment to improving your body position in the water. Building a bigger engine does not help if you are dragging your butt through the water. Focusing on improving your technique does not imply doing drills all the time, but it does mean constantly thinking of your stroke mechanics and working to make stroke improvements during each and every interval and set.

Key Stroke Issues

Ever watch elite swimmers? The key elements of modern freestyle are:

◆ Horizontal body with no vertical shoulder movement on entry.

◆ Immediate catch with vertical alignment of hand, wrist, and forearm—minimal downward pressure post-entry and rapid transition to horizontal pull. This is a clear limiter for virtually all triathletes.

◆ Head down at all times (look down or to the side when breathing).

◆ Hips and shoulders rotate together and to the same degree.

◆ Legs are kept within the body shadow.

◆ Kick rotates with hips.

◆ Upper arm aligned with shoulders for pull and recovery (tough for swimmers who have inflexible shoulders).

◆ Streamlined feet.

For the novice swimmer, the first movement following entry is to push the arm down—this is particularly common in swimmers with weak deltoids and shoulder rotators. Pushing the arm down lifts the upper body and drops the hips. This position feels comfortable because the head comes out of the water and the face is exposed for the breath. Although the swimmer is comfortable, he or she slows greatly at every breath.

Learning to keep your head in the water will help you keep your hips higher and make you faster. If you have trouble getting to the air, force yourself to rotate your hips, then your chin, a little farther. A good cue for this technique is to "breathe from your hips."

The paragraphs below discuss the major technical challenges facing triathletes and some ideas for addressing them. How do you know if these issues apply to you? The quickest and most effective way to find out is to have a friend videotape you from the front, back, and side while swimming freestyle. If you have never seen yourself swim, it will likely prove to be a shocking experience. Take heart in the fact that the more technical issues you have with your stroke, the easier it will be for you to improve . . . if you are committed to technical improvement.

Balance: Improved balance and high hips are the quickest way to faster times. Side-kicking drills can be very useful to improve your overall balance as well as your comfort in the water. These drills are discussed in more detail below.

Head position: It is instinct for us to want to have our whole head out of the water when we breathe. It is also instinct to want to be completely vertical when breathing. Both of these urges are present in all swimmers; the only difference is the magnitude of stress required to make them apparent. When swimming, your head should be steady, in line with the spine, and looking down at all times. The breath cycle is initiated by the hips and shoulders rotating together and completed with a slight head rotation that is led by the chin. Focus on keeping your head down, as this position will keep your hips up. If you lift your head when you breathe, correcting this error should be your sole objective until you have mastered the technique!

When breathing, remember to swivel your head and rotate your chin up for air, then turn your chin back down to swim and exhale, always keeping your head in the water. Hips lead your chin. By starting at the hips, you get a solid rotation and also engage your trunk and back in the stroke.

Exhale underwater: If you find that you don't have enough time to breathe or that you are not getting a full breath, then ensure that you are exhaling in the water. If you try to exhale, then inhale with your face out of the water, you may get only a partial inhalation. As soon as you are able to get a full breath, the urge to lift your head will be reduced.

Offside arm: In an attempt to push their heads out of the water, many swimmers will push down with their offside arm when breathing. Remember to let your leading hand float for a little bit when breathing.

Pressing the T: If you have a tendency to drag your butt through the water (uphill swimming), keep your head down and focus on pressing your chest down in the water while maintaining a long body line (think about a T with the top running between your shoulders). Many swimmers think they are pressing the chest downward when they are really leaning their heads, so watch for this mistake.

Distance per stroke: Focus on a long, relaxed, smooth stroke. Count your strokes and try to maximize distance per stroke.

Hand entry: Swimmers who have a tendency to cross over should focus on "skating" from hip to hip. Swim as if you are on two rails, rotating from rail to rail.

Legs together: For scissor-kickers, this is an excellent time to relax and work on keeping your legs in your body shadow. Swimmers typically split their legs when they are uncomfortable rotating or breathing. Improving your in-water comfort through balance drills can quite often eliminate this challenge. Another useful technique is to create a set of "shackles" from rubber tubing. The ankles are given enough room to kick, but the tubing prevents a large split in the legs.

The Progression

There is a progression of skills to learn in the water that should be established prior to endurance and ME work. These drills are best mastered in order and done frequently. The first two things for any swimmer to master are balance and body rotation. For any time of the year, sets that include bilateral breathing, single-stroke change, and triple-stroke change are beneficial. A complete (and highly recommended) explanation of many of these drills can be found in Terry Laughlin's "Total Immersion" series of books and videos. Terry's teaching methods have helped thousands of adults become better, more confident swimmers.

Remember that the most important part of these drills is learning to improve your balance, body position, and in-water comfort. A pull-buoy gives you an artificial aid for achieving better body position, and for this reason is not recommended when drilling. When learning these drills, many athletes will benefit from the use of short fins. As your technical competence improves, you should perform the drills without fins.

Practical examples of how to incorporate these drills are included in Appendix C.

Balance

Most triathletes have balance as a limiter. How do you know if your balance is not a limiter? If you can swim all but your toughest main sets with three-stroke breathing; you are comfortable with five-stroke breathing; and you can swim hard with offside, two-stroke breathing, then you are likely a well-balanced swimmer. Until you are in this stage, you are likely to gain materially from working to improve your balance. As we need to be relaxed to learn any new skills, you should always do your drills at a comfortable pace.

It is best not to use any swim gear, such as fins or kickboards, for balance drills; however, you can begin the side-kicking drills with fins. Most athletes will find that after a few weeks, they do not need fins. In fact, being able to comfortably do these drills without fins is a clear indication of improved balance.

Drills to improve balance consist primarily of learning to balance and breathe while kicking and moving through different orientations. Most athletes will find the following progression beneficial to improving their balance; all of these drills are done while maintaining a relaxed kick.

Back Kick: Start by kicking on your back with your hands at your side. Kick at a relaxed pace and breathe calmly. Push your shoulders down and feel your hips lift. Become comfortable with having your goggles slightly underwater, with only your mouth and nose out of the water.

Back Kick Twist: Keep your head still and face pointing up at all times. Rotate your hips and shoulders together so that your body moves to a 45-degree angle. Pause for at least three breaths on each side and when you return to the middle.

Back Kick Twist Down: Establish a relaxed position on your back, rotate to your side, stabilize, now swivel your chin so that you are looking straight down at the bottom of the pool, swivel your chin back up, stabilize, and move back to the middle. Now do the same thing on the other side.

Back Kick Change: This is the same drill as the preceding one, but now you change sides by rolling across your front (rather than onto your back). If you have trouble with the transition, then pause on your front and slow the movement down.

Some tips for the drills:

◆ Make sure you are doing transitions in both directions. You will quickly notice that you have a side and a rotational direction that feels more comfortable. Work to improve your limiting side for the most technical gains.

◆ Remember that your goal is to become balanced at all times of the rotation. Your speed down the pool is meaningless.

◆ Keep your intensity down and rest periods long. You want to have absolutely perfect technique. You may think that the intensity is too low, but the concentration required for perfect swimming will leave you fatigued. Let your bike and run training take care of your cardiovascular needs. Successful long-distance swimming is about having the lowest energy consumption for a given pace.

◆ Relax your face and neck, particularly when you are breathing. Muscular tension lowers economy of movement.

◆ If you find that you are not traveling in a straight line, then you are likely curving your body toward the direction that you are going. In other words, you have a banana shape, with your hips being pushed away from your body.

Once you have mastered these drills, you will be ready to move on to the more difficult side-kick drills.

Side-Kick: With both arms at your sides, kick on your side for an entire length of the pool. Rotate your chin to breathe while keeping your head aligned with your spine and your body in alignment (think surfboard rather than noodle). When you are well balanced, you will be able to spend the majority of the time with your face down in the water. Your goal is to increase your comfort until you need only swivel your chin to breathe.

Side-Kick Extended: Extend your low arm outward, and keep it aligned with your body (6 to 8 inches under the water). If your arm is at the surface, your hips are likely low in the water. This drill is easier than the preceding one. Remember that you will get significant balance benefits from the arms-at-side version before progressing.

Body Rotation: Triathletes are overachievers and set high expectations for themselves. Be conscious that you will have a tendency to rush your skills work. Slow down, enjoy the sessions, and master the previous section before continuing.

Single-Stroke Change: Start as you did for Side-Kick Extended and change sides by doing a single stroke. Transition as if you are moving between two rails. Settle, take at least three breaths, and transition back. Repeat as you move down the pool.

Three-Stroke Change: The same as Single-Stroke Change except three transitions are made between each set of breaths.

With the two preceding drills, start by keeping the head down during the transition, pausing, then taking three (or more) breaths to settle (using the chin-swivel method and keeping the face in the water). Once you are comfortable with this technique, transition directly to a breath and follow with two additional "swivel breaths." Once you are able to do Three-Stroke Change with a single breath on each side you have achieved three-stroke bilateral breathing. Congratulations! Further notes on bilateral breathing appear later in this chapter.

Stroke Mechanics

It is quite easy to spot athletes who have mastered the side-kick drills. They have excellent balance, are relaxed in the water, and get good distance per stroke. At this stage in your development (and not before), it makes sense to begin to focus on your overall stroke mechanics as well as your muscular endurance. What about endurance? You may not have realized it, but you will have been building it throughout your balance and body rotation drills.

Rich Strauss has been kind enough to contribute his views on this topic later in this chapter. Once you are comfortable and aligned, you are ready for some "propulsive swimming" (see sidebar).

Bilateral Breathing

The swim in an ironman-distance race typically accounts for less than 10 percent of your race day. Although your swim time will have only a limited impact on your overall result, minimizing the energy cost of your swim is a key training objective.

Bilateral breathing is one of the quickest ways for an experienced swimmer to increase swimming efficiency. Bilateral breathing refers to breathing on an odd stroke count, typically every third stroke. Experienced athletes will find that they can breathe bilaterally quite comfortably up to a heart-rate Zone 3 level of intensity. Although extensive use of bilateral breathing is recommended for training, breathing every cycle is recommended for racing.

When you start bilateral breathing, it can be very difficult to relax. If you are having trouble, keep the interval length short and stick with it. Eventually, you will be able to extend the interval. Remember your goals—if you are training to relax or to build base endurance, keep the pace easy. It is far easier to relax when the aerobic stress of the exercise is low. It is very difficult to improve your economy (in any sport) when there is tension in your body. Pay particular attention to your face, neck, and shoulders.

The principal benefits of learning to master bilateral breathing are:

Improved technique: With bilateral breathing, you will initially be forced to slow down, giving you the opportunity to work on your stroke mechanics. Some athletes will become quite comfortable with going slowly. If you happen to be one of these athletes, thinking about speeding your "hip drive" can be an excellent way to increase your speed while maintaining balance and stroke length. For long-distance athletes, it can be quite beneficial to use longer interval distances (200 to 500 meters) that include faster segments combined with bilateral, active-recovery segments.

Propulsive Swimming and the Catch

Athletes often wonder when they should begin doing fewer drills and more swimming. There is a pace that is the line between swimming for technique and swimming for speed and fitness. This pace is about 18.5 to 19 minutes per 1,000 meters (long course), or about 1:51 to 1:54 per 100 meters. If you want to express it as a "swim golf" score, the goal would be sub-90, or less than 45 strokes (for 50 meters) and about 45 seconds.

In other words, if you are slower than these times, there are far more gains to be made by focusing on technique than on fitness. Once you cross this line in the sand, your swimming performance becomes more a function of propulsive skills and swimming fitness. This is not to say that once you break 18 minutes for a 1,000-meter time trial, you have a pass to never do drills again. Rather, you would be justified in doing an increasing amount of fitness-oriented swimming in place of dedicated drill work.

Before this point, you should focus on balance drills to develop a good horizontal body position and "side swimming"—spending as much time as possible on your side and presenting less surface area to the water. Refer to "The Progression" section for drills.

After you have become proficient with these drills, what next? Let's learn how to get the most power out of your stroke.

THE CATCH—WHERE POWER BEGINS

When your hand enters the water, your palm is down toward the bottom of the pool. If you start pulling now, without doing anything else, you will be directing force downward and lifting your body rather than moving your body forward. This movement would continue until the natural sweep of your arm stroke eventually directs forces rearward.

The correct idea is to get your palm from "down" to "facing rearward" (and thus pushing you forward) as quickly as possible.

The proper way to do this is by bending the elbow, or "catching" the water as soon as possible. This would be analogous in cycling to "rolling the barrel" at the top of your pedal stroke and beginning to apply power at noon rather than waiting until 2 or 3 o'clock.

Illustration of a Proper Catch

At a table or desk, stick your left arm out directly in front of you, arm parallel to the table, palm down.

Now bend your left elbow (without moving your upper arm), and touch your left fingertips to the desk in front of you. Your forearm is probably at a 45-degree angle from your upper arm.

Notice three things:

1. Your elbow is high and has not moved significantly.
2. Your elbow is directly above or on top of your hand (relatively speaking— you get the idea).

3. Your "paddle" essentially includes your hand and your forearm. This is very important.

With your fingers still on the desk and elbow up high, now just let your elbow drop. This is referred to as a poor catch, dropping the elbow, slipping the front of your stroke, etc.

Two things to notice here:
1. Your elbow is leading your hand as you pull.
2. You have lost your forearm as a paddle.

Combining the Catch with Your Pull

Now put your arm out directly to the left, parallel to the ground, palm down. Turn your head left so that you are looking at your hand.

Without moving your elbow or upper arm, bend your elbow and forearm as you did before.

This position combines the elements of:
1. An aggressive shoulder roll—shoulder is pointing down at the bottom of the pool, belly facing the side wall.
2. Proper head position—looking down.
3. Aggressive catch.

HOW TO GET IT: FIST DRILL AND OTHER IDEAS

Fist Drill: Swim with a closed fist, normal to fast arm speed, no fins. Visualize two things:
1. There is a barrel on top of the water, and you are trying to reach over and around it, to carry it in your arm. This will help you get the high elbow discussed above.
2. Imagine that your forearm is a paddle. Swim with your forearm, not your hand.

Perform this drill for two to three lengths, then open your hand in the middle of the pool. You should feel the increase in power.

After you have done this drill a few times and return to normal swimming, these two ideas will help you maintain your high-elbow, aggressive catch:

Over the Barrel: Maintain this feeling of reaching over a barrel as you swim.

Fingers Down: Put your left arm out in front of you, palm down. Now point your hand downward, bending at the wrist while the rest of your arm remains in place. Duplicate this in the pool by pointing your fingers to the bottom as soon as possible. The rest of your catch will fall into place.

Beginning to practice these skills is the line between "balance swimming" and "propulsive swimming." If your body position and balance are not correct, it doesn't make sense to develop these propulsive skills. However, if your body position is dialed in, then this aggressive catch is where the money is. Swimmers spend years refining this one small aspect of their strokes.

SOURCE:
Rich Strauss, U.S.A.T. and U.S.A. Cycling Certified Coach, Head Triathlon Coach, Team in Training, Los Angeles Eastside Team, www.cruciblefitness.com, rich@cruciblefitness.com

Offside improvement: Nearly every athlete can improve the efficiency of his or her "away" arm when breathing. Swimming bilaterally helps you even your stroke. When you are completely comfortable with bilateral swimming, try some swimming while breathing every cycle on your offside. Not only will you learn a lot about your stroke, you will also gain the ability to swim comfortably on your offside. This can be very useful in a race situation where you may need to breathe away from swells, splashing, or waves. It also lets you check out your competition and landmarks located on your offside.

Improved stroke and balance: Stroke imbalances are very easy to detect when swimming bilaterally. Once these areas are discovered, it is far easier for you to correct them. For example, you may notice your hand pulling wide when breathing onside and not breathing offside. Your offside now becomes a role model to correct your onside stroke more quickly.

Improved timing: Bilateral breathing has a smooth rhythm and helps develop stroke and kick timing. It is also beneficial to the timing of flip turns because it offers you the opportunity to breathe on either side coming into the turn.

Improved breath control: The breath control that you learn from bilateral swimming will enable you to improve your flip turns. Why are turns important? Because they enable you to swim with stronger swimmers, maintain your workout momentum (particularly when swimming short course), draft faster swimmers in group time trials, and improve your streamlining and balance. Being comfortable with a moderate amount of oxygen debt is very useful for race starts, rounding marker buoys, and bridging forward to a faster group of swimmers.

Improved rotation: Many athletes find that they rotate well to their breathing side, then "flatten out" without rotating at all to their offside. A flat stroke can increase the load on your shoulder and result in swimmer's shoulder. With more rotation to both sides, you are able to pull through your stroke much more easily and increase the power of your stroke.

Confidence: The feeling of breathlessness that you may experience in the water is not a lack of oxygen; rather, it is a buildup of carbon dioxide. Learning to live with this sensation is an important skill for swim starts, turns, and pool swimming. Knowing that you can swim bilaterally is a real confidence booster if you miss a few breaths during a race. It will also help your threshold performance when swimming hard and breathing every cycle.

There is some discussion in swimming circles regarding whether or not bilateral swimming improves lung capacity. There is no substantial research to support the concept of bilateral breathing as a technique to improve lung capacity or lung function. However, it does increase an athlete's carbon dioxide tolerance and breath control. Both of these skills transfer to other sports. Rather than training the body to get more oxygen out of each breath, bilateral breathing teaches the athlete to breathe fully while maintaining a relaxed focus on stroke mechanics.

Stretch Cords

When you are ready to start Propulsive Swimming, you are likely to find that your catch is your key limiter. The quicker you are able to rotate your shoulder and set up the pull, the better. All athletes can afford to be stronger in the initial phase of their catch. If you are already swimming three times per week, then you will likely benefit from one or two stretch-cord sessions of 10 to 15 minutes per week.

You must use perfect form at all times with these exercises (or any technical drill, for that matter). Focus on technique before trying to move quickly or under load. The learning progression for any new skill or movement pattern is the same:

◆ Learn the movement pattern slowly.
◆ Add speed.
◆ Add resistance.
◆ Perform under stress.

When learning the Half Pull, keep the movement slow and controlled with very light resistance. Then add speed to the Half Pull. Then add resistance to the Half Pull. Then add the Full Pull and slow it down again. Then add speed, then add resistance. Maintain the same pattern for all the exercises. Your long-term goal should be to train the muscles so you can bring the quickness of the catch into your swim stroke. Also, remember to control the "negative" portion of the exercises. Work your muscles in both directions.

Start with light-resistance stretch cords. You can always make the exercise harder (if needed) by moving away from the tie point. In addition to strength, the cords give you the benefit of being able to train your muscle firing patterns without having to worry about balance and breathing. You can find stretch cords at the sports shops of most large swimming pools, at sports medicine clinics, and through mail-order vendors.

The first two stretch-cord exercises are the most important for swimmers. Full Pulls should not be attempted until the Half Pulls are mastered.

Figure 5.1

Figure 5.2

Figure 5.3

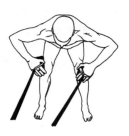

Figure 5.4

Half Pulls

Tie cords slightly above waist height and extend your arms until the cords are just tight. The elbow stays perfectly still while the forearm rotates forward and down. The elbow stays high and still; the hand remains aligned with the forearm; the arm, forearm, and hand all rotate slightly inward. The elbow does not move back; all movement is done by rotating the forearms. The goal is to build front-end strength. Look down with a neutral head position and maintain hand and forearm alignment.

Figures 5.1 and 5.2 demonstrate the Half Pull starting position. The goal is alignment of hip, shoulder, and wrist at the start. Figures 5.3 and 5.4 demonstrate the Half Pull ending position.

Forward Rotations

Kneel or stand with your back to the cords. Cords should be tied at the same height as shoulders. Arms are extended straight out, bent at the elbow, and the forearm is perpendicular to the shoulders and upper arm, making an "L" on each side. The elbow stays perfectly still while the forearm rotates forward through 90 degrees.

Figure 5.5 demonstrates the starting position, and Figure 5.6 demonstrates the ending position.

Figure 5.5

Figure 5.6

Figure 5.7

Full Pulls

Catch simulation with pull-through. Tie cords slightly above waist height and face the tie. Bend at the waist. With both arms, catch, pull, and push through. The pull should follow an hourglass pattern. Keep the elbows high and focus on a quick catch.

Repeat the first two positions as in Half Pulls. Figures 5.7 and 5.8 demonstrate the pull-through. Figures 5.9 and 5.10 demonstrate the final position of the full pull. Throughout this exercise, the hands are always pointing straight down and the palm is always facing straight back.

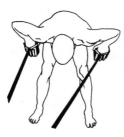

Figure 5.8

Figure 5.9

Figure 5.10

Standing Straight Arm

Face away from the tie point, both arms straight with hands overhead; alternating arms, move each arm in a semicircle from 12 to 6 o'clock. See Figure 5.11.

Triceps Extensions

Face away from the tie point, elbows high and in close, and extend hands to do a triceps extension. The goal is to keep the elbows high and tight. Do three sets: 60 seconds on, 60 seconds off, 50 seconds on, 50 seconds off, 40 seconds on, 40 seconds off. Those with a limited range of motion in their hips and back may benefit from a higher tie point. Athletes must hold 100 percent perfect form at all times. It is most important to maintain a high elbow.

Figure 5.12 demonstrates the starting position of the triceps extension; Figure 5.13 demonstrates the ending position of the triceps extension.

Figure 5.11

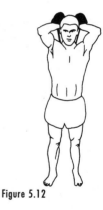

Figure 5.12

Figure 5.13

Recovery Drill

Face away from the tie point, bend at the waist, and look into a mirror. Strengthen your recovery by "swimming" while using the cords to create resistance on the recovery portion of your stroke. This drill is particularly effective for athletes (commonly female) who become fatigued when swimming in wetsuits. Figure 5.14 demonstrates a front view of the recovery drill; Figure 5.15 shows a side view of the recovery drill.

Figure 5.14

Not every triathlete can afford a set of swim cords, so a simple solution to your dry-land training requirements is "sock swimming." Start by placing 8 to 24 ounces of fishing weights into two athletic socks and tying a loop into the top of each sock. Bend at the waist and "swim" freestyle while watching your form in a mirror. Maintain a high elbow throughout the swim stroke. Sock swimming can be done in sets of 8 to 20 minutes' duration. Maintain your cadence throughout the "swim." Lift your cadence for the final 20 seconds of each minute and for the final minute of each set. This workout is surprisingly tough and an effective way to maintain your swimming muscles when you are unable to get to a pool.

Figure 5.15

The Kick and Swim Fins

The Kick: Many triathletes believe that in order to swim faster, they need to kick harder. For nearly every triathlete body type, the kick is secondary. The muscles used for kicking are big muscles that consume large amounts of oxygen and energy relative to their propulsive benefit. In addition, the limited ankle flexibility in most triathletes further limits the effectiveness of their kicks. For most of us, increased speed comes from technique, balance, and stroke mechanics, not the kick.

However, using your kick during technique swims can be beneficial to learn balance and comfort in the water. Through focused-technique swims on form, balance, and comfort, your kick will naturally improve, as will your body position. You can also work on ankle flexibility and kick sets—both are the keys to improved kicking. Belly kicks with long fins and a kickboard will help with ankle flexibility—as will stretching.

There is a portion of the triathlon population that will benefit from a strong kick. These athletes are typically male, below average height, and muscular with very low body fat. For these athletes, a solid kick is essential to swim at a high level. The lean, large legs of this body type cause the hips and legs to drop, and an effective kick is therefore a prerequisite for effective nonwetsuit swimming.

Depending on your ironman-distance swim times, a stronger kick might knock a minute out of your swim. Most triathletes may have a better return on investment by working on their bike and run instead.

Kick sets can be most useful when they are used to rest the upper body—for example, following a long pull set—or to improve balance—for example, the Side-Kick drills.

Swimming with Fins: The main benefits of swimming with fins are improved body position, better ankle flexibility, and better speed. Kick sets with long fins are also an opportunity to work on core stability, especially the fly kick done on your back. For all swimmers, particularly novice swimmers, fins are useful in the following situations:

◆ Balance drills for swimmers with weak kicks—short fins are best; try to go fin free as soon as possible.

◆ Front-end stroke drills—fins will help you relax and focus on the front end of your stroke. No more than 50 percent (maximum) of drilling should be done with fins.

◆ Fly-kick sets—done on the front, side, and back, this is an excellent core workout.

◆ Recovery sets—200 to 400 meters of easy swimming between harder sets.

◆ Long-axis-stroke drills for advanced swimmers.

If balance is your key limiter (as discussed earlier), avoid fins and pull-buoys.

The Other Strokes

As you approach the fitness and skills required for, say, a 60-minute ironman-distance swim, you will find the other strokes to be a useful addition to your training. By "other strokes" we mean backstroke, breaststroke, and fly.

Of the four strokes, improving your backstroke is the most useful in improving your freestyle. The primary reason is the similarity in critical success factors, most importantly long-axis balance and smooth body rotation.

When swimming backstroke, the ideal entry point is at 11 and 1 o'clock. However, more important than entry location is a quick, straight-arm recovery. A quick recovery with the hand entering pinky finger first will nearly always result in a straight-arm. Drive your arm deep, bend your elbow, and push as much water as possible straight down toward your feet.

Very strong swimmers, those with sub-60-minute ironman-distance swim times, are likely to benefit from adding the fly stroke to improve their aerobic power and muscular endurance. The fly stroke is fantastic once you learn to swim it properly.

Breaststroke is beneficial because of the similarity of breaststroke and freestyle catches are similiar. Athletes with a history of knee problems should substitute a fly kick for the traditional whip kick.

Mastering all four strokes improves your swimming agility and strength, leading to improved economy.

Building Endurance

An excellent way to build endurance is to swim regularly in a long-course (50-meter) pool. Endurance swimming is typically done at a pace that is 5 to 10 seconds slower per 100 meters than your 1,000-meter best average time-trial pace (T[1]+5–10s per 100). Keep in mind that when swimming endurance it is beneficial to insert some short, faster efforts into the workout.

When focusing on endurance, it is best to slow down and build your long-workout duration. Frequency is also very important; we recommend swimming three to four times per week.

An endurance swim session follows. This should be a technique-oriented session that builds your base endurance. As with all endurance swims, this is best done in a long-course pool.

Warm-up: Bilateral swimming
- 50/100/150 meters . . . upward to a peak, then . . . 150/100/50 meters downward
- 5 to 10 seconds' rest at the end of each interval
- Pyramid to a peak based on length of desired warm-up

Main set: 400-meter sets (repeat as desired)
- Odds—4 x 100 done on 15 seconds rest: 1 and 2 are steady, 3 is moderately hard, and 4 is easy
- Evens—400 bilateral breathing, easy to steady on 20 seconds' rest

Cool-down: 200 meters nonfreestyle

To get the most benefit from your endurance swims, always work on a technical limiter. Plan in advance which items will be worked on during which swims. Hold perfect form the whole way. Further endurance swims are listed in Appendix C.

Muscular Endurance

Muscular endurance (ME) is the ability to maintain a steady pace for long durations. Many athletes can swim quite fast 50- and 100-meter sets, but their major challenge is bringing that speed into 400-, 800-, and 1,500-meter distances. This is where muscular endurance comes into play.

During the Base period, your primary focus should be technical improvement and building base endurance. As you enter your Build period, a moderate amount of focused ME swimming that mimics the demands of your key races should be added. Remember that there is no point in swimming hard before you are able to swim well. In an ironman-distance swim, economy dominates power.

Here is an example of an ME workout:

◆ 600 freestyle; start easy and build to steady for the last 200 to 300 meters

◆ 5 x 200 alternate 25-meter fly with 175-meter freestyle, steady on 15 seconds' rest

◆ 4 x 300 done as:

　　300 band only, moderately hard on 30 seconds' rest

　　300 freestyle, steady on 30 seconds' rest

　　300 pull-buoy/band, moderately hard on 30 seconds' rest

　　300 freestyle, steady on 30 seconds' rest

◆ 1 x 100 backstroke, easy

◆ 4 x 300, done as above

◆ 1 x 100 backstroke, easy

◆ 2 x 50 freestyle, hard

◆ 200 freestyle, easy cool-down

It is very important to be able to maintain form when doing this type of work; otherwise it is counterproductive.

Are you ready for Pull Sets? More important than your speed is your stroke mechanics. An athlete with huge power, poor form, and excellent speed will likely ingrain his or her poor form by doing Pull Sets. On the other hand, a slower athlete with excellent form could use Pull Sets to build strength and muscular endurance.

For these sets, you have three main pieces of gear: a pull-buoy, paddles, and a band. The pull-buoy goes between your legs, the band around your ankles, and the paddles on your hands. You can mix and match the equipment for various levels of intensity (see Table 5.1). Pull Sets with "all gear" means using all three pieces of equipment. Swimmers with a history of shoulder problems should be very careful using paddles and bands.

The following is an ME set that incorporates pulling. The set, 12 x 200, is executed as:

◆ 3 x 200 pull-buoy, breathing every fifth stroke on 20 seconds' rest

◆ 3 x 200 pull-buoy/band, breathing every third stroke on 20 seconds' rest

◆ 3 x 200 pull-buoy/band, descending—steady on 10 seconds' rest, moderately hard on 20 seconds' rest, hard on 30 seconds' rest

◆ 3 x 200, no gear, building each 50 meters to moderately hard on 30 seconds' rest

Further examples of ME swim workouts can be found in Appendix C.

Table 5.1 Swim Equipment

Gear	Pros	Cons	Useful for . . .	Risky for . . .
Band	Increased resistance	Reduces body rotation Legs drop	Building strength—typically in combination with pull-buoy	Athletes with shoulder problems Band-only swimming useful only for the strongest swimmers
Paddles	Increased feel for catch phase Increased feel for hand entry	Very easy to overload shoulders if stroke mechanics are not excellent	Building strength Learning proper catch phase Increasing hand speed through the water Building increased force Improving feel for water	Athletes with shoulder problems Athletes with poor stroke mechanics
Pull-buoy	Lifts hips Enables easier focus on front end of stroke	Removal of aid can result in poor body position	Building strength in combination with band Working on front-end stroke mechanics	Athletes with balance as a swim limiter
Fins	Enable faster speed through the water Lift hips and enable better body position for a variety of drills	Removal of aid can result in poor body position	Working on front-end stroke mechanics Recovery swimming Long-axis drills Fly-kick drills Balance drills if a weak kicker (best with short fins) Improving ankle flexibility	Athletes with balance as a swim limiter
Kickboard	Makes kick sets more comfortable	"Belly" flutter kick not swim-specific; most long-axis kicking occurs on the side	Variety of longer kick sets	

SOURCES   Laughlin, Terry. *Total Immersion.* New York: Fireside.   Maglischo, Ernest W. *Swimming Even Faster.* Mountain View, CA: Mayfield Publishing Company.   U.S.A. Swimming. *Progressions for Athlete and Coach Development.* Hong Kong: U.S.A. Swimming.

Pros and Cons of Squad Training

There are many advantages to swimming with a squad or masters' group. Squad training offers a structured workout for athletes of all levels as well as having a coach on deck to ensure that you are swimming correctly. Your squad or masters' coach is the best person to evaluate the impact of technical changes because he or she can see what is happening with your overall stroke and form.

As well as having a coach to oversee and recommend drills for improvement, squad training is beneficial when you are looking to train at a higher level. Leading a lane with other swimmers just off your toes is a good incentive to help you push your efforts. A little friendly competition can make training more fun and mentally easier and help avoid burnout. Keep in mind, however, that you should go only as fast as your ability to maintain good form.

The power of demonstration is also a powerful learning tool, and swimming with technically proficient swimmers gives you a visual picture to follow. However, the opposite effect can be true when swimming with novice swimmers.

This issue leads to the drawbacks of squad training. Novice swimmers nearly always swim too hard, and many masters' coaches (and athletes) have no interest in working on technique. This attitude makes it difficult for you to learn and master correct form before adding speed into the equation. Novice swimmers are better off sticking to a slower lane and developing solid skills before advancing.

Remember that any session with others always includes an element of compromise, and the temptation to sacrifice form for the sake of speed can be great. Control and maturity are needed to avoid overdoing it. Hammering each workout will quickly lead to a performance plateau. Although all-out 50s and 100s on short rest intervals are fun, to reach your swimming potential, balance the mixture of technical, endurance, and faster work.

Recommended Reading

Laughlin, Terry. *Butterfly and Breaststroke the TI Way: Waterproof Drill Guide*. New Paltz, NY: Total Immersion, Inc., 2002.

———. *Swimming Made Easy: The Total Immersion Way for Any Swimmer to Achieve Fluency, Ease, and Speed in Any Stroke*. New Paltz, NY: Swimware, Inc., 2001.

———. *Total Immersion Pool Primer for Freestyle and Backstroke: The TI Way*. New Paltz, NY: Total Immersion, Inc., 2000.

———. *Triathlon Swimming Made Easy: How Anyone Can Succeed in Triathlon (or Open-Water Swimming) with Total Immersion*. New Paltz, NY: Total Immersion, Inc., 2002.

Laughlin, Terry, and John Delves. *Total Immersion: The Revolutionary Way to Swim Better, Faster, and Easier*. New York: Fireside, 1996.

Maglischo, Ernest W. *Swimming Even Faster*, 2nd ed. New York: McGraw-Hill, 1993.

Chapter 6

Training for the Bike

> Cycling is a blue-collar sport. You gotta do the miles.
>
> —Jonas Colting,
> Swedish champion triathlete

Although cycling accounts for roughly half of your race day, it forms the core of an effective training strategy for all long-distance triathletes. In fact, a deep love of cycling is a fundamental requirement for successful long-distance racing.

A triathlete's cycling season tends to mirror the life cycle of an athlete. We will discuss training strategies in detail later, but it is useful to have an overview of a typical year of training. The initial focus of each season is easy endurance cycling, where riding is done at low intensity. Endurance rides are supplemented with skills sessions. This low-intensity period typically lasts from three to six months and is an excellent complement to a focused strength-training program. The overall goal of this period is to increase cycling economy, enhance overall aerobic fitness, and prepare the body for the tougher work to come later in the season. If you are new to ironman-distance racing, this type of training can form up to 65 percent of your total training volume for the entire year. A strong cycling endurance base is the platform upon which your entire season will be built. Until you are confident about your ability to complete your race distance, your training should be heavily biased toward endurance-based cycling.

Once you have established your endurance platform, and following the completion of all high-intensity strength training, you will be ready to begin adding moderate amounts of ME work. It often takes four to eight weeks to receive the full cycling benefits of your high-intensity strength work. For this reason, the transition to sport-specific strength work (ME training) is normally planned for no later than eleven weeks prior to an A-priority race.

Novices should remember that the transition from an endurance focus to an ME focus is gradual. If you have any doubts about your overall endurance, it is best to postpone (or cancel) the transition to ME training. It is pointless to be able to ride hard if you lack the overall endurance for the entire event. Ironman-distance racing is about having the ability to sustain a moderate speed for a very long time. Top-end speed and anaerobic endurance are not requirements for success—at any end of the field.

Muscular endurance for the bike is best described as the ability to push a big gear for a long time. Specific ME strategies are addressed below. For athletes from the middle of the pack forward, cycling muscular endurance is typically their number-one limiter.

Elite and stronger cyclists may benefit from the higher-intensity workout and training strategies addressed later in this chapter. Novices and midpack athletes are best served by maintaining a near-total focus on endurance and ME cycling. It is possible to put together a very fast race with the right combination of this kind of training.

Equipment Considerations

Even if your goal is to finish an ironman-distance race, you are going to be spending a lot of time in the saddle. Your number-one equipment priority should be getting yourself a bike that fits. Probably the most common, and expensive, errors made by new triathletes relate to their first bike purchase. Here are some things to remember:

- ◆ Spend less than your budget. If you like the sport, you will want to upgrade and/or purchase race wheels and other accessories. You can drop a lot of money on your bike, and it is best to learn more about your needs before spending freely.
- ◆ When purchasing a bike, consider only comfort, safety, and value. Don't get caught up in the debates on frame materials or the latest paint job. A mass-market bike from a reliable manufacturer is the safest bet for your first season.
- ◆ There is only one cycling accessory you really need—aerobars. Race wheels and other "go-faster" products can wait until you are more experienced. If you are not constrained by budget, then feel free to have a little fun with the toys. However, remember that strength training, a smart training program, and a set of aerobars are worth more than all the other aero devices combined.
- ◆ Unless you have excellent flexibility, be very cautious with aggressive cycling positions. This tip is valid for experienced athletes as well. Many short-course athletes find their positions to be too extreme for long-distance training and racing. We discuss this topic in more detail below. All athletes should remember that the rider accounts for almost all of the total air resistance on the bike. Although aero wheels

and frames can save time, the largest gains are made by making yourself comfortable, powerful, and aerodynamic. This is the easiest form of free speed available.

You need only two triathletes to start a debate on frame materials, frame manufacturers, wheel sizes, shifting configurations, etc. If you notice the wide range of equipment and positions used in our sport, then you will quickly conclude that there are no right answers. In setting up your position, remember that nothing matters as much as achieving one that is comfortable. Many of us start with a bike position that is too aggressive for our experience, flexibility, and body structure. By aggressive, we mean the position of the shoulders relative to the hip joint. The lower the shoulders relative to the hips, the more aggressive the position.

There are four important starting points to any good long-distance bike position. In order of importance, they are:

1. Safety: The athlete is stable and able to control the bike easily.

2. Comfort: The athlete is comfortable and able to maintain the aero position for the duration of the ride. The transition from biking to running is smooth. A very aggressive position is useless if you can't hold it for the entire ride or have trouble running.

3. Power: The position enables the athlete to optimize power generation.

4. Aerodynamics: The position has superior aerodynamic properties.

For all athletes, there is a trade-off between power and aerodynamics. When you need to make a choice between these two, you are usually best served by choosing power. It takes a lot of aero to overcome any material loss in power.

Keep in mind that there is no right bike or right position. Correct position can vary considerably from one person to the next, even if they appear to be the same size. As the pros and elite age-groupers show, a wide range of setups can be both comfortable and powerful. Go to any long-distance race and take a look at the athletes. You may notice that many are very stretched out on their bike frames and have their elbows a long way in front of their shoulders. This position can be quite aero; however, almost all of us have a relative weakness in our lower backs, and this position often results in low-back pain.

Back pain is one of the most common ailments that affects long-distance triathletes. Not only is it uncomfortable, it is aerodynamically costly to sit up or come off the aerobars. If you suffer from back pain, there are four things you should consider:

1. Are you riding enough on the aerobars? You need to build experience with riding long periods on the bars without long breaks. In the final seven weeks before key races, insert long aerobar rides into your training plan. Briefly stretch every 15 to 20 minutes while riding, but aside from that, spend the entire time on your aerobars. Even at an easy pace, these sessions are quite demanding.

2. How good is your flexibility? Tightness in the hips and pelvis is a leading cause of back pain. When back problems arise, a focused, consistent stretching program will help. This plan should encompass all of the main muscle groups of the hip region (hamstrings, hip flexors, back extensors, glutes, quads, adductors). A flexibility imbalance can be just as troublesome as a lack of flexibility. A simple flexibility progression is described in Appendix E.

3. How are you treating hills? If you are at risk for back pain, you should always remain seated on climbs. Standing, particularly when pushing a big gear, will increase the strain through your lower back.

4. How hard do you ride early in the bike leg? The transition from swimming to cycling can be stressful on the body. Following an ironman-distance swim, it is easy to lock up your hamstrings and irritate your back. Athletes at risk include those who tend to kick very hard when sighting. This places considerable strain on the low back; combine that with some hard early riding, and back pain can be the result.

What is the correct shifting configuration for you? The bar-end shifters on bullhorns take a fair amount of skill to shift. Most novice athletes with bar ends do not shift enough, which typically means they are pushing too high a gear. With the front chain rings, they frequently shift too late, resulting in dropped chains. Bar-end shifting is useful for flat courses, but if you live in a hilly area, ride frequently with groups of roadies, or do a significant amount of nonaerobar riding, then you should consider whether Shimano Total Integration shifting might be for you. STI shifting combines the shifters with the brake levels.

Generally, the steeper setups that are appropriate for bullhorns don't climb as well as the more moderate bikes that are appropriate for STI shifting. For this reason, most athletes will find that a more traditional road setup is more powerful and comfortable in the hills.

The final decision is a personal one, and no matter what you decide, there will be plenty of athletes who agree and disagree with your selection. So long as your bike is both safe and comfortable, you'll be fine.

Getting "Dialed In"

The methods described here are starting points for your eventual correct setup. You may want to experiment with adjustments, keeping in mind that it's best (and biomechanically safest) to make incremental changes. This approach is especially important if you have ridden in one position for a long time. A half-inch change in your saddle height, even though it may eventually improve your position, will feel strange at first and is likely to cause discomfort. We recommend making no more than .25-inch adjustments per week.

Bike fit starts from the feet up. After your cleats are set, adjust the saddle, followed by the handlebars. Once these three are correctly positioned, you will ride more economically and comfortably, which translates into faster bike splits.

Cleat Position

The starting point for cleat position is placement of the pedal axle directly beneath the ball of the foot. This "neutral" position works well for many riders. For long-distance time trials, we recommend that you consider moving the cleat slightly toward the heel. As the cleat is moved back, more force is transferred to the pedal. The trade-off is that cadence slows, which can result in an ultimate loss of power when sudden changes in velocity are necessary (not an issue for long-course triathlon). Start by making a quarter-inch adjustment from neutral and see how it feels after several rides before going any farther.

Find the ball of your foot with your cycling shoes on, mark it on the lateral side of each shoe, and adjust each cleat individually. On an indoor trainer, clip in to your pedals while someone checks to see if the marks are over the spindles. Aligning the marks with the axles puts you in the neutral position.

Saddle Position and Height

For an aero position, your saddle fore-aft adjustment depends on the length of your thigh and flexibility of your hips and lower back. Establish a neutral saddle position by placing your bike on an indoor trainer, and then level it using a carpenter's level on the top tube. Spin for a few minutes to warm up. Then, with the pedal in the 3 or 9 o'clock position, drop a plumb line from the knob on the outside of your leg just below the knee (head of the fibula). When the line intersects the pedal axle, the saddle is neutral.

Moving the saddle forward of neutral by as much as a half inch may make you more comfortable and improve your power and aerodynamics. The saddle should be parallel to the floor, or slightly tipped down at the nose for comfort. If your flexibility is excellent, and you opt for an aggressive handlebar position, then you may find that you slip forward slightly on your saddle. This can be corrected by giving the saddle a very slight upward tilt.

Your saddle height has the most effect on power output. The easiest way to make adjustments is to place yourself in the aero position and have your shoes unclipped. Place your unclipped

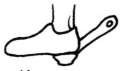

Figure 6.1

heel on the pedal at the bottom of the stroke (crank arm lined up with the seat tube; see Figure 6.1), and set the saddle to neutral position by adjusting the height until your knee is straight. Note that as the saddle goes up, it also moves back, and as it is lowered, it shifts forward slightly. For every 2 centimeters (cm) it moves up, it must also move forward about 1 cm. Likewise, if you lower it 2 cm, move it back by about 1 cm.

Handlebar Height, Reach, and Angle

One of the best investments you can make in setup equipment is an adjustable stem. It allows you to make a wide range of small changes in position to produce the most exact position needed for aerodynamics and comfort. It also allows for changes throughout the season.

When the top of the handlebars is about 1 inch below the high point of the saddle, you are in neutral position. Determine this by extending a yardstick from the saddle top out to the handlebars and leveling it with a carpenter's level. By measuring the distance between the yardstick and the handlebars, you can set the stem height. Depending on your flexibility, the handlebars can be raised or lowered by an inch. As the handlebars are lowered, you may need to move the saddle forward, opening the angle between the thigh and trunk. Otherwise, you may experience discomfort through your hip region.

Correct handlebar reach, or stem length, places your ear over your elbow in the aero position. A rough gauge of this is that the distance from the nose of the saddle to the back of the handlebars should be about 1 to 1.5 inches longer than the distance from the back of your elbow to the end of your extended fingers.

When the up-and-down angle of the aerobars is neutral, the bottom of your hand is below the bend in your elbow, and the top of your hand is above it. As always, small adjustments from neutral may improve your comfort.

The Aggressive Fit

Stronger athletes with superior flexibility, lean body type, and a good range of motion may want to consider a more aggressive race position. This section lays out a number of areas in which you can increase the race effectiveness of your setup and riding technique. We are grateful to John Cobb of Bicycle Sports for his assistance and education.

Body position has a direct impact on power. More specifically, the most aerodynamic position is almost always inferior in terms of power generation. For a quick illustration, you will need an indoor trainer and a Power-Tap or some other power-output measuring device. Place your bike on an indoor trainer and ride with the aerobar pads about two-thirds of the way back from your wrist. Increase the resistance to the point where you are putting out 350 to 400 watts, then move your arms until the aerobar pads are nearly under your elbows (stretching you out and making you more aero). You will instantly lose about 50 watts of power—you're working just as hard, but your watts will simply disappear. To put this in context, 50 watts of power can be up to 30 minutes in an ironman-distance bike leg. If you are a strong rider, learning to get the most out of your setup could be the difference between a podium finish and missing the rolldown.

Why such a clear loss of power? What happens is that the "longer" position takes out the large muscle groups of the upper body (arms, shoulders, and back) as well as reducing the impact of your core strength. You are unable to engage your full muscle mass and therefore lose power. In addition, for a given level of power output, your legs will be working harder. This is a key consideration for long-distance triathlon because you need to run when you leave the bike. Being able to effectively bring the upper body into the cycling leg gives you an advantage.

Remember that you can trade quite a bit of aero for a more powerful position. Powerful riders do not need to be as concerned with aerodynamics. For example, witness the success (and position) of riders such as Jurgen Zack and Miguel Indurain.

Many of the aero positions can rob riders of valuable wattage. It's not so much the frame geometry as how the overall configuration relates to the rider's biomechanics. In some cases, experienced riders can improve their performance simply by changing their positions. By changing their positions, athletes are able to break through to a new level in their riding. Just as in weight lifting, experienced athletes can overcome plateaus by using a radical change in training stimuli.

Riders who have reached a plateau can often benefit from a change in position, if only to help stimulate new muscular adaptations. If you have not reached a plateau, start with the traditional TT setup that we outlined in the previous section. This is something that most age-group triathletes should keep in mind. A comfortable, traditional setup is probably the best starting point for you.

Many athletes wonder how flat their backs need to be. What is optimal? There has been much written on the goal of getting the back as flat as possible, but remember that the goal is to have the scapula flat, not the entire back. The spine sits in a wind shadow behind the head, so as long as any arch in your back is behind your head, it is less important (especially if you are more powerful). Remember that your goal should be to get your scapula as flat as possible, not necessarily to get your shoulders as low as possible. The more aggressive your position, the more stressful it will be on your digestion. Given that comfortable eating and drinking are fundamental to long-course race performance, you should be very cautious with highly aggressive positions.

Where should you place your elbows? The elbows need only protect the legs. Once again, there has been much written in regard to aerobar width. Until recently, the conventional wisdom was that the more narrow the elbows, the more aero the position. However, recent wind-tunnel analysis has shown that there is no need to get your pads nearly side by side. The elbows can be fairly wide so long as they shadow the legs. You can set this position by checking the placement of your elbow relative to your knee when at the top of your pedal stroke (12 o'clock). A wider elbow position opens the chest, with positive impacts on lung capacity and rider comfort.

Set your aerobar angle with reference to the bottom of the forearm. Throughout the bike-fit process, the goal is to minimize air disturbance over the body. With the forearm, this implies a position parallel to the ground that avoids pushing any air down into the legs. Go to any bike rack on race day, and you will see that there is a wide variation in aerobar height and forearm angle. Again, the prevailing belief has been that a slight upward angle (15 degrees) is best because it would help "guide" the air down and around the body. The faster the air moves across the body the better—and trying to "steer" the air is counterproductive.

Now that you've made all those adjustments, you won't want something like a bottle cage catching the air that you've worked so hard to avoid. The best type of bottle cage depends on your bike frame—some are better on the downtube, some are better behind the seat, and some bikes may even be better with no bottle cages mounted at all. In that case, a CamelBak is the best option. For bike frames where a behind-the-seat cage is superior to a frame mount, models that place the bottles low and behind the seat are the best choice. Ensure that your rear-mount cage doesn't leave your bottles sitting high and exposed to the wind coming off your back.

All these tips are great, but ultimately, go with what feels right to you. Test your setup well in advance of race day, and resist the urge to go for the last few percentage points of aero. There are many stories of elite athletes who DNF'd key races owing to a little race-week tinkering. Optimize your setup early in the season, and stick with it.

Finally, the "cleaner" your frame, the better. Front-end bottle mounts and gear and food bags are useful for novice athletes. However, these products create unnecessary drag. Check out the bikes of the most experienced riders, and you will see that they use as clean a setup as possible.

Gearing

As coaches, we often hear the question, "What gearing do you recommend?" Many new cyclists spend a lot of time in their big chainrings and use a gear at the top of the cluster. When confronted with a steep hill, they run out of gears and are forced to rapidly switch from the big chainring to the small chainring. Suddenly they are "spinning air" as the gear ratio dives—this is the leading cause of dropped chains in races. Learning how to efficiently shift is an essential skill for all athletes.

The big chainring can quite often seem smoother, which is one of the reasons that novice cyclists use it. However, developing good shifting habits will be an asset in your races. For elite athletes, the little things add up, and you won't want to give away any unnecessary time.

Recommended gearing is individual to each athlete's abilities as well as the topography of each individual race course. Before getting into general suggestions, let's first explain the gearing lingo.

Starting with your wheels, the general standard for 700c (27-inch) wheels is 53/39 up front, and the general standard for 650c (26-inch) wheels is 55/42 up front. The most common gearing on a bike with 700c wheels is 53/39 and 12-25. What does that mean? Generally, the first pair (or any pair separated by a slash) is the number of teeth in the front chainrings. The second pair (or any pair separated by a hyphen) is the range of teeth in the rear cassette. As an example, 53/39 refers to the front chainrings. The big ring has 53 teeth, and the small ring has 39 teeth. The 12-25 number refers to the rear cassette. The smallest cog has 12 teeth, and the largest cog has 25 teeth.

To find out what you currently ride, go to your bike and count the teeth on the two front chainrings. Next, count the teeth on the smallest gear on your rear cluster, then count the teeth on the largest gear on your rear cluster.

Once you know what gearing you have, it's time to learn about how your gears are combined into an effective shifting pattern. For example, for a flat ride you may prefer the 53/21 with the big ring and the 39/15 with the small ring. By comparing the ratios, you can determine if you are riding the "same" gear. Let's illustrate with an example. Your biggest gear might be 53/11. That gives you a gear ratio of 4.82—for each turn of the cranks, the rear wheel will turn 4.82 times. Your smallest gear might be 39/25, giving you a gear ratio of 1.56—for each turn of the cranks, the rear wheel will turn 1.56 times.

When cyclists talk about "gearing up," they mean moving from a low gear ratio to a high gear ratio. New cyclists can find this terminology confusing because "gearing up" means shifting "down" the rear cluster (i.e., 53/15 is 3.53, and 53/11 is 4.82). Shift down the cluster (from the 15 to the 11) and therefore increase the gear ratio—you have "geared up." Gearing down is the same thing in reverse. The sidebar gives a sample shifting pattern for a basic shifting pattern. See the end of this chapter for a Web link to an online gearing calculator.

When it comes to race day, always try to ensure that you have a "bail-out" gear. You may not need or use that last gear, but having it can be your saving grace if you get your pacing off or blow up late in the bike leg. On most North American Ironman® courses, a 53/39 and 12-25 is generally enough gears for most age-group athletes. Cyclists in the 5-hour range for an ironman-distance bike split typically ride an 11-21 on the rear, and cyclists in the 6-hour range could use an 11-23. These figures are for the average athlete on an average course and refer to 700c bike frames.

Standard Gearing Table

Gears on Rear Cassette	SCR Ratios	BCR Ratios
23	1.70	2.30
21	1.86	2.52
19	2.05	2.79
17	2.29	3.12
16	2.44	3.31
15	2.60	3.53
14	2.79	3.79
13	3.00	4.08
12	3.25	4.42

SCR (small chainring) = 39 teeth.
BCR (big chainring) = 53 teeth.

The 53/19 and the 39/14 gears are equivalent, so this is the point where the athlete should move between the big and small chainrings.

When gearing up, an athlete would shift from the 39/15 to the 53/19.

When gearing down, an athlete would shift from the 53/17 to the 39/14.

Stages of Cycling Development

Before we discuss the details of how to train for an ironman-distance bike leg, it is essential that you understand our bike-training philosophy as well as the physiological requirements for long-course cycling success.

Our experience is that the bike is the biomechanically safest and most effective place for an athlete to build his or her aerobic base. Most athletes will be able to safely tolerate weekly cycling volume that is double or triple their run volume. Overall race endurance is the key limiter for the majority of long-course athletes, which implies a lot of riding.

In reviewing the "average" ironman-distance bike leg, there are three physiological components required for success.

1. Race endurance: the ability to complete the swim and bike legs and to run for a long time

2. Climbing: the ability to minimize the energy cost of riding (not racing) all climbs as efficiently as possible

3. Time trialing: the ability to push a big gear for a long time in flat and rolling terrain

Each of these components is best addressed by a different training focus, and most athletes will be addressing them to a varying degree throughout their athletic careers. Our experience is that most athletes have the greatest gains from eliminating these potential limiters in the order of endurance, force, and then muscular endurance. These three physiological attributes relate directly to race endurance, climbing, and time trialing, respectively.

How is long-course racing different from long-distance cycle racing, and what does this imply for you?

Anaerobic endurance: If you are dropped during a bike race, your chances of success are greatly reduced. Cyclists need to be able to endure, and recover from, frequent bouts of high-intensity riding. Triathlon cycling is a steady-state, sub-threshold event. The patience and maturity to avoid high intensity are a limiting factor for many athletes.

Pacing: Although a single rider can impact the pace of a long-distance cycle race, the overall pace of a bike race is governed more by group dynamics than by the personal decision of any one rider. In triathlon, the intelligent athlete is typically the one who is able to avoid the temptation of dueling with the athletes around him or her.

The finish line: Although it may seem obvious, remember that you will be running a marathon when you get off your bike. Triathletes who "race" the bike leg tend to walk their run leg, which is very costly in terms of overall time.

The sections below follow the development of a triathlete who is new to the sport of cycling. The three sections describe the overall life cycle of a novice cyclist and the seasonal periodization of an experienced cyclist. The more experienced you become as a cyclist, the more your training should become focused on your personal race limiters.

Stage 1: Endurance, Skills, and Technique

The most important component in your cycling development is to build the endurance necessary to complete your race distance. At the same time that you are building your aerobic engine, you can be improving your bike-handling skills and technique. Technical improvements have a direct benefit on your cycling economy and efficiency and lead to more successful long-distance racing.

Volume

The core of your week is your long, slow distance (LSD) session, and you will want to plan on building your ride up to 5 to 6 hours. Build your session and overall volume slowly. Two or three weeks forward, one week of consolidation, and then repeat. A good rule of thumb is to limit increases to 10 percent in terms of long workout duration and/or weekly volume. The body will not be rushed, and even if you are racing early in the season, you will have plenty of time to prepare yourself.

You will receive a lot of advice on appropriate workout distances and durations. Listen to your own body, and be conservative on the long stuff. This approach will enable you to recover quickly, maintain consistency, and avoid injury. The two most likely times for injury are during high-intensity training and when you run long after a long ride. We recommend avoiding these kinds of sessions.

Long, slow distance

LSD cycling is the most effective way to improve overall endurance, giving you the base fitness required to compete at the ironman-distance level. The less experience you have with the distance, the more importance you should place on endurance training. For experienced athletes, the best time to build endurance is through the winter months into spring. Summer is generally the time for more focused ME cycling work.

"How long is long?" is a frequent question. For cycling, "long" starts at 2 hours. Your goals and experience should guide your decisions on bike volume. A novice athlete with a goal to finish will have different "longs" than an experienced athlete who is trying to place in his or her age group.

For athletes who are new to long-course training, it is best to slowly build their long bike up to 5 to 6 hours. The reason for building up that duration slowly is that numerous physiological benefits accrue from a gradual increase in your endurance abilities. A tip for going "really long" on the bike is that you want your butt to give out before your legs. In other words, you are doing a workout in which intensity and average speed do not matter. Your goal is to train the physiological systems involved in going very long.

Endurance rides start in heart-rate Zone 1 and will sometimes end up in heart-rate Zone 2 owing to cardiac drift. For a fit athlete, the entire ride will quite often be in heart-rate Zone 1. During your Base period (and throughout the year), do a portion of your endurance training at an easy pace. When you head into the late Build and Peak periods, you can increase the pace as you prepare your body to go faster.

In the early and middle Base periods, build your endurance with rides that focus on easy to steady pacing. Take this seriously—frequent racing (formal and in training) in the early season will limit your endurance gains and greatly increase your risk of burnout. Limit your "megarides" to two or three per month. Keep them slow, and gradually increase your boundaries. Consistent weekday rides are far better than an extra couple of hours on the weekend.

For novice riders, it is best to stick to flat terrain and very gentle hills where you stay seated while climbing. The resulting heart-rate spikes mean that no long or tough climbs are recommended when a novice is building overall endurance building.

Cycling economy

In the exercise physiology lab, economy is a rating of submaximal work output in relation to oxygen consumed. For example, if we tested two riders with the same VO_2max and discovered that Rider A used less oxygen at 300 watts than Rider B, we would say that Rider A was more economical. Since Rider A wastes less energy in pedaling a bike, we could also surmise that Rider A is capable of riding longer at any given speed before becoming fatigued owing to this greater economy. That's quite an advantage in long-course racing. The longer the race, the greater this advantage becomes.

Economical pedaling comes from the split-second timing of muscle contractions and relaxations. Throughout the pedal stroke, scores of muscles must fire, some for longer than others, and then relax. These muscle recruitment patterns are initiated by signals from the central nervous system and are automatic but can be improved. When the nervous system is enervating muscles in intricate harmony, it's like the New York Philharmonic Orchestra. Elegant. A nervous system firing muscles at slightly the wrong times is more like a junior high school band. Amateurish.

More than likely, your pedaling economy is somewhere between elegant and amateurish. To improve your skills, you need to think while you pedal. This means drills (specific cycling drills are discussed in Chapter 4). Winter is a great time to develop your pedaling skills since winter weather for most is not suited to outdoor riding.

There are two keys to improved economy. One is to refine the movements that take place at the top and bottom of the stroke, when the leg must shift from "up and back" to "forward and down," with the reverse situation at the bottom of the stroke. At the top of the stroke, the foot should feel as if it is pushing forward in the shoe. At the bottom, you should get the sense that mud is being scraped from the shoe.

The other key is to focus on the relaxation part of the pedal stroke. Tensing more muscles than are needed to apply force to the pedals is wasteful and uneconomical. Start with the muscles you have the most control over—the face and fingers. Once you can relax them, try relaxing your calves and toes while spinning. The idea is to activate only the muscles needed when they're needed. No more, no less.

The following equipment may help you become a more economical rider.

◆ **Spinning bikes:** The bikes used in health clubs typically have a heavy flywheel with adjustable resistance. The flywheel minimizes leg-speed variations while pedaling and keeps your stroke smooth. Although you can get some benefit from using these bikes, be careful with spinning workouts; they can be a training disaster under the guidance of an overenthusiastic exercise leader. You don't need to be in race shape in February (unless you live in Australia). Keep the intensity in check and work on your pedaling economy.

◆ **Fixed-gear bikes:** To set up a fixed-gear bike, remove the derailleurs and shifters from an old frame. Have an older-style freewheel body welded, or buy a track-hub wheel. Select a gear that puts you at about 90 rpm on the flats when riding easily—this is probably in the range of 39-42 x 15-19 gearing. Ride only on flat to gently rolling courses. Be cautious at first—you'll have to unlearn old coasting habits such as standing on the pedals to stretch and pausing to sit back down.

◆ **CompuTrainer SpinScan:** If you are fortunate enough to have a CompuTrainer to train on, you can use the SpinScan mode to improve economy. By pedaling in this mode while watching the monitor, you can vary left-right leg output and force application to the pedal and see the result immediately. Isolated-leg training, with one leg at a time doing all of the work, is an excellent drill with this equipment. The idea of drills with the SpinScan is to lower the peaks and raise the valleys of your power curve.

◆ **On the road:** Of course, all of these ideas have only one purpose—to make you more economical at pedaling in the real world of the road. It doesn't matter how proficient you become at any of these exercises if the gains don't translate to your bike in a race. During the winter months, think about what you're doing on the road. Is your pedal stroke relaxed even when the tempo picks up? Are you making smooth transitions at the top and bottom of the stroke? Are you pedaling at the high end of your cadence comfort range? By spring you should be answering "yes" to all of these questions.

Bike-handling skills are discussed in Chapter 4.

Stage 2: Overall Strength

As you begin to establish your endurance base, you will want to begin increasing your muscular endurance using hills and steady long rides in heart-rate Zone 2.

Muscular endurance in hilly terrain

The goal of a hilly ride is typically to build muscular endurance. Novice athletes should begin these sessions on routes that offer an hour of easy terrain to warm up and then move to gentle rollers. You will want to work over these rollers keeping your heart rate in Zone 2 and your cadence low, around 60 rpm. Dropping your cadence any lower than 60 rpm can add excessive load on your knees, which can lead to injury or inflammation. Experienced athletes should incorporate longer, steady climbs maintaining heart-rate Zone 3. In the Base period, the downhill and flat terrain in these rides is typically done at an easy pace. The key focus is building climbing-specific strength.

Group rides

As the racing season approaches, many athletes benefit from riding in a group. Many athletes may avoid group rides because they may feel they aren't up to group speed, lack group skills, or prefer to ride solo. For those who may be new to group riding, the best way to learn is to start with a smaller group of friends. Have your experienced training buddies explain what you need to know. When riding with a new group, it is best to be conservative and work just like everyone else.

Those who prefer to ride solo will find that riding with a fellow athlete or small group will enable them to maintain their focus as they get stronger. Four to five hours of steady riding is much easier when you have someone pushing you from behind, or if you are sitting on the wheel of a much stronger rider. You will get benefits from both types of rides.

Following are a few basic guidelines for group riding:

◆ Always ride single file.

◆ Never half-wheel the person in front of you. Half-wheeling is when the leading edge of your front wheel is in front of the trailing edge of the leader's back wheel. It is highly dangerous because you can clip wheels. Even if you are riding in fierce crosswinds and trying to set up an echelon (riding to the side, and back, of the leading rider to sit in their wind shadow), it isn't worth the risk until you have excellent bike-handling skills.

◆ When riding at the front, increase and decrease speed gradually. Always continue to pedal when going downhill.

◆ Even if you think you are speeding up when you come out of the saddle, you are likely slowing down. This change has implications for athletes on your wheel.

◆ When drafting, the safest place for your hands is on your brake hoods. If you are team time-trialing (riding on your aerobars), you need a very safe course and a lot of confidence in the other athletes in the group as well as your own skills. It is highly risky to draft without your hands on the brakes.

◆ When you peel off the front, peel into the wind. The next rider in line should build into his or her turn gradually.

◆ If you are riding with stronger riders, don't feel that you have to take a turn. If you are going to sit in, make it clear to the others what your plans are and work out whether you are going to cycle through the group or simply stay at the back. Having a weaker cyclist cycle through can slow down the ride; some riders may prefer that you simply stay at the back and out of the way. Leave your ego behind if you have doubts about your stamina. It is far better to draft than blow to pieces halfway through the ride.

◆ If you are much stronger than the rest of the group, take longer turns at the front, or even ride the whole time at the front. There is a huge difference between being at the front and sitting in the group. You can get a very solid ride by leading, and the riders behind you will need to match only 60 to 70 percent of your power output.

◆ If you are riding with roadies, it is polite to leave your aerobars at home.

Because cycling is fundamentally a power-based sport, incorporating year-round strength training into the regimen will benefit nearly every triathlete's cycling performance.

Stage 3: Time-Trial Strength

Most strong cyclists will find that time-trial strength is their key limiter. ME interval sessions, cruise intervals, and big-gear work are the best sessions to address this limiter. The brick workouts in Appendix A can be used as bike-only ME workouts.

Which workout to choose? Here are some tips for selecting the right session for your needs and the time of the year.

◆ Early in the season, interval duration and intensity should be shorter and lower.

◆ For long-course racing, most athletes will benefit from building toward longer, sub-threshold intervals.

◆ Athletes who are force-limited will benefit from intervals that incorporate large-gear, low-cadence work. When doing strength-oriented intervals, keep your heart rate down and focus on making smooth, powerful circles.

◆ If your greatest limiter is the ability to focus, then 5- to 25-km subthreshold time trials can be an excellent way to enhance focus.

◆ If focus or endurance is your greatest limiter, then high-intensity intervals should be avoided; you will reap greater rewards from consistent steady rides that incorporate cruise intervals (periods of faster, subthreshold riding during a longer workout).

◆ Your economy will benefit from interval training at the limits of your comfortable cadence range (both high and low).

◆ The most effective interval session for ironman-distance racing is a series of moderate intervals incorporated into an endurance-oriented BT workout. Examples of these sessions are included in Appendix A.

Interval Guidelines

As heart rate significantly lags behind effort, those of us who like to use our heart-rate monitors for training have to learn to incorporate RPE when doing intervals. Probably the most common mistake with interval (ME) work is going too hard. An overenthusiastic athlete can blow the entire set by starting too fast.

Pacing: To get the best results, build into each interval and each set. If you are aiming for a heart-rate target, then you will need to be very patient at the start of each interval and each set. Control your effort and build toward the target at the end of the interval. Pushing extremely hard early in the set or interval is not needed. Just as in a race, split the work effort into quarters.

1. In the first quarter, your body is fresh and free of lactate; the goal is to hold back.

2. In the second quarter, maintain your goal interval pace/effort.

3. The third quarter is when most people have a dip in output, and this is where you should focus on maintaining your effort while holding perfect form.

4. The final quarter can be tough if the interval intensity is high. However, for ironman-distance racing, we are rarely doing very high-output intervals. If you have paced yourself through the first 75 percent of the repetition, then the quiet satisfaction of a solid repeat should bring you home.

Intensity: If you are like most triathletes, deep down you probably think that 10 x 7 minutes (flat out) on 5 seconds' rest is "better" than 6 x 5 minutes (build to threshold) on 75 seconds' rest. Note that the "better" set has longer interval duration, higher intensity, and shorter rest.

Many sports scientists have spent time analyzing the optimal mix of intensity, duration, and recovery. The good news is that we do not have to completely fry ourselves to get the physiological adaptations we desire. This is particularly true for ironman-distance training, where most athletes are close to their recovery limits.

Feelings of nausea and deep fatigue are signs that you have pushed too hard. All-out intervals are not required to get the physiological changes you are seeking. High-intensity sessions all too often result in extended recovery periods and poor technique.

Temperament: Intervals are a great way to get a look at how you are likely to perform in a race situation.

◆ Do you fade toward the end of the main set? You will need to focus on mental toughness or better front-end pacing.

◆ Do you consistently fry yourself in the first few repeats? You will need to leave your ego at the race start.

◆ Do you want to quit in the middle, struggle through, then feel great at the end? You will likely benefit from visualizing strong performance in the middle of a race.

Many athletes have suffered from of going too hard too early in a race. Learning to control yourself in training is an important part of hitting the right effort levels on game day.

Sense of pace: Most strong cyclists have an inbuilt sense of what pace they are going. They don't need a clock or heart-rate monitor; they just "know." Different-paced intervals are excellent for helping the athlete learn a sense of pace. It can be quite beneficial for all athletes to do pace work on measured courses. Intervals are the perfect time to develop your sense of different paces.

Nutrition: Ever wonder if your stomach will be able to handle a certain sports drink in an ironman-distance race? Drink 1.5 liters of it before a 40-km time trial and you'll have an idea of how you'll fare. Ever wonder what it is like to eat solid foods at the end of an ironman-distance bike? Insert 5 x 3 minutes hard on 1-minute recovery at the 3-hour mark of a steady-state endurance ride. As soon as your breathing has slowed after the intervals, start eating and see how you feel. These are somewhat extreme examples of how you can use intervals to "test" your nutrition.

Safety: Doing hard bike intervals outdoors is probably the most dangerous activity that we do as triathletes. Traveling at high speed on the aerobars is risky. The following are a few pointers to remember.

◆ Always wear a helmet. It is amazing how otherwise sane athletes leave their helmets at home (or even take them off). To illustrate this point, drop a cantaloupe from a height of six feet onto the road. Now picture the same scene with the cantaloupe starting at a speed of 20 to 45 mph.

◆ Never do intervals in the dark, and if you are riding in the dark, use lights and wear reflective clothing. The right equipment will improve your chances of being seen. Once you get used to riding safely, you'll feel naked without your protective gear. High-quality LED flashers are inexpensive and greatly increase your visibility.

◆ Assume that you are invisible. A triathlete moving at high speed on the aerobars doesn't present a lot of frontal area for a driver to see. Always assume that the person in the car doesn't see you. It's better to lose a bit of a repeat than to spend weeks recovering from a Superman impersonation across someone's hood.

◆ Keep your head up. This advice may seem obvious, but you often see cyclists riding with their head down. It's not just cars that can get you—it's also joggers, pedestrians, potholes, ditches, other cyclists, etc.

◆ Review your route in advance. Warm up by riding through the entire interval route. That way you will be able to spot any potential trouble spots in advance.

◆ Be aware of the location of all traffic, particularly cars that are approaching you from behind, and know what all the vehicles in your area are doing.

Key Sessions

Given cycling's nonimpact nature, you will have a much better tolerance for cycling intensity than running intensity.

When incorporating higher-intensity riding into your training plan, remember that most self-coached athletes do much too much intensity and volume and tend to keep themselves in a constant state of overreaching with periodic flirtations with overtraining. Often they train at intensities that are inappropriate for ironman-distance training. You should seldom be at heart rates in Zone 4 to Zone 5a, even on your hardest rides.

In fact, learning to control intensity and using heart rate to prevent going anaerobic during a race, especially on hills, is one of the keys to successful racing. If you go anaerobic in a race, there is an increased chance that your stomach will shut down, forcing you to slow in the latter stages of the race. This situation needs to be rehearsed in training so pacing discipline becomes routine.

If you frequently go anaerobic in training, some studies have shown that it may actually be detrimental to your aerobic capacities.

Muscular Endurance Training Sessions

For building early-season ME, we recommend indoor-trainer sessions, starting after the completion of the highest-intensity phase of your strength program. The following eight-week protocol can be used for these sessions and should be adjusted to your own personal limiters or race-season goals. Athletes who live in temperate climates can do these sessions outdoors.

◆ Start intervals easily, and build into each effort. Be particularly careful with the first 45 seconds, as legs will be relatively lactate free and heart rate lags behind effort.

◆ Use RPE in conjunction with power and heart-rate value. The goal of these sessions is to build toward hard efforts. Maximum-effort intervals are not required.

- The goal should be to increase intensity through the session. Finish strong; save a little for the last part of the session. Focus on the third and fourth intervals of each set.
- Rest interval (RI) should be easy spinning. Maintain form.
- Never push into deep pain. Learning to tell the difference between normal "training pain" and "preinjury pain" takes time. Be cautious, and back off if there is any uncertainty.
- Alternate between a "climbing" and an "aero" bike position. The appropriate mix of position will depend on the nature of early-season race courses and your personal limiters.
- Hold perfect form—relaxed face, jaw, and shoulders; proper back alignment; smooth leg drive; and eyes open. You want to train with perfect form so it will translate to the road and races.
- Intervals are best done after a 20- to 40-minute warm-up that includes several 15- to 30-second pickups to threshold effort (not heart rate).
- Follow your interval session with some easy spinning and a stretching session (at least 10 minutes).
- Use your own judgment on the cadence guidelines. For example, Athlete A, who is a good spinner, might use 90 to 95 rpm as normal, but Athlete B, who is a grinder, would use 80 to 85 rpm as normal. Riders with force as a limiter will benefit from lower cadence intervals, while riders seeking to lift their comfortable cadence will benefit from higher cadence intervals.
- Be "reasonable" with all guidelines, in particular heart rate and cadence guidelines.

Table 6.1 outlines a structure for ME training sessions.

Late Base and Build Period Muscular Endurance Sessions

After this eight-week program, athletes will be ready to start their race-specific preparations. The purpose of these sessions is to build subthreshold cycling power and prepare you for the specific demands of your A-priority race. These sessions should begin seven to eleven weeks out from your first A-priority race of the season.

Most athletes will benefit from a transition run after these sessions. Novices and athletes who take longer to recover should run for only 10 to 20 minutes while focusing on cadence and smooth running form. Experienced athletes can turn these sessions into race-simulation workouts by adding 45 to 90 minutes of running following the bike sessions. Elite and very strong athletes should build to a tempo finish (heart-rate Zone 3) for the run.

Examples of ME brick sessions can be found in Appendix A.

Table 6.1 ME Trainer Sessions

Week	Main Set	Intensity	Cadence
1	Set A 5x3 minutes on 1-minute RI	1. End at low heart-rate Zone 3	1. Normal
		2. End at middle heart-rate Zone 3	2. Faster
		3. End at upper heart-rate Zone 3	3. Slower
		4. End at lower heart-rate Zone 4	4. Faster
		5. Build to heart-rate Zone 4 in first 45 seconds and hold	5. Normal
2	Set B 5x3 minutes on 1-minute RI	1. End at middle heart-rate Zone 3	1. Normal
		2. End at upper heart-rate Zone 3	2. Faster
		3. End at lower heart-rate Zone 4	3. Slower
		4. End at upper heart-rate Zone 4	4. Faster
		5. Build to heart-rate Zone 5a in first 45 seconds and hold	5. Normal
3	Two sets of 5x3 minutes on 1-minute RI Repeat with 15+ minutes of heart-rate Zone 1/2 riding between sets	Both sets at Set A Intensity	1. Faster
			2. Slower
			3. Faster
			4. Slower
			5. Normal
4	Heart Rate or Power Testing		
5	Two sets of 5x3 minutes on 1-minute RI Repeat with 15+ minutes of heart-rate Zone 1/2 riding between sets	1 at Set A intensity	1. Faster
		2 at Set B intensity	2. Slower
			3. Faster
			4. Slower
			5. Normal

Week	Main Set	Intensity	Cadence
6	Two sets of 5x3 minutes on 1-minute RI	Both sets at Set B intensity	1. Faster
			2. Slower
	Repeat with 15+ minutes of heart-rate Zone 1/2 riding between sets		3. Faster
			4. Slower
			5. Normal
7	Set C	Use Set B intensity	1. Faster
	5x5 minutes on 90-second RI		2. Slower
			3. Faster
			4. Slower
			5. Normal
8	Heart-rate or power testing		

Note: Further indoor training ideas can be found in Appendix D.

Training with Power

With the advent of portable power measurement devices, the field of "power training" is set to undergo a transformation as athletes and coaches learn the best way to use this unique training tool.

This section focuses on techniques and methods that work in the field. Our goal is to present a methodology that is effective and applicable across a wide range of athletes and abilities. Undoubtedly, these methods will be refined and replaced by superior techniques in the years to come. In making this topic easier to interpret, we have simplified certain technical and physiological aspects of power-based training.

The principal benefits of heart-rate training are that the equipment is readily available, easy to operate, and affordable. Indeed, a heart-rate monitor and a set of aerobars are probably the two best investments for novice triathletes—once they have goggles, a bike, and running shoes! Like all training methods, heart-rate training has its limitations, and often we may find that we are a little too focused on our numbers.

One of the immediate benefits of using a powermeter is that you are provided with a new source of data to incorporate into training. Power responds differently than heart rate and can encourage an athlete to think outside the heart-rate "box." A powermeter provides an instantaneous check of performance. Powermeters express performance in the form of watts. The greater your wattage, the more power you are generating and the faster you will travel for a given set of external conditions.

There are several areas in which power-based training can be an effective supplement to heart-rate-based systems (nearly all commercially available powermeters incorporate a heart-rate function). Power-based training is most effective in these areas:

◆ Early in a workout, and a race, athletes will tend to underestimate how hard they are working. A well-rested athlete will be able to produce significant wattage and/or lactate levels without immediately elevating his or her heart rate. Powermeters are quite useful for regulating early ride intensity and quickly showing the impact of power spikes or surges.

◆ When used in conjunction with a heart-rate monitor, powermeters are extremely useful for steady-state training. At the start of a long race or workout, an athlete can have confidence that, despite a lower heart rate, he or she is working at the correct intensity. Previously, coaches could only advise their athletes to "go easy" or "hold back" at the start of a race or training session. With powermeters, a specific power range can be determined in advance.

◆ In general, the time lag between effort and cardiac response is between 20 seconds and 2 minutes, depending on how early or late in the workout that heart rate is being monitored. This lag in cardiac response means that for short-duration efforts (intervals, in particular), heart rate is a poor indicator of actual work being done.

◆ Although nearly every athlete can produce a heart-rate profile that rises while climbing, it takes practice to produce an even power profile over a climb. Typically, a "power novice" will generate his or her highest power output in the first 20 to 40 seconds of a climb. Following the peak output, power then declines (as heart rate and blood lactate levels climb). This athlete may be under the impression that a higher heart rate implies increasing power output. A powermeter will quickly show whether this is the case and help this athlete learn to climb more efficiently.

◆ Regular use of a powermeter enables an athlete to quickly realize when he or she is accumulating excessive fatigue within a training block. When an athlete is tired, it quickly shows in the power numbers. A lower-than-usual power-to-heart-rate ratio and a higher perceived effort for a given level of power are clear indicators that an athlete should consider additional rest.

Power-based training, like any system, has its own limitations. Power is most effective when used in conjunction with the full range of training variables available to an athlete (principally heart rate, pace, RPE, and cadence). In general, the shorter the workout or race duration and the fitter the athlete, the greater the role "feel" plays for an athlete. By "feel" we mean perception of effort. However, as you will find, fairly high-wattage figures can initially feel very easy to a highly motivated and rested athlete.

The techniques presented in the following sections are a summary of what Gordo uses in his training as well as the training programs that we use for our athletes who have access to powermeters. For a more complete explanation of this topic, refer to the recommended readings at the end of this chapter. You are highly encouraged to review a copy of Joe's "Training with Power Guide," available online at the Power-Tap website. These are the most common questions raised by athletes concerning power zones and power testing.

Why use a 30-minute time trial? The power methodology presented has been designed to be consistent with the training system outlined in this book. As your most frequent cycling test is a 30-minute time trial, your average power for this test is the starting point for discussing power zones. Although taxing, the test duration is short enough to be repeated every four to eight weeks to track your progress.

When should I test? Power testing is best done toward the end of a recovery week and more than forty-eight hours after a strength-training or BT session. Athletes should prepare themselves by using a thorough warm-up prior to testing (see "Warming Up" sidebar).

What is a CP30 value? The average power generated across any time period is referred to as an athlete's "critical power." So the 30-minute average-power test would yield a 30-minute critical-power value; this value is referred to as "CP30." Like any best average test, critical-power testing is most accurate when you are able to hold the average power with as small a variation as possible. If you blow up midtest, then the results will likely be inaccurate. For this reason, we recommend that you build into your tests and start a little easier than your anticipated best effort. Remember that you'll have a long career to improve your CP numbers!

Warming Up

Prior to any time trial, race, or test, you will generate the best results if you are able to complete a thorough warm-up. An effective warm-up for a time trial of any duration follows:

Step 1: Ride 40 minutes, easy to steady pace. While riding, survey the course and build to 80 to 100 percent of CP30 (threshold perceived effort) on some short rollers. Ensure that there is no significant lactate accumulation during this period of the warm-up.

Step 2: Take a short bathroom break, and, if it is a hot day, have a good drink.

Step 3: Ride 20 minutes, steady pace. While riding, insert four to five efforts on long recoveries. The efforts should be done in time-trial position, roughly twenty pedal revolutions that build to a cadence of 100 to 120 rpm and power output of 150 to 165 percent of CP30 (hard to very hard perceived effort). Again, ensure that there is no large lactate accumulation. Efforts should last just until you notice a change in your breathing pattern.

Step 4: Following the completion of the final effort, take a 2- to 5-minute break. During the break, focus on goals for the test or race. If the session is to last longer than 15 minutes, eat a small, highly glycemic snack and have another drink. Once the drink and snack have settled, start the session.

What is a CP30 range? Like heart-rate-based training, power values can be used to determine training zones. The training zone for a given CP value is 5 percent above and below the test average. For example, an athlete with a CP30 of 200 would have a CP30 zone of 190 to 210.

How does power change over CP duration? A good rule of thumb is that average power decreases by 5 percent as duration doubles. So an athlete with a CP30 of 200 would be expected to have a CP60 of 190 (95 percent of CP30). The farther you get from a test value, and the more anaerobic a test becomes, the less accurate this estimation procedure becomes. For example, your CP60 would be a poor predictor of your CP6.

Are any other CP figures useful for the long-course athlete? Our experience to date shows CP30 as the most useful data point for long-course athletes. CP30 is a reasonable estimation of threshold power and easy to test. However, athletes will benefit from developing an understanding of their individual power profiles across a range of durations, intensities, and terrain.

For elite and strong cyclists, the CP12 value is a reasonable measurement of anaerobic endurance and can provide useful information for racing shorter distances. However, anaerobic endurance is rarely a performance limiter for long-course racing, so this test is more important for a short-course athlete. Although it can be useful to track power output in race situations and training, there is limited value to power testing for any duration longer than 30 minutes.

Table 6.2 is a rough guideline for heart-rate and critical-power zones. As you will quickly discover, heart-rate-intensity zones do not track directly to critical-power zones. This discrepancy is due to the variation in muscular endurance seen in the spectrum of athletes (from elite to novice). Also included in the table is qualitative pace description of each power zone.

Table 6.2 Heart-Rate and Critical-Power Zones

Heart-Rate Zone	Critical-Power Zone	Pace Description
5c	CP0.2–CP1	max effort
5b	CP6	very hard
5a	CP30	hard to very hard
4	CP60	mod-hard to hard
3	CP90	mod-hard
2	CP180–CP240	steady
1	half of CP12	easy

Table 6.3 provides a more qualitative description of a range of aerobic training zones relative to CP30. Due to the challenges of relating power directly to heart rate, the values given in the table do not specifically match the heart-rate estimations in Table 6.2.

Table 6.3 Aerobic Training Zones to CP30

Zone Description	Percentage of CP30	Pace Description
Threshold	100	hard to very hard
Cruise intervals	90–100	hard
Sprint-distance triathlon	90–95	hard
Olympic-distance triathlon	85–90	hard
Half-ironman-distance triathlon	80–87	mod-hard to hard
Intensive endurance (long ride)	73–80	steady to mod-hard
Base endurance (long ride)	67–73	easy to steady
Easy training	< 67	easy

The percentages in Table 6.3 relate to averages across the entire workout. For longer sessions, you will find that perceived exertion increases as session duration increases. For example, a 2-hour ride at 75 percent of CP30 will ultimately feel completely different than a 4-hour ride at the same power output.

If you are planning to race long distance on power, it is essential that you perform race-simulation workouts that mimic your planned power strategy. An "easy" power level in the first hour of a race can prove to be quite strenuous after 5 to 6 hours of riding. If you have any doubts about the appropriate pace, effort, or power, then it is best to start the ride at a slightly easier level than your goal effort.

Long-distance racing is about getting from A to B as quickly and efficiently as possible. Once the training is done, your physiological potential is essentially determined by your talent, preparations, and taper. At this stage, your actual race performance will be dominated by your ability to execute an effective race strategy. Efficiency and pacing are critical success factors for every athlete's race strategy. Racing with power can enhance your ability to maximize your performance for a given level of fitness.

Triathletes who are able to use their watts in the most efficient manner will get the most speed for a given level of effort. In general, a simple rule for efficient riding is to hold back when moving at faster-than-average speed and work a little harder when moving at slower-than-average speed.

However, you need to be cautious about how you define "average speed" and be particularly wary of working "a little harder" when riding into a sustained headwind. On a bike, resistance is a function of air speed rather than ground speed. From an aerodynamic viewpoint, an athlete riding into a sustained headwind is traveling at a substantially faster speed than his or her speedometer indicates. Experience (and watts) will help you decide on an appropriate level of effort. In a headwind, it can be comforting to see that despite a "slow" pace, a reasonable amount of power is being produced.

In order to fully utilize the benefits of power, you should have a clear understanding of the most important areas of your course. Pay particular attention to the length, duration, and grade of all climbs and the distances that must be ridden in areas that may be exposed to high winds (head-, tail-, or cross-).

Consider your race strategy for each key section. Your strategy should be based on prior race performance as well as the results of your key race-simulation workouts. As of this writing, racing long-course triathlons with power is a very new field, and reliable data are still hard to come by. As a result, it is wise to base your strategy on your personal training experiences rather than the pacing recommendations of others. Still, here are some tips for you to consider:

◆ A properly trained athlete will be able to average 65 to 70 percent of CP30 for the duration of a 6-hour ride. However, this figure is highly variable due to individual muscular endurance as well as an athlete's ability to push during a CP30 test.

◆ For short climbs of up to 5 minutes' duration, athletes should consider an effort ceiling of 95 to 105 percent of CP30.

◆ For longer climbs, consider an effort ceiling of 85 to 95 percent of CP30.

◆ For all climbs, it is very important to "save some watts" for cresting the apex of the climb. Novices tend to have their highest watts at the base of a climb. The intelligent athlete will have his or her highest watts over the top of a climb and accelerate down the back side. Experienced power users know that higher lactate levels can be cleared during the descent and after the rider has returned to cruising speed.

These guidelines are merely a starting point for helping develop your own race strategy, a strategy that should be field tested well in advance of race day. Highly trained elite athletes may be able to sustain levels up to 5 percent above these guidelines. Novice athletes should consider racing at, or below, the bottom end of these guidelines. It's also worth noting that many of our sport's strongest cyclists train extensively with power and then race using a mixture of RPE and heart rate.

As an ironman-distance race extracts a severe penalty for early pacing mistakes, you should start each race conservatively and build your pace through the second half of the race. Walking even a single mile of the marathon can negate a lot of hard work on the bike!

The single greatest benefit of using power for long-course racing is learning how to best moderate your effort. Even if you race without your powermeter, the knowledge that you will gain in training will prove highly valuable come race day.

Recommended Reading

Baker, A. *The Essential Cyclist*. New York: Lyons Press, 1998.

Bernhardt, G. *The Female Cyclist: Gearing Up a Level*. Boulder, CO: VeloPress, 1999.

Borysewicz, E. *Bicycle Road Racing*. Brattleboro, VT: Velo News, 1985.

Burke, E. *Serious Cycling*. Champaign, IL: Human Kinetics, 1995.

Burney, S. *Cyclo-Cross Training and Technique*. Boulder, CO: VeloPress, 1996.

Friel, J. *Cycling Past 50*. Champaign, IL: Human Kinetics, 1998.

——. *The Cyclist's Training Bible*. Boulder, CO: VeloPress, 1996.

——. *The Mountain Biker's Training Bible*. Boulder, CO: VeloPress, 2000.

——. *The Triathlete's Training Bible*. Boulder, CO: VeloPress, 1998.

LeMond, G. *Greg LeMond's Complete Book of Bicycling*. New York: Perigee Books, 1987.

Niles, R. *Time-Saving Training for Multisport Athletes*. Champaign, IL: Human Kinetics, 1997.

Phinney, D., and C. Carpenter. *Training for Cycling*. New York: Perigee Books, 1992.

Skilbeck, P. *Single-Track Mind*. Boulder, CO: VeloPress, 1996.

Sleamaker, R., and R. Browning. *Serious Training for Endurance Athletes*. Champaign, IL: Human Kinetics, 1996.

Sources

Bernhardt, G., *The Female Cyclist: Gearing Up a Level*. VeloPress, 1999.

Bishop, D., and D. G. Jenkins. The Influence of Recovery Duration between Periods of Exercise on the Critical Power Function. *European Journal of Applied Physiology* 72 (1–2) (1995): 115–120.

Bishop, D., D. G. Jenkins, and A. Howard. The Critical Power Function Is Dependent on the Duration of the Predictive Exercise Tests Chosen. *International Journal of Sports Medicine* 19 (2) (1998): 125–129.

Clingelleffer, A., L. R. McNaughton, and B. Davoren. The Use of Critical Power as a Determinant for Establishing the Onset of Blood Lactate Accumulation. *European Journal of Applied Physiology* 68 (2): 182–187.

Gaesser, G. A., T. J. Carnevale, A. Garfinkel, et al. Estimation of Critical Power with Nonlinear and Linear Models. *Medicine and Science in Sports and Exercise* 27 (10): 1430–1438.

Hawley, J. A., and T. D. Noakes. Peak Power Output Predicts Maximal Oxygen Uptake and Performance Time in Trained Cyclists. *European Journal of Applied Physiology* 65 (1) (1992): 79–83.

Herman, E. A., H. G. Knuttgen, P. N. Frykman, and J. F. Patton. Exercise Endurance Time as a Function of Percent Maximal Power Production. *Medicine and Science in Sports and Exercise* 19 (5) (1987): 480–485.

Hill, D. W. The Critical Power: A Review. *Sports Medicine* 16 (4) (1993): 237–254.

Hill, D. W., and J. C. Smith. A Method to Ensure the Accuracy of Estimates of Anaerobic Capacity Derived Using the Critical Power Concept. *Journal of Sports Medicine and Physical Fitness* 34 (1) (1994): 23–37.

Hopkins, S. R., and D. C. McKenzie. The Laboratory Assessment of Endurance Performance in Cyclists. *Canadian Journal of Applied Physiology* 19 (3) (1994): 266–274.

Housh, D. J., T. J. Housh, and S. M. Bauge. The Accuracy of the Critical Power Test for Predicting Time to Exhaustion during Cycle Ergometry. *Ergonomics* 32 (8) (1989): 997–1004.

Housh, T. J., H. A. deVries, D. J. Housh, et al. The Relationship between Critical Power and the Onset of Blood Lactate Accumulation. *Journal of Sports Medicine and Physical Fitness* 31 (1) (1991): 31–36.

Jenkins, D. G., and B. M. Quigley. Blood Lactate in Trained Cyclists during Cycle Ergometry at Critical Power. *European Journal of Applied Physiology* 61 (3–4) (1990): 278–283.

———. Endurance Training Enhances Critical Power. *Medicine and Science in Sports and Exercise* 24 (11) (1992): 1283–1289.

McLellan, T. M., and K. S. Cheung. 1992. A Comparative Evaluation of the Individual Anaerobic Threshold and the Critical Power. *Medicine and Science in Sports and Exercise* 24 (5) (1992): 543–550.

Moritani, T., A. Nagata, H. A. deVries, and M. Muro. Critical Power as a Measure of Physical Work Capacity and Anaerobic Threshold. *Ergonomics* 24 (5) (1981): 339–350.

Morton, R. H. Alternative Forms of the Critical Power Test for Ramp Exercise. *Ergonomics* 40 (5) (1997): 511–514.

———. Critical Power Test for Ramp Exercise. *European Journal of Applied Physiology* 69 (5) (1994): 435–438.

———. Ramp and Constant Power Trials Produce Equivalent Critical Power Estimates. *Medicine and Science in Sports and Exercise* 29 (6) (1997): 833–836.

——. The Relationship between Power Output and Endurance: A Brief Review. *European Journal of Applied Physiology* 73 (6) (1996): 491–502.

——. A 3-Parameter Critical Power Model. *Ergonomics* 39 (4) (1996): 611–619.

Vandewalle, H., J. F. Vautier, M. Kachouri, et al. Work-Exhaustion Time Relationships and the Critical Power Concept: A Critical Review. *Journal of Sports Medicine and Physical Fitness* 37 (2) (1997): 89–102.

Websites

Bicycle Gear Inch and Shifting Pattern Calculator:
http://www.panix.com/~jbarrm/cycal/cycal.30f.html.

Chapter 7

Training for the Run

Of the three sports in triathlon, running is the most stressful on the body. It is also the sport that appears to cause the majority of injuries in both novice and experienced athletes. For this reason, you should approach run training with caution.

Stages of Running Development

The four stages below follow the life cycle of the development of a runner. They can also provide ideas for structuring your season if you are an experienced runner.

There are many ways to successfully train for running, and you should remain sensitive to the signals you receive from your body. With running in particular, your body typically gives numerous early-warning messages in advance of an injury occurring. Knowing when to back off is a valuable skill, whether you are a novice or an elite runner.

Stage 1: Learning to Run

The primary goal in this stage of training is to strengthen connective tissues and prepare your body for the stresses of the longer sessions in Stage 2. This process is enhanced by strength training, particularly if you are a novice, a cyclist, or a swimmer.

A secondary goal of this stage (and an important focus for all athletes) is technical improvement. Though the overall intensity of this stage is low, you will be able to maintain your quickness, enhance economy, and improve form through using speed drills such as Strides, One-Leg drills, high-cadence rides, and technique exercises (see Chapter 4 for skills descriptions and sample workouts).

The training focus of this stage is frequency, with three to four runs per week. Each run should last from 20 to 45 minutes. At least one of these runs is a short transition run following a bike ride, generally 15 to 30 minutes. The purpose of this transition run (this combination is also known as a "brick," "combination," or "transition" workout) is to teach your body to quickly move from cycling to running. You do not need to run long or fast (that may come later). What you need to do is run until your muscles successfully change from cycling to running. These runs have the shortest duration.

If you are looking to speed your adaptation through this stage, you can supplement run training with hiking or backpacking and trekking, all of which are excellent ways to build endurance and complement run training (see Chapter 3 for a discussion of limiters).

All runs should be done in heart-rate Zones 1 and 2. If you are a novice, you may feel that this pace is too slow to produce any benefit. However, this stage of running development is essential to have a long, healthy, and successful running career.

The length of time that you spend in Stage 1 is highly variable, ranging from three to six months (if you are a fit cyclist or swimmer) to several years if you are a novice and/or overweight. As a guideline, if you are new to running, you should spend a minimum of six months in this stage of development.

Stage 2: Building Endurance

The goal of Stage 2 is to build the endurance necessary to complete (rather than compete) the run portion of your event.

Once your running base has been established, you can safely extend the duration of your longest run each week. The duration of your long run should increase by 5 to 10 percent (5 to 15 minutes) each week in your training cycle. Your long run should be significantly reduced during recovery weeks.

Once your long run has been built up to between 90 and 150 minutes, you should consider extending the duration of your second-longest run. Typically, if you are slow to recover or have running as a key limiter, you will find greater benefits from two moderate runs than one megarun. The principal reason is recovery. The marginal benefit of a run over 2.5 hours is outweighed by the extended recovery period that is required.

When you are seeking to build endurance, the duration of your workout is more important than the overall intensity. Whenever you are extending your "endurance envelope," intensity should be kept down and your focus should be on holding excellent form for the entire workout. Long runs provide an excellent opportunity to program strong running technique into the neuromuscular system. These programs are what will reappear when you are under stress in a race situation.

Once you are able to comfortably run the desired duration, intensity can be steadily increased. The most effective way of increasing intensity is to do it gradually through a workout. For example, a 2-hour run could start in heart-rate Zone 1 and slowly build so that it finishes at the top of heart-rate Zone 2. In general, when building base endurance it is best to avoid heart-rate Zone 3 and above.

Though the main focus of this stage is to build run endurance, you should continue to focus on your transition running as well as balancing the long, slow distance work with one or two weekly Strides and skills sessions.

You should stay in Stage 2 until you have been running for at least two years. You will benefit from building your endurance base for up to five years before starting focused ME work. The body adapts slowly, and the deeper the base that you create, the harder you can work when the time is right.

Stage 3: Building Muscular Endurance

Once you have built up the endurance necessary to complete your run, the next step is starting the training necessary to compete during the run.

Long-course running is about having the ability to run following a long cycling effort. This type of running is based on strength and muscular endurance. Raw speed is not a requirement for success, but superior muscular endurance is essential. Specific ME workouts are included in Appendix A. However, here are some general ideas to incorporate into your ME run training.

Triathlons: Up to sprint distance for novices, up to Olympic distance for most age-group athletes, and up to half-ironman-distance for elite athletes.

- ◆ Run or ride after a short, intense race. For example, after a sprint duathlon, ride for 2 to 3 hours at a low to moderate intensity (heart-rate Zone 1 or 2).
- ◆ Athletes using this strategy should watch their race frequency. Even a series of "easy" races can prove physically and mentally draining for any athlete.

Hills: Gently rolling courses provide natural fartlek training as the intensity increases on the climbs and drops on the descents. Hill running (while maintaining form), like hill cycling, gives you sport-specific strength. The key is finding the right amount of volume and balancing with other training. Endurance runs in rolling terrain are very useful for building race-specific strength. Athletes should allow ample recovery time from these challenging sessions. Hills are particularly useful for athletes who are seeking to boost running economy while training their aerobic systems. You should remember that hills are useful only to the extent that good form and a reasonable intensity can be held while climbing. It doesn't take a very steep grade to promote the economy and strength benefits of hill running.

Tempo running: Running in heart-rate Zone 3. Some ideas for tempo sessions:

◆ Insert up to three intervals of 5 to 20 minutes' duration into the middle of an endurance run.

◆ Insert a tempo finish to a transition or endurance run. The intensity should build to the top of heart-rate Zone 3 by the finish. Elite runners should extend the duration of the tempo finish to between 45 and 75 minutes by the end of the Build period.

◆ A specific tempo run: Following warm-up, build to tempo pace and hold for 20 to 90 minutes.

Road races: Up to 10K for novices and half-marathons for elites and experienced age groupers. Short races enable you to place a higher level of aerobic stress on your system without compromising recovery times.

It is worth remembering that longer and harder are not necessarily better with this type of training. Combining appropriate recovery with focused sessions that gradually stretch your limits is more effective than training to the edge of fatigue or injury.

Trail running: Best in the Prep and Base periods, trail running is excellent for building complete leg strength as well as improving agility. Trail running is less appropriate in the Build period because training should simulate race conditions. See the "Cross-Training: Hiking" sidebar for more on trail running.

Even when you are focusing on building muscular endurance, it is essential to maintain your running endurance. Many strong runners find that this result can be achieved by a combination of cycling and tempo run training.

Novice runners or runners with endurance as a key limiter should remember that cycling endurance and muscular endurance are more important for long-distance triathlon. Although many athletes enjoy running fast, it is not always the best strategy for overall triathlon success. You should ensure that your run training does not compromise the quality of your bike training.

In planning their seasons, experienced runners can use half-marathons and 10Ks for building intensive aerobic endurance. Spring half-marathons are particularly useful because pace and heart-rate data provide an excellent indicator of running fitness. Half-marathon efforts measure running fitness without major muscular damage or long recovery periods.

Two final things to remember: (1) Avoid high-intensity running when strength training is at a high intensity; and (2) when building muscular endurance for long-distance triathlon, keep the overall intensity below threshold for the quickest recovery. High-intensity running is for only the strongest athletes, and the marginal benefit is not worth the injury and recovery considerations for most athletes. Until your run splits are in the top 10 percent of your age group, ME work is the safest way to build triathlon run speed.

Stage 4: Building Superior Threshold Speed, Elites

What follows is the final stage of a runner's development. This kind of training is only appropriate for athletes with all of the following characteristics:

◆ You have been running without injury for at least the last twelve months.

◆ You have successfully completed twelve months of muscular endurance training.

◆ You recover well from your hard sessions and do not have endurance (bike or run) as a key limiter.

◆ You consistently place in the top 10 percent of your age group.

There are many ways to build running speed, and the protocol that follows is an effective one for certain athletes. You should take the guidelines in this section and interpret them in the context of your specific goals and limiters. What follows is a summary of the key points for this type of training. Readers who are interested in further information should review the "Recommended Reading" section.

The first step is to determine your VO_2max pace. Here is a sample protocol for the test, which should be completed at a 400-meter track.

An extensive warm-up of 30 to 45 minutes, for example:

◆ Run 800 meters easy.

◆ Run 1,600 to 3,000 meters with a mix of easy, steady, and running drills.

◆ Eight Strides with walk-back recovery. Strides are best done barefoot on grass. Do thirty left-foot strikes, run at 800-meter-race pace, focus on perfect form, about 19 seconds per repetition (95 rpm cadence). Walk-back is essential to drop heart rate.

◆ Run 800 meters easy, with builds to test effort.

◆ Fully recover for 3 to 5 minutes.

Following the deep warm-up, run 6 minutes at the fastest continuous pace possible; the goal should be to have even or slightly faster splits each lap. Athletes should note the total distance completed in meters. VO_2max pace is then determined by dividing 142,000 by the total distance traveled (in meters). For example, an athlete who covers 1,600 meters in 6 minutes has an estimated VO_2max pace of 88.75 seconds per 400 meters (142,000/1,600 = 88.75). Your VO_2max pace is also referred to as your sustained speed (SS) pace. VO_2max testing is a maximum-effort test that should be completed only by the strongest athletes who have complete confidence in their ability to finish safely.

Armed with VO_2max pace information, athletes have the ability to build training sessions that incorporate anaerobic endurance work. Typically, this kind of training will start in the late Base period and extend to the beginning or middle of the Build period.

Cross-Training: Hiking

For those with running as their greatest limiter, the early Base period is an excellent time for longer, low-intensity walking and running sessions. Hiking and trail running provide the opportunity to

◆ improve running economy
◆ strengthen running-specific connective tissues
◆ build base endurance

The most important thing to remember is that these sessions should be done at an easy pace and designed to gradually stretch your endurance. Trail running also provides an opportunity to improve your running economy. Trails, specifically inclines, give you the opportunity to shorten your stride and increase cadence while building greater leg strength.

TRAIL TIPS

Form: Whether running uphill or downhill, maintain proper running form. Particular attention should be paid to the alignment of the foot and knee.

Technical improvement: Longer, low-intensity sessions are an ideal time to remove running flaws. There is a low level of training stress, leaving you free to focus on your personal limiters such as cadence, arm carriage, pelvic and hip stability, foot strike, or body alignment.

Hydration: As the Base period generally occurs in the cooler months of the year, hydration needs are reduced. However, it is still important to maintain adequate hydration, particularly on long sessions. Products such as the CamelBak are an excellent way to carry fluids on the trail.

Nutrition: Long, low-intensity sessions are an excellent way to promote fat burning if you are looking to improve your body composition. You should always bring plenty of food when hitting the trails. However, most will be able to get away with 100 to 300 calories per hour, depending on the duration of the hike.

Duration: You will get an appropriate workout from a hike lasting 2 to 6 hours. When trail running, a session of 1 to 4 hours is appropriate, depending on the severity of the terrain. As a general rule, go long rather than fast.

Terrain: Soft surface and rolling terrain with a variety of climbs lasting between 10 and 30 minutes provide an opportunity to build "whole-leg" strength. A wide variety of grades will utilize the full range of running muscles. On steeper terrain, you should remember to keep your heart rate and exertion under control; even elite runners will walk hills.

Downhill running: Even when using a short, rapid stride, downhill running is quite stressful. You may benefit from inserting walking breaks of 2 to 10 minutes into each 10- to 20-minute period of downhill running. When running downhill, focus on a relaxed body and maintaining a high, comfortable cadence. It is best to avoid striding out, as this can overload the leg muscles and soft tissues of the joints. Use extreme caution with downhill running if you are a novice runner.

Running with packs: Avoid running with a pack on your back, as it can overload the knees and lead to injury.

Considerations when weight lifting: Hiking and trail running are complementary to the early phases of your strength program. However, because of the risk of overloading the lower body, longer run sessions should not be undertaken when you are in a heavy strength-training phase.

Clothing: Cycling clothing can be quite useful on the trail. A long-sleeved bike jersey will provide pockets for trail maps, food, and other supplies. In order to avoid the contents bouncing or spilling onto the trail, pull a set of tights up and over the pockets. A hat and thin windbreaker are excellent items to bring on any excursions in the cooler months.

Partners: Hiking is a great time to bring along the kids or a nontriathlon partner. A heavy pack can be a great equalizer for even the strongest athlete.

Here are some sample workouts:

Workout 1: 10 to 15 minutes done as 30 seconds at SS pace and 30 seconds at 50 percent of SS pace.

Workout 2: 10 to 15 x 400 meters done as 200 meters at SS pace and 200 meters steady.

Workout 3: 3, 6, or 9 x 400 meters descending at SS pace + 4 seconds, SS pace + 2 seconds, SS pace (repeat if desired). Interval time is 3 minutes, or such length as gives approximately a 1:1 work:rest ratio.

Workout 4: 3 to 5 x 1,000 meters at SS pace with equal recovery time.

The purpose of this kind of training is to increase VO_2max, increase threshold pace, and improve running economy. Some important points to remember with this kind of training:

Once per week: As a long-distance triathlete, you need to do only one of these sessions every seven to ten days. Increased frequency will result in lower-quality sessions in the rest of your training week.

Moderate volume leads to the best results: Studies have shown that 10 to 15 minutes of this type of work once a week is sufficient to achieve results, with improving threshold speed as well as economy. Early sessions should be done at 4 to 10 seconds per 400 meters over SS pace. You should gradually increase the speed and the workload.

Focus on technique: You will find that by focusing on form and relaxing, the pace is challenging but comfortable. If you are experiencing trouble hitting target pacing, then either your splits are too challenging, you need additional recovery, or you may be starting each interval too quickly.

Timing: As mentioned earlier, this type of training should be started eight to fifteen weeks before your first A-priority race of the year.

Pacing: If you are a strong runner, then you will be able to run these sessions at faster-than-SS pace. Research shows that running at a faster pace is not necessary and will only prolong recovery times. Stick to your VO_2max pace; you will get the same benefit and recover more quickly.

Warm-up and cool-down: Hard BT sessions are best done later in the day following a deep warm-up. In addition to the warm-up outlined above, you may benefit from 20 to 30 minutes of easy cycling prior to arriving at the track. Core conditioning work and running skills can be incorporated into the warm-up to more effectively use your time. Following the main set, a proper cool-down, including light stretching, will help promote recovery. You should also plan your nutrition needs in advance of this session.

Testing: If you plan to do more than four weeks of this type of training, then you should repeat the 6-minute test every four to six weeks. It bears repeating that if you are new to running or injury prone, then the risks of this training far outweigh the benefits.

After four to eight weeks of VO$_2$max training, athletes should begin to focus more on threshold and subthreshold running; this involves extending the interval duration and lowering the intensity and pace of the sessions. Sample sessions include:

Workout 1: 6 to 12 x 800/400 continuous where the 800s are done at fresh marathon goal race pace less 90 to 120 seconds per mile and the 400s are done on the same total split. For example, if your goal is to run a 3:10 ironman-distance marathon, the mile pace would be 5:15 to 5:45, and the workout split for the 800/400 would be 2:37 to 2:52.

Workout 2: 6- to 12-mile repeats done at goal race pace less 30 to 45 seconds per mile with light jogging recovery. Recovery interval should last 25 to 35 percent of the work interval.

Workout 3: 3 to 5 x 2,000 meters at 10K race pace with 400 meters easy jogging for recovery.

Athletes should aim for 25 to 40 minutes of work intervals. A good guideline for overall session duration is that athletes should finish each main set knowing that they could have done one more interval at goal intensity. If you miss a split or if your form falls apart, then it is best to call it a day and head home.

Short of an all-out effort in a short-course race, the sessions above are the highest-intensity work that you will be undertaking. They offer incremental speed gains and involve a high degree of biomechanical and recovery risk. Please use caution when attempting these workouts.

Key Issues

The role of nutrition: Probably the single greatest thing that most age-group athletes can do in order to improve their run performance is to improve their nutrition strategy. Ideas on this topic are included in Chapter 12.

The role of economy: There aren't many sources of "free speed" in sport, but running economy is an easy way to maximize performance from an existing aerobic base. Chapter 4 discusses good running form. To promote economy, you should incorporate Strides into your weekly program. In addition, pay particular attention to your running form toward the end of long runs or when you are running off the bike.

Running tired: Many coaches and athletes believe that it is beneficial to learn how to "run tired," so they schedule long runs for the day following long rides. This training does benefit a few, but it is accompanied by a greatly increased risk of injury and illness. For this reason, you will see both safer and more rapid results from starting your key running BT workouts as fresh as possible. If running is a limiter for you, then this approach is even more important. The benefits of training fresh are higher-quality sessions and more rapid recovery times.

Marathon running for nonelite athletes: Many ironman-distance triath-letes are tempted to improve their running by competing in early-season marathons. However, because of the training time lost owing to the taper and subsequent race recovery, this strategy is a poor one for most triathletes. If your key limiter is running endurance, focus on your nutrition and long endurance sessions. If your key limiter is running muscular endurance, you can often achieve a substantial improvement by targeting an early-season half-marathon and using an appropriate mix of sustained speed and ME sessions.

"Recovery" runs: Given the stresses associated with running (at any speed), running workouts should rarely be used for active-recovery sessions. Recovery workouts are best done on the bike, in the pool, or in another nonimpact activity, such as yoga.

A caution regarding intensity: High-intensity running is powerful training. If you have a history of injuries or biomechanical problems, it is best to remember that a marginal gain in running speed will not matter if you are injured or miss key BT workouts. Once endurance is built, cycling muscular endurance should be the number-one focus for all endurance athletes.

The 3-hour run: Some athletes like to include 3-hour, or longer, runs in their training program. You should exercise caution in using runs of this duration, as recovery times are normally 48 to 72 hours. There are very diminishing returns from running longer than 2.5 hours. The reason is the risk of extended recovery being required after the session, as well as the risk of injury. Therefore, cycling and swimming BT workouts can be adversely impacted. It is far better to do a 2-hour run and be able to get back on your training program after a single recovery day. Consistent training is the most important aspect of preparing for an ultra-endurance event. Long endurance sessions are best done on the bike or as a combination workout.

Running is a very important part of ironman-distance racing. However, a quick review of any set of race results will show that raw speed is not a requirement for race success. What is required is a long apprenticeship that safely builds endurance and speed as the body adapts to constant training. If you seek shortcuts, then injury is a likely result. Persistence and patience are the essential attributes of success.

Recommended Reading

Noakes, Tim. *Lore of Running*. Champaign, IL: Human Kinetics, 1991.

Chapter 8

Training the Mind

Do you think my
muscles have anything
to do with my being
faster and stronger?
—Morpheus, *The Matrix*

So much of long-distance triathlon is related to the power of the mind, yet how often do we take the time to train our minds? The mind is a powerful ally, but it can also be a formidable adversary. The techniques in this chapter are designed to help you control your mind and, in doing so, achieve an elite mind-set to maximize your race performance. The beauty of these techniques is that everyone can improve their performance through their application. Why? Because it's all in your head!

Before getting into this chapter, it is recommended that you spend some quality time considering these three things:

1. Your long-term goals from the sport of triathlon as well as the other key areas of your life (such as work, family, community, friends, and other interests)

2. The level of commitment you are able to give to the achievement of your triathlon goals

3. The "price" you are willing to pay in order to achieve your goals

Be as honest as possible in making this assessment. One of the most effective ways to develop these goals is to sit down and write for 15 minutes each morning. Write down whatever comes to mind, resist the urge to judge, and save everything. After 7 to 28 days of these sessions, go back through your notes and highlight items that repeat. Then create a short list of overall goals. You can find out more about this technique in a book by Julia Cameron called *The Artist's Way* (see "Recommended Reading").

Why are these three items important in a chapter on mental training? These are the main reasons:

◆ The subconscious mind is highly attuned and will quickly see through anything other than true commitment. You should strive for total commitment to whatever level of dedication you believe is appropriate.

◆ Athletic success is only one component of a fulfilling life. The size of this component varies from person to person. You will be most successful when your athletic goals sit in harmony with your life goals.

◆ In order to maximize the benefits from implementing the techniques discussed below, your mind needs to be in a state of harmony. Harmony is best achieved when your life goals are working in concert with each other.

Being Your Goals

Probably the quickest method for achieving any goal is to "be" that goal. This means that you should aim to replicate as many things as possible that are consistent with your goals. For example, if your goal is to be the very best, then you could do the following:

Eat like a champion: Dedicate yourself to following a suitable nutrition strategy.

Train like a champion: Focus on high-quality BT workouts. Training hard is often the easiest task for a highly motivated athlete.

Recover like a champion: Know when to back off, and ensure adequate levels of sleep each night. An inability to listen to the body's signals has been the downfall of many athletes. Champions are sensitive to all aspects of their health and know that rest is their ally.

Behave like a champion: Strong ethics are highly valuable. If you follow a well-developed set of ethics, you will find it much easier to achieve harmony. Always remember that success does not imply arrogance.

Be a champion: Walk like a champion, talk like a champion, stand like a champion—in as many areas as possible, behave consistently with your goals.

Many athletes have a fear of truly committing to their goals. It is important to remember that seeking excellence is never something that should cause you embarrassment. When you are on a path of excellence that balances the aspects of your life goals, success is close at hand.

Many athletes feel that they have to hide their successes, often out of a fear of the response of others. In some cultures, friends, peers, and others belittle or undermine an athlete's goals. In this situation, the time spent considering your goals is highly valuable. It is much harder for people to harm us when we are working toward our goal in harmony. The most stinging comments often arise when people remind us that we have strayed from our path.

What Do You Control?

What is the greatest obstacle that stands between you and the things you desire? Money? Education? Social status? Genetics? Time? Opportunity?

None of the above! The greatest obstacle that we face is ourselves, and more specifically, our doubting selves. The doubting self is the little voice inside all our heads that says, "You can't," "You'd better not," and "You'll never make it."

There are only two things that are under your direct control: your words and your actions. You may think that these are easy to control, but sit down at a race and actually listen to what people are saying. "I'm so out of shape." "I haven't done enough training." "There's no way I am going to finish." Some may say that these people are releasing pre-race tension. It is probably more accurate to say that they are programming failure.

Mentally strong athletes understand that the body will follow where the mind leads it, and they are careful where they lead their minds. By controlling your words and actions, you eventually become your goals. Your words and deeds become such a habit that your mind has no choice but to follow.

Successful athletes have the ability to focus on the areas that are under their control and let go of factors that are beyond their control. In long-distance racing, the following are examples of factors that are not under your control:

◆ weather
◆ competition
◆ equipment (flats, unexpected mechanical issues)
◆ swim conditions (surf, temperature, currents, course accuracy)
◆ bike conditions (wind, temperature, road debris, other riders, vehicles)
◆ run conditions (cloud cover, temperature, terrain, other runners)
◆ aid stations (volunteers, supplies, location)

Though every effort should be made to become as informed as possible, you would be wise to spend very little time focusing on factors that are outside your control. Given the nature of long-distance triathlon, challenges will appear in every race. You will be best served by focusing on the items that you can control:

◆ pacing
◆ nutrition
◆ hydration
◆ equipment (appropriate, serviceable)
◆ technique (form, cadence, economy)
◆ preparation (race strategy, course knowledge, training)

The "controllables" are the factors that lead to improved race performance. The "uncontrollables" are best left alone, as they either have no direct impact on you or impact all athletes evenly.

Learning to "Push"

Many find it difficult to maintain a "fighting spirit" for an entire race. Quite often you may be disappointed that you cannot push for the entire duration of a long-course event. The truth of the matter is that this is a very hard skill to master. It can take years of practice to be able to push on when the mind wants to ease off.

How do you learn to push? Probably the most effective method is to start small and then build up. Train the body and the mind to remain focused for a shorter period, and then expand outward. One of the most useful aspects of short-course racing is that it trains you to endure high levels of intensity.

Indeed, the layout of a typical season is well suited to learning to push. The early season's focus on endurance, technique, and strength requires little in the way of intense mental focus. Early in the race season, you will have a series of C-priority races, some of which will be shorter in length. By midseason, you will be mixing shorter races with BT and race-simulation workouts. All of these sessions will help you build the skills necessary to race mentally strong.

Another factor you should remember is that every individual has a unique breaking point. For this reason, a conservative early pace can pay large dividends. One should never underestimate the psychological impact of being stronger than one's competitors late in the race. This is a concept of mental pacing as well as physical pacing.

Key Words and Signs

An effective technique for preparing to race is to use certain key words during training. Words such as *power, control, pace, endure, jump, push, calm,* and *breathe* can be used to invoke a certain state. Choose your own words and then incorporate them into key moments of your training. The words can then become a preprogrammed performance cue that you can summon at the appropriate time in a race.

A Little Bit on Fear

All athletes experience pre-race jitters—the people who look calm at races are probably doing their best to "be" their goals! Here is a progression that works for many people when they find themselves face-to-face with fear.

Acceptance: Accept the fact that you are nervous, or even scared. Accept yourself for being scared and know the it is perfectly natural.

Channeling: After you have acknowledged your fear, focus on where it is taking root physically. For example, many people experience shortness of breath when they are scared. If you are one of these people, then some trunk and abdominal stretching combined with a short period of deep breathing will quickly make you feel better. By breaking fear's physical chain, you will be able to regain your focus. This technique of fear management can easily be built into any pre-race routine.

Perspective: There is nothing like context to help deal with the doubting self. Quite often this side of our personalities will attempt to take over our minds when we are feeling stressed. At these times, it is useful to pause and remember that it's only a race! The worst-case scenario is that you learn something new about your current limits—hardly a disaster. An obvious exception to this rule would be if you find yourself in a situation where your personal safety is at risk (such as a swim in rough surf). In those situations, caution is the best course of action. There will always be another race.

Reflection: Take some time to identify the source of the fear. Quite often a solution presents itself as soon as the source is identified.

Naming: Once the source of the fear is identified and acknowledged, it can be quite effective to name the fear. An example of this might be athletes who have a fear of racing in the wind. Perhaps they give the wind a name, Mr. Blowhard. In their pre-race visualization, they talk with Mr. Blowhard and explain that there is nothing he can do to disrupt their races. By making the fear tangible, the athletes are able to address it with thought-specific visualization.

Listing: As with naming, there are many benefits to writing fear down because the action makes the issues clearer. Write a list of risks, fears, and concerns and rate them on a scale of 1 to 10. When under stress, the mind can blow things out of proportion, so it helps to decide the rank of situations in advance. Then make a two-column list: At the top of one column is "Risk/Fear" and at the top of the other is "Solution." Use all the resources at your disposal (books, the Internet, experienced athletes, online forums, friends, coaches) to find a solution for every risk. There are some risks (most noncontrollables) for which the only solution is to accept the risk.

Humor: Another effective method for dealing with fears is to treat them with humor. When we are able to view our fears, flaws, and failings with compassion, they are much easier to bear. This does not imply a lessening in our resolve to improve; however, it does imply having patience with our imperfections.

Action: Ultimately, the only way to deal with any persistent fear is to face it down, to turn to it and say, "You are not going to beat me." It can take tremendous strength of spirit to truly face our fears, but the payback is enormous.

In combating fear, remember that the goal is not to remove all fear but to acknowledge the fear and achieve superior performance notwithstanding its presence. Fear makes us feel alive. It heightens our arousal and challenges us to be our best. Rather than overcoming all fear, learn to dance with your fears, all the while becoming stronger in both body and spirit.

Your Mind and Racing

It is very common to have two conversations going on in your head as you roll toward your A-priority race.

Conversation 1 is your mind telling you that you are woefully unprepared and you will surely crash and burn. Hogwash! Remember this . . . when you are at the track . . . when you are in a pack . . . when you are at the pool . . . when you are naked in front of the mirror . . . when you are on the start line . . . say this to yourself when you need confidence: "My body did the training. I belong." We all need to boost our confidence!

Conversation 2 is your taper telling you that you can win your age group; qualify for Kona, knock one, two, or three (!) hours off your personal record; or crush the course record. Maybe you race farther back in the pack and catch yourself thinking about a daylight finish when two months earlier your goal was simply to cross the finish line with a smile. When this happens, stop and think back to what your goals were when you signed up for the race. These are the goals that you have been working toward for the last three to nine months. These should be the goals around which you have built your season.

Both of these conversations are natural, and it is worth sitting down and having a rational discussion with your mind. It is important to focus on your original goals. If you have set them properly, you are now very, very close to achieving them. You have done the training, and all you need to do is stay calm and execute your plan.

During a race, you may find either of these conversations starting again. There are normally two directions of diversion: (1) fixation, and (2) splitting. Fixation is an obsession on an element that is in the past or out of your control (other athletes, a flat tire, the weather). Splitting is when you start that internal conversation ("You can't do it"/"You can do it"). Fixation and splitting are signals that you have become diverted from your focus. Once you have diverted, economy, decisions, and timing all deteriorate. By spotting the diversion early, you can refocus on a task orientation.

If you keep your goals reasonable (yet challenging), your mind will be your friend throughout race day as you hit your targets and perform. Even if things don't work out, you'll be able to know that you are doing the best that you can do. If you have the desire to be the best, you must be willing to serve an apprenticeship. It takes a very long time to become a master at any skill. Typically, those who are new to the sport place too much pressure on themselves to perform at a high level. By realizing that an apprenticeship is required, and committing to paying your dues over the long term, you will enjoy the journey more and enable yourself to achieve a higher level of ultimate performance.

Try this exercise before your next A-priority race to help clear your mind. Say, "I feel the best I've ever felt." Write down the first thought or feeling you get from this statement. Then write, "OK" beside it and sign it off. Continue until your mind is empty.

If you are truly feeling the best that you have ever felt, your mind will be empty. The statement will just be true and float in the air. The mind will feel no compulsion to prove a true statement. It is very important to say the statement aloud and write down the response (if any). When there is doubt, accept and clear the doubt.

Other examples:

"I love myself and truly enjoy my life."

"My body is strong and powerful."

"I am going to race the best that I have ever raced."

Key Races

How do you define success? Time related? Finish position? The way to define a successful race is whether you did your best throughout it. When we focus on doing our best at each moment during the race, a successful outcome is much more likely. This has been the secret to many athletes' best races—a sharp focus on the present. The past is gone, and the future will take care of itself. If you focus only on doing your best (right now), then every race, every session, every moment can be a success.

How do you build a strong focus? Try focusing on your breathing. Feel the air moving in and out of your lungs. When you are centered on your breath, it is more difficult for your mind to generate those thoughts we'd prefer to do without. It is a technique that you can use on the bike and when running. In the water, think about the feel of the water moving against your body as well as the feel of the water against your forearms.

The Mind's Eye

A technique used by almost all elite athletes is visualization. Visualization can be used to

◆ increase the probability of positive outcomes

◆ create comfort and reduce anxiety

◆ improve technical skills

There are two main styles of visualization called the Movie Screen and Video Camera. Movie Screen visualization is when you are watching yourself perform as if you are outside your body. The goal is to run a movie of your desired outcome. Video Camera visualization is when you picture the scene from within yourself, as if you are looking out through the lens of a camera.

No matter which style you prefer, you should try to picture as many aspects of the scene as possible—what the setting looks like, the quality of the sunlight, the color of the water, and the people around you. The goal should be to create as realistic a scene as possible.

In the final two weeks before an A-priority race, spend 10 minutes per day visualizing key aspects of the race and positive outcomes. Pay particular attention to reinforcing positive images regarding any area of concern. A good time for this type of visualization is when lying in bed.

Athletes who have the opportunity to train alongside technically proficient athletes should use these opportunities to create mental images of excellent form and economy. These images can be replayed during visualization sessions.

In addition to evening visualization, you can use the last 10 minutes before you fall asleep to focus on one thing that was good about that day's workout. Play that one good thing over in your mind, and relive the experience as you fall asleep. This technique can be used by athletes who experience confidence issues.

Improving Mental Strength

Almost every athlete would like to improve his or her mental conditioning. The difficulty most of us face is finding a formula for achieving success. What follows are some practical ideas for improving your mental strength.

In a book by Edward O. Wilson called *Consilience* (see "Recommended Reading") are some novel concepts about the mind, genes, free will, and thoughts. Wilson believes that the mind is a powerful analog computer—a series of arrays that are constantly running various scenarios. The ability to generate and interpret successful scenarios is what determines intelligence and a person's adaptability within his or her environment.

One key implication of the "brain as array" model is that the scenarios upon which we focus (the scenarios that are repeated most often) are the ones that are most likely to become our "reality." Just as we train our neuromuscular pathways, we can train our neurological pathways. Though it is difficult to control our thoughts (particularly if our computer is running a wide range of them at any given time), we can control a few things.

Exercising control over the written word is probably the easiest level of control. Writing is a deliberate act, less subject to habits. Our diaries, e-mails, training logs, etc., are areas where we can use the written word to help strengthen our desired thought patterns and outcome.

Controlling our speech is a more advanced level of control and subject to a higher degree of habit. Words, particularly about the self, are very powerful guides to patterns. The first step to verbalizing our intentions is to say them out loud when we are alone. State the goal, desire, or intended outcome. Note the thoughts immediately after you've made your statement. Some people like to write these down and place a little "OK" beside the notes. This practice can be a useful tool for uncovering your biases as well as clues to your current self-image. The purpose of the "OK" is to acknowledge the validity of any thought that we may have (a simple acknowledgment of self-acceptance).

If we can't write it or say it, then odds are that it will be quite difficult to do it. Many of us have a fear that if we write down or speak our goals, we will be devastated if we don't hit them. This is an irrational fear. There is really only one "failure" that cannot be overcome—death. Everything else is only as serious as we want to make it.

Seeing as we are already thinking our goals, what is the difference between thinking and writing or saying them? The act of writing and speaking our goals makes them real. It can also flush out issues around the goals. If we are having trouble making our goals concrete, we should examine the source of our trouble—the source of our fear.

If you feel nervous about making your goals concrete, or if you have experienced difficulty dealing with the opinions of others, you are likely to be best served by keeping your goals to yourself or only sharing them with trusted advisers (such as your coach, physician, or nutritionist or another member of your athletic network).

Though a weak self-image is a common challenge, the opposite can also occur when an athlete is subject to goal inflation regarding targets that are too challenging. As a rule, goals should be challenging and achievable. When an athlete is constantly falling short of his or her goals, either the goals are too challenging or the athlete's mental skills need sharpening. An example of this is the athlete who excels in training only to underperform on race day.

After we have gained experience with controlling written and spoken words, the next step is to work on our attention and focus. The first step is to begin to note where we spend most of our time—what we are actually thinking about (positive outcomes, negative outcomes, past injustices, future fears). One way to track these thoughts is to keep a short diary that contains thoughts, feelings, and filters along with a note summarizing what triggered them. By first understanding our existing patterns, filters, and triggers, it will be easier to move our patterns toward our desired outcomes. The results of this exercise are almost always surprising.

Of course, all of these exercises assume that we know where we want to go! Once we have a plan for our desired outcomes, we should take every opportunity to support this direction through words and actions that are consistent with our game plan. When situations arise that are inconsistent with the plan, it is best to calmly move on toward our goals. Classic examples are sickness, injury, and concerns over current fitness levels. Sitting on the couch worrying about the results of a time trial or about the fitness lost during a recent illness will not move us toward our goals. Learning from our challenges and taking concrete actions will lead to achievement.

Preparing to Race

DURING TRAINING

◆ Write a list of your reasons for doing the race.
◆ Write a list of your life priorities.
◆ Write a list of your goals for the race.
◆ Ensure that all of the above are in harmony.
◆ Ensure that your partner/family/work/friends support your goals.

RACE PREPARATION

◆ Issues list—two columns (issue, solution).
◆ Get solutions to issues from experienced athletes and coaches.
◆ Take action early to address outstanding issues.
◆ Write things down—identified issues are normally minor and easily addressed.
◆ Ensure that thought patterns support goals—spoken and written words should be in complete alignment with life and race goals.
◆ Use visualization techniques to reduce stress and improve probability of success.

RACE STRATEGY

◆ Create a written race strategy that covers pacing, hydration and nutrition, equipment lists, transitions, and contingency issues.
◆ During Race Week, review the race strategy daily.
◆ Race strategy should include as much detail as possible.
◆ Pace should be effort based, not time based. External factors can affect time goals (flats, etc.), but effort goals are independent and 100 percent controllable by you, the athlete.

RACE WEEK

◆ Beware of goal inflation—maintain perspective.
◆ Avoid that "one last" megasession.
◆ Rest and prepare mentally.
◆ If you make any mistakes, do "too little."
◆ Ensure that you have 30 to 60 minutes' quiet time each day.
◆ Remember that changes in sleep patterns are normal.

DURING THE RACE

◆ Focus on the present—maintain a task orientation.
◆ Leave the past behind.
◆ Take the race in pieces, little chunks.
◆ Move forward at all times.
◆ Manage the emotional cycles (hold back in the peaks, endure the valleys).
◆ If you find yourself obsessing or flip-flopping, it's a sign you need to refocus.
◆ CONTROL THE CONTROLLABLES—leave all externals alone.

The Power of Belief

All of the techniques in this chapter are designed to enhance your self-belief. Ultimately, the beliefs that you have in your preparations, your experience, and your race strategy are the key determinants of your mental strength on race day.

Long-course racing presents hurdles for every athlete on race day. The extent to which you prepare your mind will determine how well you do in navigating the challenges that will inevitably arise.

Recommended Reading

Armstrong, Lance. *It's Not about the Bike: My Journey Back to Life*. New York: G. P. Putnam and Sons, 2000.

Cameron, Julia. *The Artists' Way: A Spiritual Path to Higher Creativity*. New York: Jeremy P. Tarcher/Putnam, 2002.

Castaneda, Carlos. *The Wheel of Time: The Shamans of Ancient Mexico, Their Thoughts about Life, Death and the Universe*. New York: Washington Square Press, 2001.

Hogg, John M. *Mental Skills for Swim Coaches*. Edmonton, Alberta: Sport Excel Publishing, 1995.

Moore, Thomas. *Care of the Soul: A Guide for Cultivating Depth and Sacredness in Everyday Life*. New York: HarperCollins Publishers, 1994.

Tolle, Eckhart. *The Power of Now: A Guide to Spiritual Enlightenment*. Novato, CA: New World Library, 1999.

Wilson, Edward O. *Consilience: The Unity of Knowledge*. New York: Random House, 1999.

Chapter 9

Tapering for the Ironman Distance

Don't leave your race
out on the Queen K
during the week before
the event.
— Dave Scott, six-time
world champion

Probably the greatest misconception about tapering for an ironman-distance race is that all an athlete needs to do is kick back and drop the volume, and a peak performance will result. This idea is a long way from the truth. It is best to look at a three-week taper in two components. The first component is the two-week period referred to as the Peak period. The goal of this period is to start the process of bringing you to a physiological peak for your ironman-distance race. The second component is Race Week.

The Peak Period

The two most important elements of the Peak period are intensity and recovery.

Intensity: Because of the reduced volume associated with the Peak period, it is important to maintain intensity. Basically, you are trading a little endurance for (you hope) a significant increase in race performance. Maintaining intensity is the critical element of achieving these desired changes.

Recovery: Remember that the overriding goal for the Peak period is to prepare the body to race. A key element of this preparation is eliminating all training fatigue. The ideal Peak period schedule has you eager to complete each workout and worried that you are not doing enough. If you are fresh for every session, you are on track. If you are arriving at

Finishing Your Build Period

The Build period ends with a race-simulation workout, typically 2.5 to 3.5 hours on the bike, followed by 90 minutes of running. If convenient, it is okay to swim before the bike. However, a swim is not essential.

If you are working on improving your endurance, the pacing of the race-simulation workouts should be Zone 1 early, building into Zone 2. This pacing will apply to many athletes preparing for their first ironman-distance race. These athletes might consider being at the top end of the recommended duration. More volume and less intensity would make sense for an athlete seeking to improve his or her endurance. Following are pacing thoughts for athletes who have a strong endurance base leading into this race-simulation workout.

We recommend that most athletes hold back at the start of the bike. You will be rested and likely think that you can go faster. It is an excellent time to practice the huge discipline that you will need during the early part of the ironman-distance bike. After the first 15 miles of the bike, gradually build to a pace faster than ironman-distance race pace. The last 15 minutes of the bike should be done hard, in Zone 4. Push a big gear and ride hard.

Bike-to-run transition should be a race simulation as well. Get all your gear in a bag as quickly as possible.

If you rode hard, your legs will be loaded and stiff as you begin your run—just like in an ironman-distance race. For the first 2 to 3 miles, focus on a high cadence and getting your step back. Then sit in Zone 3 (faster than ironman-distance pace). Finish the last 30 minutes of the run working hard (top of Zone 3 to Zone 4).

Post-workout recovery food and stretching are very important.

your BT workouts tired, additional recovery should be your highest priority.

Scheduling Peak Period Workouts

Most athletes will have completed a race-simulation BT on the weekend before the start of Peak Week 1 (see sidebar, "Finishing Your Build Period"). For this reason, the start of the week should be light in terms of both volume and intensity. The key goal for the start of the week should be to remove all residual Build period fatigue.

Since the idea is to do a race-intensity or mini-race-simulation workout every 72 to 96 hours in the Peak period, there will typically be two race-simulation BTs planned for each week. Working athletes are likely to be under time constraints during the week, and therefore, Week 1's longer BT should be scheduled for the weekend.

BT 1 (Peak Week 1, no. 1): Scheduled for Wednesday or Thursday, this session is normally the shorter BT of the week and lasts for 2 to 3.5 hours, depending on recovery. As the shorter session, this workout should incorporate an element of maintenance for your key strengths. If you have not fully recovered from the Build period, this session should be changed to an aerobic maintenance workout. Normally, the running aspect of the race-simulation brick is limited to 30 to 45 minutes with a tempo finish (heart-rate Zone 3 or close to half-ironman-distance race pace).

BT 2 (Peak Week 1, no. 2): Scheduled for Saturday or Sunday, this is the key BT of the Peak period. It is likely the last opportunity to add material fitness and therefore should address your greatest personal limiter. This session is normally 3 to 4 hours long with 45 to 60 minutes of running. After you establish your running legs, the workout should build to a tempo finish, similar to BT 1.

BT 3 (Peak Week 2, no. 1): Scheduled for Wednesday or Thursday of Week 2, this workout should be done at goal ironman-distance race pace (or slightly faster). If you are recovering well, you will benefit from inserting blocks of 10 to 30 minutes of heart-rate Zone 3 efforts into the bike and run legs. The total duration of this session is normally 2 to 3 hours, with 30 to 45 minutes of running—it is likely to be counterproductive to run longer than 45 minutes.

BT 4 (Peak Week 2, no. 2): This workout is scheduled for the final weekend before the race. It is normally done with full race setup (clothing, wheels, etc.) and includes a large percentage of ME work. Typical duration is 90 to 120 minutes, including 30 minutes of running—again, running longer is likely to be counterproductive.

All other workouts are secondary to the main period goals of maintaining intensity and ensuring recovery. The recommended approach to swimming and strength training is discussed later in this chapter.

Important Peak-Week Considerations for All Athletes

All workouts should start with a period of heart-rate Zone 1 effort. This allows you to warm up and simulates the discipline that will be required at the start of the ironman-distance bike leg. Typically, this "easier" period lasts for the first 20 to 25 percent of the scheduled bike leg.

Hydrate at target race consumption. This is particularly important for athletes living in cooler climates who may be racing in hot weather.

All workouts should incorporate an element of sublactate threshold ME work. For most athletes, heart-rate Zone 3 intensity is sufficient.

The overall goal of the BT workouts is to prepare the body to race, so many athletes wonder if it makes sense to train in the hottest part of the day. There is a trade-off between slower BT sessions owing to the heat and the acclimatization benefit of midday training. Most athletes will have sufficient heat training from the Build period so that, on balance, it makes sense to avoid the hottest part of the day and maximize average training speed.

As the race draws near, if you are feeling tired before or during a session, eliminate the session or cut it short. It is essential that you are totally fresh at the end of Peak Week 2.

In order to simulate the "heavy legs" sensation experienced at the start of the marathon, you should include 10 to 15 minutes of harder effort (heart-rate Zones 3 to 4) at the end of the bike for at least two of the race-simulation BT workouts. At the start of the run leg of each race-simulation BT, focus on cadence and maintaining good form. The goal of the first 10 to 15 minutes of the transition run should be to establish a steady, comfortable tempo.

All transitions should be as quick as possible, with transition gear laid out in race fashion (typically bagged).

If you have had problems holding back early in the race, you should schedule one BT workout per week in which the bike is done at target ironman-distance pace. The run in this session could be a faster, ME-oriented session. Typically, the longer BT workout each week should be done in terrain that closely mimics the race venue. The exception is if you have a critical limiter in one particular area (for example, hill climbing, rollers, or flat riding). You would likely achieve greater benefits from focusing your longer BT session on your critical limiter.

Common Issues during the Peak Period

Many athletes have a very strong urge to get one last megasession completed. If this training period is working as intended, you will start to feel fresh and have high energy levels. At this stage, it can be tempting for the highly motivated athlete to go long. This is a mistake. It is far better to go fast than to go long. Energy should be saved for race day.

Probably the most dangerous urge is the desire to run long. Running is the most physically stressful of all three sports and therefore should be approached with the most caution. If you have running endurance as a key limiter, it might make sense to plan a 90- to 120-minute run for BT 1. For most athletes, a long run less than 16 to 18 days before an ironman-distance race is counterproductive.

If you have been doing regular strength-maintenance work during the season, continue to lift once a week during the Peak period. Schedule strength training in such a way that it does not impair the quality of the BT sessions. The final strength session in Peak Week 2 should be lighter than usual—perhaps only one set of each exercise.

Most athletes will benefit from maintaining their "normal" swimming schedule during the Peak period (one longer swim, one faster swim, one technique swim). Athletes swimming four times a week or more should incorporate at least one open-water swim per week. Those swimming three times per week or less should incorporate an open-water swim into Peak Week 2. Athletes who have difficulty with open-water swims should continue with the weekly open-water swims that were started during the Build period. Open-water swims (that are nonrecovery in nature) should include 20- to 45-minute blocks of continuous swimming at goal ironman-distance effort. These workouts are an excellent time to work on your drafting technique as well as sighting skills.

The day after every BT workout should either be a total rest day or a very light, technique-oriented day. No weights or hard swimming should be scheduled for this day. Sleep is an important element of recovery, and many athletes experience sleep disruption during the Peak period. Here are some strategies for encouraging a good night's sleep:

◆ reducing daily caffeine intake (see Chapter 12 for thoughts on caffeine)
◆ not exercising late in the day
◆ a hot shower or bath before bed
◆ a short evening walk followed by a gentle stretching session
◆ increased carbohydrate intake for dinner
◆ going to bed and waking at the same time each day

As training volume is reduced, you will want to focus on your nutrition and lower your overall caloric intake. This practice is particularly relevant for Peak Week 2. Most athletes will have become used to a high intake of food during the Build period. Considerable discipline can be required to ensure that you arrive at Race Week with your desired body composition. Replacing energy-dense food sources with fresh fruits and vegetables can be one strategy for dealing with appetite challenges. Great care should be taken with the nutrition strategy for the period before, during, and after key BT sessions. These sessions are very important, and you should ensure that you have sufficient carbohydrates in your diet for optimal performance and recovery.

Almost all athletes will experience doubt about their training and potential race performance. This doubt comes from a variety of areas, including residual fatigue from the Build period, pre-race nerves, and the normal doubts that everyone experiences from time to time. A good strategy for combating these fears is to review your training log and remember the large number of quality sessions that have been completed.

Novices

Novice athletes (or athletes with endurance as their greatest limiter) will likely benefit from reducing the length of (or eliminating completely) the midweek BT workout and extending the length of the first Peak Week weekend BT to 4.5 hours. In order to compensate for the additional weekend volume, reduce the average intensity of the weekend BT. Typically, this session would start in heart-rate Zone 1 and build to Zone 2.

Elite Age-Groupers

Stronger athletes will want to consider a number of additional factors during the Peak period, such as the possibility of a half-ironman-distance race at the end of Build period 2 (Week 4) or an Olympic-distance race at the end of Peak Week 1. You may also consider the possibility of a third, shorter BT session in one of the two Peak Weeks. Just be sure to keep these BT workouts separated by seventy-two or more hours. It may require some schedule juggling on your part to fit all of these workouts in.

Strong swimmers should simulate the swim start with main sets incorporating longer intervals that start at threshold pace and move to ironman-distance race pace (see Appendix C for swim workout suggestions).

Stronger athletes will likely be able to handle a total workout volume of 3 to 4 hours and should consider extending the duration of the first BT session in Peak Week 1. The focus should be muscular endurance.

Increasing the intensity of the BT sessions is particularly relevant for the bike, in which stronger athletes will be able to average a heart-rate Zone 3 effort for rides of 2 to 4 hours' duration.

Use pace instead of heart rate for the running element of the race-simulation bricks. Typically, athletes will be able to hold a pace of 20 to 40 seconds per mile faster than goal ironman-distance race pace. The appropriate pace will vary with the duration of each BT workout's running component, as well as an individual's personal profile.

Race Week

All athletes share one goal for Race Week: to arrive at the start line in the best condition possible. Recovery is paramount in all decisions made during Race Week.

Scheduling Race-Week Workouts

What follows is an outline of a standard Race-Week strategy for a Sunday race. Athletes racing on a Saturday should adjust all comments forward by one day.

Following the completion of the final BT workout on the weekend before Race Week, you will likely want to take a break from cycling and running on **Monday**. For this reason, it is typically best to schedule a swim of 45 to 60 minutes. Ideally, this will be an open-water swim at the race venue. The main set of this workout should be six intervals of 90 seconds. The intervals should be swum at threshold pace on a rest interval of 30 to 60 seconds. In addition, the workout should include 10 to 20 minutes of continuous swimming at target race effort. The rest of the workout should include technique work that focuses on balance and stroke-length drills.

The main workout on **Tuesday** is a run session lasting 30 to 45 minutes. This workout should include an easy warm-up followed by four to eight Strides with walking recoveries. The main set of this workout should be five intervals of 90 seconds' duration. The intervals should be run at threshold pace on a rest interval of 3 minutes. Focus on maintaining perfect form and a smooth cadence at all times during this workout.

The secondary workout for Tuesday is a light spin that is completed before the evening meal. This workout is optional, and its intensity should be low.

On **Wednesday**, the main workout is a bike session of 30 to 45 minutes' duration. This should be an easy ride that includes four threshold intervals of 90 seconds' duration. Recovery should consist of easy riding. These intervals can be spread throughout the ride or done on 30- to 60-second recovery intervals.

The secondary workout for Wednesday is an easy swim of 30 to 45 minutes. If you are already at the race venue, you should swim on the course, ideally at the race start time. This workout should be used to note landmarks as well as the swim exit. Be sure to note any underwater hazards at the swim start and finish.

Thursday's key session is an easy brick four threshold intervals of 90 seconds. The intervals should be evenly split between the bike and the run. The duration of the brick should be 60 to 90 minutes. This session is an excellent opportunity to ride the run course and note any significant climbs.

As on Wednesday, the secondary workout is an optional easy swim of 20 to 40 minutes.

Friday should be a total rest day on which you can take care of registration formalities, final equipment checks, and race briefings. This is a good day to get away from the crowds by driving the bike and run courses. Stronger athletes should consider scheduling a light swim or ride.

Following the break on Friday, you should schedule a swim, bike, and run session that lasts 45 to 60 minutes (total). This session is best done in the morning on **Saturday**. This entire session should be done at an easy pace with three to four 30-second pickups inserted into the bike and the run. The pickups should consist of some brief faster work. Their purpose is to stimulate fast-twitch muscle fibers and ensure that you feel fresh on race day. After this workout, tighten all bolts on your bike. This is a good day to focus on rest. Restful activities include options such as watching television, going to a movie matinee, and taking a guided bus tour of the area.

Sunday is race day, and some important considerations for race day are discussed below.

Important Race-Week Considerations

Ideally, you should arrive at the race site four to seven days prior to racing. This schedule allows plenty of time to recover from the journey and prepare for the race. Athletes traveling across time zones should allow one day for each time zone crossed. See the "Pre-race and Race-Day Checklist" sidebar for preparation tips.

Maintain your normal hydration routine. If you are flying to the race venue, be sure to remain hydrated on your flight because the lack of humidity on aircraft can result in dehydration.

Race-Week training volume is likely to be one-quarter to one-third of normal workloads. For this reason, you will be best served by reducing your caloric intake. Here are some ideas for achieving this result.

Pre-race and Race-Day Checklist

PRE-RACE
◆ Take bike to local bike shop for checkup.
◆ Ensure that all supplies are stocked in advance.
◆ Take care of any last-minute emergencies.
◆ Pack all transition bags.
◆ Pack all special needs bags.

RACE DAY
◆ Wake three to four hours before race start.
◆ Eat breakfast and begin mental preparations.
◆ Double-check special needs bags.
◆ Gather swim start gear.
◆ Prepare post-race recovery drink for dry-clothes bag.
◆ Add anything you'll want post-race in dry-clothes bag.
◆ Arrive at race site at least two hours prior to race start.
◆ Double-check bike and transition bags.
◆ Find a quiet place to collect your thoughts prior to race start.
◆ Smile and enjoy the day ahead.

◆ Use only water during Race-Week sessions—avoid sports drinks, energy bars, and gels.
◆ When hungry, increase consumption of fresh fruits and vegetables that are low on the glycemic index.
◆ Eat smaller, more frequent meals.
◆ Reduce consumption of energy-dense foods, typically those with a high sugar and fat content or dry carbohydrate foods such as crackers and pretzels.
◆ Don't overeat at the pre-race dinner—save it for the awards banquet.

Bike maintenance is best carried out during the Peak period, well before arrival at the race site. To ensure that everything is in working order, all Race Week workouts should be done using full race setup (wheels and all accessories). If you arrive at the race venue late in the week, you should schedule an additional easy ride to ensure that your bike is fully functional.

Spend at least 15 minutes per day mentally running through your race strategy as well as visualizing a positive outcome to any anticipated race-day challenges.

Use your spare time during Race Week to increase the amount of stretching that you do. Stretching should be gentle and targeted at keeping you limber. It is most important to stretch during the period of travel to the race site (particularly when long periods of sitting are required).

Two days prior to race start, begin increasing your sodium intake if you are racing in hot climates. Approximately 18 hours prior to race start, move to a low-fiber diet.

Common Issues during the Race-Week Period

Most athletes will experience a change in their sleep patterns during Race Week. Some athletes will have a desire to sleep more, and others will experience a significant reduction in their need for sleep. Owing to reduced training volume, most athletes will be best served by eliminating all naps. This approach will make it easier to maintain normal sleeping patterns. Even if you can't sleep at night, it is beneficial to spend the time lying down—visualization and relaxation exercises are an excellent way to pass the time.

Keep your workout intensity in check. If the taper has worked as intended, you will feel very strong during the final workouts of Race Week. It is very important to hold back and avoid the urge to increase the duration and intensity of Race-Week sessions. Energy is best saved for race day, and it is not possible to add any fitness.

Don't worry if doubt creeps in. Most athletes will experience periods of self-doubt during Race Week. These are normal, especially with the extra amount of spare time from reduced training. Here are some tips for counteracting self-doubt:

◆ Make a list of issues. Beside each issue, write out a strategy for dealing with it.
◆ Think back and recall key BT sessions. Remember the hard work and preparation you have done.

◆ Know that an element of doubt is normal. Acknowledge the feeling, but remain focused on the weeks of preparation that you have completed.

◆ Discuss concerns with experienced athletes. Veterans of previous races are an excellent source of information as well as coping strategies.

Try to avoid crowds. Many athletes find it draining to spend time in large groups of people during Race Week. There is a constant nervous tension surrounding most competitors that can be emotionally and physically exhausting. Consider allocating a block of quiet time each day. Reading a book, watching a movie, or doing some other activity away from the race venue can help maintain energy levels.

Be aware of goal inflation, and maintain perspective on your race goals. The taper, the crowds, and the overall race atmosphere can lead to goal inflation. It is essential to maintain a positive outlook during race day, and it can be mentally challenging to "stay in the game" when your race goals exceed your athletic ability.

Keep your daily schedules light. Do your best to minimize all work and social commitments during Race Week. Stressful and fatiguing situations should be avoided as much as possible.

Novices (or any athletes who feel fatigued during Race Week) should consider eliminating the optional bike sessions and training at the low end of indicated workout duration. If you arrive early at the race venue, you will likely benefit from the acclimatization effect of the additional morning swims, but the duration should be kept short and the intensity low.

Athletes racing their first ironman-distance race should keep their time goals, if any, to themselves. Without any previous race experience over the distance, it is hard to accurately predict race performance. Most athletes are 1 to 2 hours slower than they anticipate. Race strategies are discussed in detail in Chapter 10.

Racing Long

Twenty miles of hope
and six miles of reality.
— Cameron Brown,
Ironman® champion

Ironman-distance racing is the most challenging physical undertaking that most athletes will undertake in their athletic careers. As such, it should be approached with both respect and humility. Many excellent athletes have been humbled by the challenges presented by this awesome event. The following series of tips is designed to help you get the most out of a day that should be one of the most unique experiences of your life.

The Swim

The swim start can be crazy, with many people in close proximity. At each race, experienced athletes will be a valuable source of information for the best place to start. Seek these veterans out before the race and have them explain their thoughts on the course.

Athletes who expect to swim in less than an hour should seed themselves toward the front. Athletes who expect to swim longer than 75 minutes should be toward the back. Everyone else should be in the middle. For your first ironman-distance swim, it is best to be a bit wide and a little too far back.

The swim should feel very easy to you. The combination of race adrenaline and the taper will have you very ready to race. Athletes almost always believe that they are swimming very easy. However, if you wear a heart-rate monitor, you will be able to see (after the fact) that you were working quite hard. Once you have established yourself with a good draft, then it is best to relax and enjoy the ride. No matter what speed you swim, you want to be "cruising" for 95 percent of the swim.

If you find yourself struggling from starting too hard, use a little backstroke to relax your breathing. Then swim into some clear water and regain your composure. Once you have settled, get back into the flow and look for a draft to take you around the course.

Occasionally, you will find yourself swimming among aggressive swimmers. In this situation, it is almost always best to let those swimmers pass (and follow them if the pace is right for you). These athletes often provide an excellent draft around the course.

Strong swimmers can gain time by bridging from pack to pack as the swim establishes itself. Be wary of bridging, as even a short distance can prove challenging. This skill should be practiced in B- and C-priority races as well as in training. Knowing the distance that you can bridge is a valuable skill for open water. This skill is really appropriate for only the very strongest triathlon swimmers.

The turns are key points for any race. Most swimmers will slow as they come into the turn. In races that have a long distance before the first turn, swimmers are all forced together at the turning buoy. These two reactions provide the intelligent racer with an opportunity to improve his or her position by finding a faster draft or bridging forward to a faster group.

Remember that it is risky to swim hard at any stage. Most swimmers are best served by staying relaxed and enjoying the draft around the course. Enjoy the swim, as it is typically the easiest part of your day.

Swim-to-Bike Transition

As part of your race preparations, you should have walked the transition areas and rehearsed your swim exit. You should also have mentally and physically rehearsed what you are going to do during your first transition. This preparation should make transition very straightforward as you execute your race strategy.

Many athletes race through transitions. Given that you will have been horizontal for an hour or more, it is best to move steadily rather than speedily through transition. Going from the swim to fast running is very stressful on the body. At this stage of the race, you want to minimize the stress on your body. Rushing transition can put an undue strain on your low back, hamstrings, and digestive system. Move smoothly to your bike and settle into your ride.

The Bike

Your goals for the early part of the bike should be to settle into your cycling rhythm and start replenishing the energy that was used in the swim. Specific hydration and nutrition recommendations are discussed later in the chapter.

Early in the bike you will likely feel better than at any time in the previous three months. You will be rested, energized, and very strong. For this reason, it is crucial that you control your arousal and avoid riding too hard. You have a long day ahead, and the first 5 to 6 hours of the race should feel relatively comfortable. If you feel that you are "working" at any time early in the race, you are going too hard.

Proper early bike pacing enables you to get ahead on your nutrition and hydration strategies. This is the key benefit of early race control. Almost all athletes find that as the race progresses, it becomes more and more difficult to motivate themselves to eat. In addition, it is much easier for your body to digest food and drink while riding than running.

Ironman-distance racing is not a bike race, and it is wise to have a healthy respect for the marathon that lies ahead. For this reason, a conservative bike strategy pays dividends later in the day. There will always be athletes who take the bike out hard, and it is important to have the control to stay within one's race plan.

So how should an athlete approach the bike portion of the event? Table 10.1 offers some guidelines for the average athlete. You should adjust these guidelines based on your personal strengths and limiters. Before deciding to ride harder, please remember that athletes who are strong cyclists will almost always be tempted to use their bike leg as a "weapon." This is a serious mistake because difficulties in the run are very costly in terms of time lost. Quite often 5 to 10 minutes on the bike can be the difference between being able to put together a solid run and walking. Most athletes are best served by adopting a conservative bike strategy and putting any surplus energy into the second half of the run.

Many novice athletes who tend to do the best relative to their training note that they never exceed heart-rate Zone 2 on the bike. The entire ride is done in the lower end of their aerobic range. This is a conservative strategy that works for many athletes, particularly those who have a concern about their endurance and how they might perform in the run.

In the months prior to the race, it is quite useful to ride the course, in whole or in sections, in order to gain an understanding of the bike leg. Athletes who are unable to ride the course in advance should ensure that they drive the course prior to race day. Note landmarks around the 30-, 60-, and 90-mile marks to help you remember to control your effort during the race.

You should plan ahead for the weather that you may face. Even in summer, and even in many races in temperate climates, it is possible to have very cold and wet conditions. In the tropics, it is important to keep your clothing wet during the bike to stay cool. In locations where the sun is fierce, wear sunscreen and UV-protective clothing.

Table 10.1 Pacing Guidelines

Segment	Overall Goals	Effort Guidelines	Heart-Rate Guidelines	Notes
Miles 1–30	Settle into a comfortable cycling rhythm; establish food and drink strategy.	Pace should feel easy.	Once the heart rate has settled from the swim, typically upper heart-rate Zone 1.	You should be holding back through this whole segment.
Miles 31–60	A continued emphasis on nutrition and hydration as well as an overall assessment of how the day is progressing.	Pace should feel steady.	Typically, Zone 2 effort.	The goal of this stage is to maintain a steady effort at goal ironman-distance bike pace.
Miles 61–90	This is the meat of the ride. Here is where early ride pacing pays off or takes its toll. Goal should be to work a little harder than goal effort. Athletes who have paced properly will begin to move up the field.	Pace should feel steady. Hills and rollers will see efforts up to moderately hard intensity. Avoid hard intensity.	Typically, upper Zone 2 effort with short periods of Zone 3 effort when climbing.	This is the key stage and where you will have to concentrate to maintain your focus. Early ride pacing starts to pay off, and athletes receive a mental boost as they start to move through the field.
Miles 91–112	Athletes should maintain their cycling momentum and continue to eat. Almost all athletes will have lost their appetites, but continued nutrition is essential for a strong run.	Pace should feel steady to moderately hard. There will be fatigue and stiffness, but these should be manageable.	Zone 2 effort with periods of Zone 3 effort when climbing.	Athletes should maintain their focus on pacing, nutrition and aero position. Race fatigue can cause the mind to wander. Athletes should maintain task orientation.

Whether you race on wattage, heart rate, or perceived exertion, use your effort wisely. Show control when you are feeling strong, and keep your focus when you experience a bad patch. Hills and headwinds present unique challenges and will tempt you to ride harder than you planned. Remember that the mental benefit of passing people on the run far outweighs the 10 to 15 minutes that you might save by pushing on the bike.

Many athletes find that they run more comfortably if they ease off on solid food for the last 20 to 30 minutes of the bike. If you have experienced stomach problems early on the run before, then this could be a good idea. However, it is essential that you continue to consume calories, so a liquid or semisolid food source should be substituted.

Finally, there will likely be one or more periods on the bike during which you experience doubts about your race. This feeling is normal, and overcoming these challenges is a key part of what makes the race so special. These bad patches never last too long, and it is important to maintain your cycling momentum when faced with mental and physical challenges.

Bike-to-Run Transition

Many athletes spend a long time in the second transition. Unless you have a medical problem, you should move through the transition area steadily and efficiently. Even if you are walking on the run course, you are making more time than if you are sitting in transition.

If you are racing in conditions where the sun is strong, take advantage of the sunscreen that is available in the transition area. In all races, be sure to use lubrication on sensitive areas. Carrying a small tube of Vaseline can save time and enable on-the-fly lubrication.

The Run

After winning Ironman® New Zealand in 2002, Cameron Brown described the marathon as "twenty miles of hope and six miles of reality." This is an excellent approach to the run.

If you have executed your race strategy according to plan, then once you have found your running legs, you will feel

Race-Day Checklist

The day before your race, you will be required to drop off your bike and your swim-to-bike and bike-to-run transition bags. Following are basic gear and accessory suggestions.

SWIM-TO-BIKE (T1)
◆ towel (optional)
◆ cycling shoes (can be on bike)
◆ cycling helmet
◆ cycling jersey (optional if using a tri-suit; can be worn under wetsuit)
◆ sunglasses
◆ sunscreen (applied pre-race)
◆ cycling gloves (optional)
◆ cycling socks (optional)
◆ sport bar/gels/salt tabs (held together with elastic band and/or secured to bike)
◆ race belt

BIKE-TO-RUN (T2)
◆ running shorts (optional if using trisuit or Speedo)
◆ running socks (very risky to run without socks)
◆ hat or visor (useful for placing other items inside and wrapping with elastic to save time)
◆ sunscreen (applied by race volunteers)
◆ Vaseline (small tube for start of run)
◆ sport bar/gels/salt tabs
◆ race belt

SPECIAL NEEDS BAGS
On race morning, you will be required to drop off your special needs bags. There is one bag for the bike and one bag for the run. It's up to you what you put in these bags — remember that in most races, the bags will not be returned. Here are a few common ideas:
◆ favorite snack food
◆ extra sport bars/gels/salt tabs
◆ extra bike tube and CO_2 cartridge
◆ extra running shirt for warmth if running into the night
◆ letters of encouragement from friends

quite strong in the early part of the run. Many athletes find that they are able to run very fast in the early part of the marathon. Again, having patience and holding back at this stage will pay off. Early in the run, athletes should focus on maintaining a steady pace while doing their best to ensure that their nutrition and hydration needs are met.

In general, you should be able to maintain a pace that is between 40 and 90 seconds per mile slower than what you have run in a half-ironman-distance race. Better-conditioned and better-paced athletes will be at the lower end of that range. Another common run prediction formula is that a properly trained and paced athlete should be able to run within 30 to 45 minutes of a recent stand-alone marathon time.

Although it can be interesting to develop a pacing strategy in advance, most athletes will find that they are left with few options on race day. Once you leave your bike, it is best to run with a little in reserve until at least the second half of the marathon. Whether you are racing for prize money, for a slot at the World Championships, or simply for the joy of finishing, you will find that huge amounts of time can be made, or lost, in the final 6 miles of the race.

The race really begins somewhere near the end of the first half of the marathon. By this stage, everyone is feeling quite tired, and the race is starting to grind down people's resolve. The second half of the marathon is where you will find out the results of your training, pacing, nutrition, and hydration efforts. It is also where you will discover whether you have the toughness to push well beyond your comfort zone. Athletes who are looking to achieve their very best should bring all of their mental strength to bear on the final half of the marathon. It is essential to continue to eat, drink, and push right to the finish line. You never know what is happening up the road, and it is possible to make up major time and placings in the final stages of the race. Even if you have major problems, continue to press onward, as you could recover very quickly. There are many examples of elite athletes coming back to win races when their prospects appeared very dark at various times during the race.

Novices who have developed a run/walk strategy in their training and plan to use it on race day should start at the beginning of the marathon, not in the latter miles, when things are more apt to get difficult. This is a proven method that can see you to the finish line feeling good. The most important part of the run/walk strategy is ensuring that the run restarts each time. Many athletes find that once they start walking, it can be very difficult to get running (another reason why it pays to keep tight control of your pace on the bike).

Break the run into pieces if it gets hard: A good strategy can be to run from aid station to aid station. The next aid station becomes the key objective, and you are rewarded with a walking break, which you can use for eating and drinking.

Wear clothing that will see you through the heat of the late afternoon and keep you warm in the evening. Your first ironman-distance experience is not a race; it is a test of how much patience you are prepared to exercise so that you do not expire on the marathon.

Mental Toughness

Odds are that sometime during the day you are going to feel really, really bad. This feeling is normal, and things will get better if you persevere to the end. Finish at all costs, and you will thank yourself later.

Even on a good day, things will go wrong—the race has no respect for previous results. Even if your last race was good, the next one could be a challenge. Start with a series of objectives in mind, and if one is not achievable, drop down to the next. Remember to keep everything in perspective and simply move toward the finish line. Even if things get really tough, you can quite often regroup by slowing down (or even stopping) and focusing on your nutrition and hydration. Many athletes have taken breaks of 30 to 60 minutes, eaten some real food, and finished comfortably within the cutoff.

What Do I Eat and When?

The figures that many sources quote for what the body can absorb are estimates and are highly variable across the population. Some athletes can consume up to 800 calories per hour without difficulty, while others top out at 250 per hour. It is best to practice what your body can handle during training and C-priority races. Here are some guidelines for race nutrition. We recommend that you rehearse what and how much you will eat and when you will take in nutrients in training starting several weeks prior to your A-priority race. Don't experiment or try anything new in your most important race.

Pre-race

◆ Don't pig out. Eat normally.
◆ Increase table-salt intake for the 48 hours prior to race day.
◆ Hydrate normally with water. Drinking gallons of water is not required.
◆ Eighteen hours before the race start, go to a low-fiber diet.
◆ The day before the race, eat small meals frequently.
◆ On race morning, consume 600 to 1,000 calories 3 to 4 hours before the start. Target breakfast completion for 2.5 to 3 hours before race start. Two hours is okay unless you are eating a high-fat breakfast that will digest slowly (which is not recommended).

Race

◆ Drink 10 to 16 ounces of sports drink (slightly diluted), or consume one gel with half a bottle of water, 5 to 8 minutes before the race start.

Gordo's Top 10 Mistakes in Ironman Racing

10 — Did too much in the week leading up to the race.

9 — Ate too much in the week leading up to the race.

8 — Didn't check my race setup until 60 minutes before bike check-in closed (there were problems).

7 — Drank a bottle of extra-strength sport drink before the swim start.

6 — Forgot that it is normal to feel bad sometimes during the race.

5 — Ate a sport bar in T1 (water or nothing now).

4 — Mixed my sport drink too strong.

3 — Hung on to the feet of a faster swimmer for far too long.

2 — Went anaerobic in the first 400 meters of the swim.

And Gordo's #1 mistake made in ironman-distance racing . . . Rode too hard in the first 90 minutes of the bike.

◆ Consume nothing else until your heart rate has settled on the bike (5 to 20 minutes out of the first transition [T1]).

◆ Most athletes benefit from drinking half a bike bottle of water before starting to eat because it settles the stomach and ensures that the food is more easily absorbed.

◆ On the bike, consume gels, sports bars, and sports drinks as required.

◆ If you are using gels and bars, drink plenty of water to aid absorption.

◆ Eat right up to the end of the bike. On the run, anything can happen, and it is wise to have a calorie buffer.

◆ On the bike, the following schedule could be used:

    0–20 minutes: water only

    20–40: 200 calories

    40–60: 00 calories

    60–120: target 200 calories per 20 minutes

◆ The above schedule would provide 1,000 calories in the first 2 hours. As there is a deficit when you come out of the water, it is worth trying to get ahead with early calories. Appetites and concentration can lapse later in the day, so it is beneficial to have a little nutrition in the bank. If you target 500 calories per hour, you'll probably end up with 400 to 450 calories. Smaller athletes may need to reduce these quantities. Always base your race-day caloric intake on what you learned in training.

◆ The second transition (T2)—consume one or two gels if you can stomach it, and chase with water.

◆ On the run, alternate between cola/water and sports drink/water at every aid station. Start on the cola immediately. If you are peeing a lot, drop the water, but keep alternating between cola and sports drink.

◆ Many athletes can never eat anything solid or semisolid during the run.

Adjust these suggestions based on your body weight and time on the course. Middle-of-the-pack or back-of-the-pack Clydesdale men are going to need to eat significantly more than will a 165-pound athlete. In general, most men should target 450 calories per hour and most women 350 to 400 calories per hour. Please remember that these are simply guidelines—practice your nutrition extensively in B- and C-priority races as well as during your long bike sessions.

Finally, as a general rule, don't plan on anything other than liquid "survival" calories during the run, and try to consume 60 percent of your bike calories in the first half of the ride.

How Much Should I Drink?

On the bike, drink only water until your heart rate has settled, then drink one to two bike bottles of water alternated with sports drink per hour. If you are peeing more than once an hour, back off on the water and switch to sports drink. If you aren't peeing at all, increase your hydration to ensure that you finish the bike well hydrated. By the time you feel thirsty, you could already be in trouble, so you want to stay ahead when it comes to hydration. If you find yourself dehydrated, then slow immediately and increase overall hydration; the time you lose will be more than compensated by improved late-race performance.

On a hot day, you should be looking at consuming more than 1 quart per hour, though personal needs are highly variable here. Target a minimum of 1 quart per hour, and ease off if you start peeing more than once an hour. If your food source on the bike consists of gels, bars, and a liquid carbohydrate source, a higher water intake early in the bike is essential because of the concentrated nature of your food.

If you are having problems with bloating on the run and you are peeing, go to sports drink/cola only. If you feel bloated and are not peeing, take an electrolyte tablet, slow down, and go to water only.

The Role of Sodium

Athletes should look at sodium supplementation as insurance. Most athletes probably don't need it, but they feel better taking it. There are, however, certain athletes who may experience significant troubles if they don't supplement. If you think you might benefit from sodium supplementation, you should experiment during your long sessions in training. Such experimentation is highly recommended if you are new to ironman-distance racing.

Another factor to bear in mind is the sports drink that you are planning on using. Some athletes use a sports drink that contains no sodium, but to race long on that beverage (alone) would be pretty risky. In general, 400 mg of sodium per hour is enough for most athletes. Some athletes require up to 1,000 mg of sodium per hour, and others require no supplementation at all.

If you plan on supplementing, you should start as soon as you start drinking water on the bike. How much extra sodium you take in depends on how much sodium is in the sports drink and food you are consuming. By reading labels and using simple math, you can determine the quantity weeks in advance of the race. There are many commercial electrolyte sources available. Some are listed in Chapter 12.

Ironman-Distance Race Recovery

One of the most common mistakes an athlete will make is coming back too quickly after an ultra-endurance event. Many athletes have pushed themselves into an overtrained state by following an ironman-distance race with a season of short-course racing. If your body is not ready to start training again, you will receive numerous warning signals. Ignoring these signals and continuing to push will likely end in either injury or illness.

Recovery time varies from person to person and season to season. In general, most athletes will find that they require at least two months before they are able to race or train hard again. The recovery period is highly variable—it can be as short as a month or as long as six months. Additional recovery guidelines are described in Chapter 4.

One of the best methods to promote recovery is frequent massage. Although research typically doesn't support it, there is little doubt in the minds of those who use it that it is effective. Massage helps to relieve muscle tension, remove metabolic waste products, and may reduce muscle soreness following strenuous training. Most effective for your body is one massage every week throughout the year and two massages per week during your key Build periods. Acupressure and Rolfing may also be beneficial.

Chapter 11

Equipment

It's not about the bike.
— Lance Armstrong, four-time
Tour de France winner

Bikes, wheels, aerobars, wetsuits, heart-rate monitors, trainers, computers. . . . If you follow the various discussions in our sport, then you will see that endless time is devoted to analyzing the right training strategy, the right frame material, the right wheel set, etc. However, when you talk with the majority of truly elite athletes and coaches, you will discover that what it takes for athletes to reach their full potential, simply, is a lot of very consistent work over a very long time.

The role of the intelligent athlete is to channel this work into the most effective training schedule. Although some gear is needed to aid this task, there is no need to run out and spend your life's savings on every gizmo and gadget on the market.

The most important gear to begin with is a properly sized bike, a properly fitted wetsuit, quality running shoes, and a heart-rate monitor.

Choosing a Bike

To some, the choices may seem daunting—makes, geometries, wheel sizes, wheel sets, frame materials, aerobars, saddles. . . . The best advice when purchasing your first triathlon bike is to spend a lot less than your budget. It takes most athletes a few frames to figure out what works for them.

Bike fit (discussed in more detail in Chapter 6) is highly personal, and you can have success with all geometries and frame materials. Your first deciding factor should be what is most comfortable. For racing and training long, always choose comfort over aero. If you are comfortable, you will stay more aero and run better off the bike. Comfort is really all that matters for your first few ironman-distance races. By the time you are ready to get more serious, you will have logged many miles and know what style works best for you. So what choices are there?

Material: Many talk of frame materials such as titanium, carbon fiber, aluminum, and steel. It is generally accepted that carbon-fiber frames offer a more comfortable ride, titanium frames are the lightest, steel is the most responsive, and aluminum gives the harshest ride.

Although some materials have better vibration-dampening properties than others, it is worth remembering that if any material is used incorrectly, then the bike can have a harsh ride. That said, there is only one real category for choosing which frame to ride—fit. A properly fitting aluminum frame will be far more comfortable than a poorly fitting carbon-fiber frame.

Geometry: Now that you've chosen your frame, your next decision is triathlon or road geometry. Other than the obvious need for a safe bike, for long-distance training and racing, comfort is your number-one goal. Road bikes are often the most comfortable, with a 73-degree, seat-tube geometry. This arrangement is often referred to as a "relaxed" position, placing the rider a little farther back, and is the best climbing position. A bike with triathlon- or time-trial-specific geometry is more "steep," at about 78 degrees. These bikes tend to be most comfortable (and efficient) when the rider is down on the aerobars.

It would be easier if we could all afford two bikes—one triathlon-specific and one with a road frame. Since that is not possible for most of us, consider your key races, overall comfort, and training terrain when selecting the geometry most appropriate for you.

Wheel size: Once you have determined an appropriate frame and geometry, the best wheel size will be a function of fit. Never make a frame decision based on wheel size alone; the right wheel size for your height will normally be clear once you have decided on your other purchase variables.

Shifters: Your next option is shifters—drops with STI shifting or bullhorns with bar ends. A moderate-geometry bike with drops and STI shifting will be the most versatile selection for a range of terrain, races, and training environments.

Bullhorns and bar-end shifters are slightly faster for most riders on a flat course; however, the slight aero disadvantage of an STI setup can often be more than made up by the more efficient shifting and better power over short hills. Steep bikes with bullhorns and bar-end shifters aren't generally as comfortable for riding hills.

Although the STI setup is more versatile, if you were building a race-specific, time-trial-specific bike, then bullhorns and bar ends would be the way to go.

Pedals and shoes: Pedal choices range from a small, light platform to a wider, heavier platform. Pedals should be chosen wisely, as some athletes have been known to develop foot or knee problems from certain brands.

When purchasing cycling shoes, think comfort and ease of getting them on and off. Some shoes are vented, which is nice for riding and racing in hot locations. Cycling shoes should fit comfortably snugly, not tightly. When shopping for your shoes, it is best to shop at the end of the day or shortly after a long ride. Feet swell naturally throughout the day and while riding. If your shoes fit very snugly at 9 A.M. in the bike shop, chances are they will be too snug 3 hours into your 5-hour ride.

Aerobars: There are several choices for aerobars on the market. The most durable ones are generally clip-on because they are easy to put on and take off and allow you the option of adjusting the elbow pads inward or outward.

Race wheels: The next big debate is whether to use race wheels and disc wheels. Conventional wisdom is that a good set of race wheels will speed you up by 1 to 1.5 mph. The largest speed differential comes from swapping 32-spoked training wheels with a set of aero wheels. However, the greatest benefits of aero wheels only arise at high speeds in excess of 17 mph. There is limited benefit to using aero wheels if you don't have the muscular endurance to take advantage of their properties.

To disc or not to disc . . . You need to be a pretty fast ironman-distance rider to get a noticeable difference from a disc versus a deep aero wheel. Still, if you are a strong rider, then a disc will, on average, be superior to any other wheel choice.

A set of deep, or trispoke, aero wheels is an excellent all-purpose race wheel set. The only exception would be when riding in heavy or gusty crosswind conditions, as the front wheel can be difficult to control. Make sure that your skills and confidence match your wheel selection. It doesn't take much braking to give away the entire benefit from a flash set of wheels!

Helmet: Now that your bike is built, you're ready to go. Not so fast! Above all else is safety. Never leave home without your helmet. Always choose an ANSI/CSI-approved helmet with plenty of vents for cooling, especially when racing in heat or humidity. Elite athletes may do well with a more aerodynamic, ventless helmet because they don't spend as much time on the bike and tend to be very lean. If you have difficulties in the heat, then choose a well-vented helmet for your races.

When shopping for a helmet, choose one that fits snugly but not too tightly, as your head can swell slightly in heat or when your core temperature is elevated. Look for one with finely adjustable sizing.

Choosing a Wetsuit

There are three major benefits to a properly fitted wetsuit: safety, speed, and warmth. Wetsuits are buoyant, allowing you to float higher in the water, which adds a sense of security for novice open-water swimmers. Many long-distance races take place in cold waters, and a properly fitted wetsuit works as an insulator against the cold water, making you more comfortable and reducing the risk of hypothermia.

There are many brands and styles of wetsuits to choose from. Just as with your bike, choose your wetsuit based on fit and comfort. All of the established manufacturers make quality products, so if your selected suit fits well, then you are unlikely to have problems.

The first decision is between a sleeveless and a full-sleeved wetsuit. A good-fitting full suit is generally accepted as the faster choice. However, if you are more comfortable in a sleeveless suit, you are unlikely to be giving away much time. The sleeveless suit, or Long John, lets you maintain a better feel for the water. Those athletes with a high stroke count as well as less strong swimmers may find these suits more comfortable.

A good wetsuit can conserve a considerable amount of energy during an ironman-distance swim, as much as 5 minutes or more, depending on your swimming ability. The more inexperienced the swimmer, the more advantage there is to be gained.

Many athletes have the sensation of moving more slowly in a wetsuit, or think a suit that fits correctly is too tight. Ideally, your wetsuit should feel snug and almost uncomfortably tight when not in the water—it should be tight around the waist and legs, and there should be no leaks around the neck (and arms for a sleeveless suit). Once you are in the water and swimming, your suit will expand slightly and feel comfortable.

In addition to ensuring that your suit is sized correctly, it is very important to put it on correctly. Do this by slowly working the neoprene up your legs. Using socks helps to slide the suit over your feet, and rubbing a lubricant such as Body Glide or PAM on your shins (and forearms for a full suit) will aid in a speedy removal.

The suit should pull up snugly against your crotch to allow the top to fit properly. With a sleeveless suit, you need only ensure that it is pulled up your torso enough for the armholes to seal properly. With a full suit, work the arms up the same way that you worked up the legs—slowly. There should be no air pocket between the suit and your armpit when your suit is on correctly. Any excess rubber will collect above your shoulder. For maximum range of motion, it is critical to ensure that a full suit is on correctly.

Running Shoes

After all the money spent on your bike, bike accessories, measuring equipment, wetsuit, etc., running shoes are often overlooked. This oversight is a mistake because quality shoes can help you to avoid injury and lost training time.

When choosing your shoes, consider your personal biomechanical issues, such as overpronation, supination, flat feet, and high arches. Next, address comfort. The quality of your fit can make the difference between happy feet and potential injury.

Be sure to go to a running specialty store where the salespeople are runners themselves. A good running store—not your average chain store—will let you run outside in the shoes to see how they feel. They will also watch your gait and make suggestions. Choose the shoes that feel most comfortable to you—if they don't feel good at the shop, they won't feel better later at home.

As when shopping for cycling shoes, try to go late in the day after you've been on your feet a lot, as feet swell naturally throughout the day. Wear the same socks you normally run in to ensure that the shoes fit properly. If you use orthotics, then take them along as well. Ensure that there is a thumb's width between your big toe and the front of the shoe when standing.

Your shoes may be only a few months old or still have a lot of tread, but that doesn't necessarily mean they're still giving you the support you need. Shock absorption and support qualities are usually the first to go. You will want to ensure that your shoes are working for you because training for long-distance triathlons places a great deal of stress on your feet and body. Many foot and lower-leg injuries are caused by poor-fitting or overly worn running shoes.

The general rule of thumb is to replace your shoes at least every six months or after one ironman-distance race. You can also go by mileage—every 250 to 300 miles of running. To get the longest wear out of your shoes, it is wise to purchase two pairs and rotate them. Never do strength training in your current training shoes.

The life span of your shoes includes time spent walking in them; however, walking in your training shoes is not recommended. Once your shoes have reached the end of their safe training duration, they can be retired and become gym shoes. Also check with your local running-shoe store because some will buy back old shoes or donate them to charity.

Should you buy a training shoe or a racing shoe? Some athletes believe they need to change to a lighter or thinner shoe, such as a racing flat, for racing. This is acceptable for shorter races but quite risky for ultradistance racing because the risk of injury is far too great. A racing flat will save only a couple of grams in weight and 1 or 2 seconds per mile pacing—hardly justifiable when the risk of injury and extended recovery time increases substantially.

Generally, it is best to race in the shoes that you train in. If your training shoe is heavy, then visit your local running-shoe store and experiment with shoes that may be a little lighter for racing. Ensure that your race choice offers you adequate support and comfort.

Be sure to purchase any new shoes well in advance of your A-priority race in order to break them in. We do not recommend running a marathon or half-marathon in brand-new shoes. Some suggest that you should have about 100 miles on new shoes before racing a marathon, although with modern shoes, two long runs would be enough. For ironman-distance racing, you would do well to get new shoes at the beginning of your Peak period. That will be enough time to ensure that they are broken in prior to the race while maintaining their shock absorption and support qualities throughout the race.

Race Wear

What to wear on race day is a common thread in triathlon discussions—skinsuits, triki-nis, trishorts, regular cycling shorts? What works for one athlete may not necessarily work for another. Clothing should be chosen based on functionality and comfort as well as race climate and fitness levels. The longer the race distance, the more important comfort becomes.

A one-piece skinsuit is suitable for races up to a half-ironman distance, for ironman-distance races in hot or humid climates, or for elite athletes. A skinsuit will keep you cooler if you keep it wet by dumping water on yourself; however, it can become somewhat tedious to get in and out of when you make stops at the porta-potties.

A regular cycling jersey is quite comfortable and functional for long-distance racing. If you make this selection, then choose a material that aids in keeping you cool when wet. Jerseys can also be worn under your wetsuit to save changing time in transition.

Where conditions are hot, you may want to consider a top with short sleeves (as opposed to a singlet) to reduce the amount of skin exposed to the sun.

Trishorts are the most common shorts of choice. They have a slightly thinner chamois pad and can be worn for the entire race. Some athletes prefer regular cycling shorts because they offer more comfort on the long bike ride. Elite athletes often race in no more than a trikini or swimsuit. These do have some thin padding; however, they are more suitable for those closer to the front of the pack who finish the bike early.

Whatever you choose to wear on race day, use it extensively in training.

Training Aids

Heart-rate monitors: If there is one gizmo you do need, it is a heart-rate monitor (HRM). HRMs range in price and functionality from a basic model that simply shows your current heart rate to top-of-the-line models that record multiple variables and then let you download all the information to your computer for graphing and further study.

Though all the extra features can be fun, especially for the technically minded, the only features you really need are current heart rate, average heart rate, maximum heart rate, and average heart rate by split. A fifty-lap memory option is plenty for training needs.

Stationary trainers: There are several types of stationary trainers—rollers, wind, and magnetic resistance. Rollers are beneficial in learning proper balance and for spinning, and they are inexpensive. However, they do not simulate road riding and are easy to crash on. Wind and magnetic-resistance trainers are more stable because you can lock your bike down on them. These are affordable options for indoor training during long winter months.

CompuTrainer: Although it exceeds most people's budgets, a CompuTrainer is an excellent tool for riders. It is an especially valuable addition to the training equipment for athletes who live in climates with nasty winters, are preparing for an early-season race, or have an excellent base. A CompuTrainer can be used for interval sessions and power testing, giving you immediate feedback that can be adjusted during the workout.

PowerCranks: The main benefit of PowerCranks (PC) is their impact on cycling economy. Economy is a tricky thing to evaluate because improvements in economy are often obscured by changes in fitness. However, the major economy improvements come from closing the "dead spot" in the pedal stroke and in timing of the stroke—forcing your leg muscles to learn a correct firing pattern.

Athletes who are using PC should do regular speed-skills workouts to maintain muscular quickness. Athletes who tend to race with low cadences should supplement their PC use with spin-ups (high-cadence drills).

Power-Tap: Second only to an HRM, a power-measurement device is very useful. The Power-Tap is a proven powermeter. Training by power—or watts—provides more immediate feedback than an HRM and lets you know whether your efforts are having an effect on performance. Training with power is discussed in more detail in Chapter 6.

SRM: The SRM training system is similar to the Power-Tap in that it is used for collecting and analyzing power data while cycling. The system uses a special crank set that measures pedal rate, torque, and power output. As well, it displays and records heart rate, cadence, wheel speed, distance covered, ambient temperature, and energy expenditure. Though it is more expensive than the Power-Tap, the SRM system can be used with any wheel configuration. Look for competition between Power-Tap and SRM in the next few years with dropping prices.

Chapter 12

Nutrition, the Fourth Discipline

Other than training wisely, the most important things most working athletes can do to improve their performance are to get an extra hour of sleep every night and improve their nutrition. The benefits of an effective nutritional strategy flow into all areas of training and will greatly improve the quality of your life.

A few sessions with a good sports nutritionist are very valuable and recommended to any athlete seeking to improve his or her performance, recovery, or body composition. The ideal consultant will also be an athlete who has experience working with others in your sport.

There are many experts, diets, books, videos, and theories out there concerning nutrition. As an athlete you can often be left wondering what it takes to achieve your best. We have found that following the "Key Three" is the most effective way to better health and performance.

The Key Three:

1. Eliminate processed foods from your diet.

2. Obtain the majority of your energy needs from whole fruits, fresh vegetables, and lean protein.

3. Limit your use of starchy and sugary foods to during and after your longest or most intense sessions.

The "Key Three" account for nearly all of the benefits covered in the tips that follow.

Nutrition = Athletic Performance: I once mentioned to my wife that I wished I could play the saxophone as she does. She turned to me laughing and said, "Apparently not bad enough to learn how." She was absolutely correct.

— Kevin Purcell, triathlete and coach

Body Composition Management
Motivation

It is important to understand our motivation in making the food choices that we do. You may recognize some of the points below as they relate to your relationship with food.

Food as a signal: Thinking back over the years, the times when you have been making the poorest food selections may have been the times when you were under the greatest levels of stress. Stress can come from a variety of sources: training, relationships, children, work, finances, a partner's alignment with your life goals, and others. When these sources of stress are reduced, your food choices will improve.

In this sense, poor eating habits may merely be a symptom of a wider issue in your life that needs to be addressed.

Food as nourishment: Food is essential for our survival, period. There may be times when you feel a certain sense of guilt at meals. It is almost as if food has become an enemy that is preventing you from achieving your ideal self. This feeling is very dangerous because it sets up a negative cycle.

When we view food as a source of strength, it is far easier to establish a virtuous cycle in which our strong nutritional choices move us toward our ideal self. By acknowledging this flawed view of food, it will become easier to see food for what it really is: a source of energy and pleasure.

Food as self: There may also be periods in your life when you believe that you are a "good" person when you eat well and a "bad" person when you make poor food choices. Realize that you are the same person regardless of your food choices. This is important, particularly in conjunction with why we like certain types of food.

In order to gain power over food, it is best to avoid defining ourselves by the food choices we make. Once a choice has been made, it is done. Regardless of its nature, all we can do is focus on the next choice. Worrying about the past is a waste of time.

Wiring

Have you ever wondered why we like fatty or sugary foods? It's because they taste good and make us feel good (at least they give that illusion). It's not because we're losers!

It is important for you to take total responsibility for your food choices. Although it may be interesting to know everyone's personal life struggles, there is only one person who decides what you eat. With a few medical exceptions, the way you look is dictated by a huge number of tiny decisions that you make on a daily basis. In order to change ourselves, we need to take responsibility for ourselves.

What we look like today is based on decisions we have made in the past. Likewise, what we will look like tomorrow is based on decisions we start making right now. It is a classic conflict between short-term pleasure and long-term gain. When you see an elite athlete, you are looking at the result of tens of thousands of little decisions that he or she has made over many years.

What Is It Worth?

Before getting into a discussion of useful techniques, you should ask yourself how much you are willing to commit and how important improvement is to you. Why? Because there are no shortcuts, and good nutrition is a lifestyle decision. As in any endeavor, the results are completely dictated by your commitment and dedication.

Getting Started

The first step in getting started is gaining information about your current position. Start by keeping a food log for an entire week. Record what you are eating, not how much, and make an honest assessment of your current eating habits.

When you are keeping your log, be honest. Anyone can "eat right" for seven days. There is no point in fooling yourself and your advisers. In order to make changes, you need to have a realistic assessment of where you are.

Armed with the log, you are now in a great position to visit a sports nutritionist. By combining that log with your training diary, your professional adviser will be able to give you some excellent advice on how to make progress. Or you can read on . . .

Energy-Dense versus Nutrient-Dense Foods

Energy-dense foods are those that are high in calories relative to their size or volume. Some examples are cheese, whole milk, butter, French fries, burgers, sweets, energy bars, and soft drinks. These types of food can put a lot of calories into you at times when you don't need them.

There is a time and place for many energy-dense foods. However, when you are trying to lose weight, you need to know what you are eating. In general, athletes who are seeking to improve their body composition should limit their intake of energy-dense foods and increase their intake of nutrient-dense foods, such as fruits, vegetables, fish, poultry, and lean cuts of other meat. Highlight the energy-dense foods on your log.

Starting to Change

The next step is to swap half of your energy-dense choices for nutrient-dense choices. Why only half? Several reasons:

◆ We all have limited willpower, and we should apply it sparingly. The people in your life who appear to have tons of willpower are just the same as you. However, they have learned to apply their limited willpower to gradually mold themselves closer and closer to their ideal selves.

◆ Radical change does not work. We are trying to change habits that have been formed over years and, quite often, generations. This is powerful programming that needs to be adjusted.

◆ Going cold turkey is not required for results. Although this approach works for some people, they often return to their old eating habits after shedding pounds.

Our ultimate goal is to develop a healthy, long-term lifestyle that will bring out your ideal self. We want to make this long-term change in a manner that maintains your quality of life.

Reality Check

It sounds so easy—write a log, swap half your food, and presto, you'll be transformed into your perfect self. Seems hard to believe.

What we are talking about is a long-term transformation. It could take up to six months before you notice a major transformation (although your friends will notice before that). This is because our bodies change very slowly. Nature is slow, and you will need to have patience. However, if you make the changes, the results will come. There are many success stories from athletes who have followed this advice.

Tips and Suggestions

Housecleaning: Get a box and clean out all the foods that are inconsistent with achieving your ideal self. It is much easier to make excellent food choices when they are all around you. Keep plenty of fresh fruit at your office, home, car, and training sites. This makes it a lot easier for you to stick with your plan.

Treats: Think about some of your favorite foods. During or after your long sessions, treat yourself to a moderate amount of these foods. Focus on eating them slowly and consuming nutrient-dense foods with them (this helps moderate intake).

Acceptance: Constantly remind yourself that your goal is to bring out your ideal self. Visualize the person within that you are helping to strengthen and bring forward. This philosophy is useful for making positive choices in all aspects of your life. It changes your mind-set from "denying yourself a candy bar" to "feeding your ideal self a peach."

Serving: Serve your meals in the kitchen rather than having large plates of food on the table. Like many people, you are likely to continue to eat well past being hungry if there is food in front of you. When trying to improve your body composition, try the following suggestions:

◆ Use smaller plates and bowls.

◆ Eat as much as you want but to wait 5 to 10 minutes between servings.

◆ Make a conscious decision to eat slightly more slowly than usual.

◆ Increase your intake of foods that are high in fiber but relatively low in calories.

Patterns and habits: Each of us has our own particular patterns and habits that either result in poor food selections or lead us toward poor choices. Pay attention to when and why you are engaging in self-sabotage. Show yourself some compassion, and see if you can understand the motivation behind the feelings or situations that lead you down familiar paths.

Perhaps you have a habit of pizza and beers a few times each week. By changing that pattern to stir-fry at your place, you might be able to achieve better food choices and see your friends at the same time. Sometimes a simple change is all it takes.

Scales: Weighing is counterproductive for many athletes trying to improve their body composition. Why is that? Scales encourage a short-term focus, whereas nutrition is a long-term strategy. Tracking your daily weight will show artificial highs and lows (quite often based on nothing more than your hydration levels). Wake up two pounds lighter, and you are happy all day. Find out that you are up three pounds, and the world better watch out!

Scales give inaccurate feedback. What we weigh says very little about our ability as an athlete (and our worth as a person, for that matter!). Although there are a number of sports in which it is beneficial to have a high power-to-weight ratio, many athletes lose power faster than they lose weight.

Athletes who focus excessively on weight tend to underhydrate and skimp on recovery nutrition because they want to "save" the weight they just lost. In reality, the fat has been burned and food and water are necessary to replenish glycogen, rebuild muscles, and restore hydration levels—all essential in order to be able to train and burn more fat. Proper nutrition is an essential part of this virtuous circle.

Finally, and most important of all, it's not about how much you weigh. It is about how you look, how you feel, how you recover, and how you perform. A scale tells you nothing about these things (although your mind might trick you into thinking it does!).

Spend some time considering your relationship with your scale. Is it affirming your ideal self or helping the part of your mind that beats you up? You may be better off pitching it into your housecleaning box.

Go natural: Probably the easiest thing to remember is to maximize your intake of fresh fruits, fresh vegetables, fish, poultry, and lean cuts of other meat. Focus on achieving a balanced, natural diet, and you are well on your way to good health.

Cooking: Many athletes have limited time in their lives, and finding time to cook can be difficult. We all have the same amount of time. The only difference is how we use it. In order to save time, make extra quantities when you cook "healthy." That way you have leftovers for the days when you are busy.

Fat: Very low-fat diets involve a lot of stress on your system, as there is a high degree of "background hunger" associated with avoiding fats. A more moderate approach to fats

Good Fat Sources

Albacore tuna
Almonds
Avocados
Cashews
Cod-liver oil
Dark green, leafy vegetables
Flax meal
Flaxseed oil
Macadamia nuts
Mackerel
Olive oil
Olives
Pecans
Salmon
Sardines
Trout
Walnuts

works best. Include small amounts of "good" fat in your diet. Sources of good fat include small amounts of olive oil, canola oil, raw nuts and seeds, and avocados as well as substantial amounts of organic, free-range, lean meat and coldwater fish (see "Good Fat Sources" sidebar).

Starches: When choosing rice, pasta, breads, and other foods with a large amount of starch, choose foods that have been subject to minimal processing. Avoid boxed cereals, white breads, white pasta, and white rice in favor of whole-grain breads, unsweetened grain-based cereals, whole-wheat pasta, and other whole grains. Limit your consumption of starchy foods to after training, and combine them with nutrient-dense foods.

Listen to your body: Our bodies will tell us what they need. The secret is learning to interpret the signals we receive. We are often prone to misinterpret these signals. The classic one is when we feel hungry. Somehow your mind might convince you that you need a bacon cheeseburger. When you start giving yourself balanced nutrition, you will discover that you feel better and many of your cravings disappear. They will still appear from time to time, but you can better deal with them through the other strategies given earlier in this chapter.

By putting these tips into action, you will be able to realize that you don't really need all the poor food choices that you thought would make you happy. By caring for your ideal self, you will find that it will become easier and easier to make choices that support your long-term goals.

You can do it! There are many people who have been in exactly the same position as you. They were full of self-pity, self-hate, despair, and fear. Despite their doubts, they decided that enough was enough and started a journey toward their ideal self.

Make a decision today, and take it hour by hour. There will be hurdles to overcome, but the rewards are worth the dedication required. Always remember that you get a fresh start every morning and can take it one meal at a time.

Show compassion to yourself, make gradual changes, and build the habits that strengthen your ideal self. Soon you will see that it's been there all the time.

Recovery and Post-workout Nutrition

Your recovery days and weeks are the most important times in your training. If you find yourself tired the second day after a big workout, drop the volume immediately. Many folks do "just one more session" to see if they are really tired, but history has shown again and again that if you are tired, it is best to take extra rest. Remember that you can't train a tired body.

In addition to rest, food is important to aid and speed your recovery. It is very important to immediately reload the carbohydrates lost during long or intense workouts. Carbohydrates are necessary to replace spent glycogen, a primary fuel source in exercise. Protein is needed to rebuild muscle and other protein-based tissues. Fat, especially mono-unsaturated, maintains the immune system and other vital physiological systems. Also important are the micronutrients, such as vitamins and minerals, found in quality foods. Your goal should be to eat a wide variety of foods in a condition as close to their natural state as is possible while minimizing sugar and highly processed products. Appropriate amounts of water are required to prevent recovery-delaying dehydration. If any of these factors are neglected, then the time to full recovery is pushed back several hours or even days.

In the first 30 minutes post-workout (i.e., a long and/or fast workout) or of a race, use a recovery drink that contains both carbohydrates and protein in a 4:1 ratio. You can buy a commercial product such as Endurox R4, or you can make your own by adding 6 tablespoons of table sugar to 16 ounces of skimmed milk. This 30-minute period is critical. For the next 90 minutes or so, continue to focus your diet on carbohydrates, especially moderate to high-glycemic-index (GI) carbohydrates (see "Glycemic Index of Selected Foods" sidebar). After this 2-hour-or-so window, return to your normal healthy diet.

If you train two or more times a day, or have very long sessions of 5 hours or longer, you may find that you need to supplement your diet with moderate- to high-GI carbohydrates for a longer period—perhaps up to 4 hours post-workout or post-race. The exact period will depend on your unique physiology, total training load, and nutrition strategy.

When recovering, the total amount of carbohydrate is more important than the GI rating. In other words, when you finish a 6-hour session, you need to reload the right amount of grams rather than worry about the GI rating.

Eat normally after recovery-paced or skills workouts of up to 90 minutes.

Glycemic Index (GI) of Selected Foods

The GI ranks carbohydrate-containing foods according to their immediate effect on blood-sugar levels. High-GI foods elicit a fast blood-glucose response, low-GI foods a slow and sustained response. Low-GI foods are beneficial before training and competition and throughout most of your day. Medium- and high-GI foods help speed recovery during and after exercise. Total carbohydrate intake, combined with a high GI, is the most important factor in speeding recovery.

Low GI (less than 50)		Medium GI (from 50–79)		High GI (greater than 80)	
Grain-based foods					
27	Rice bran	51	Vermicelli	80	Muesli cereal
45	Barley (pearl)	58	Rice, parboiled	81	Wild rice, Saskatchewan
38	Pasta, spaghetti, protein enriched	60	All bran cereal	87	Oatmeal
		61	Spaghetti, brown, boiled 15 minutes	89	Rye bread, whole-meal
45	Spaghetti, white, boiled 5 minutes			82	Semolina bread
		63	Wheat kernels	93	Couscous
46	Fettuccine	65	Bulgur	95	Rye crispbread
48	Rye	68	Rye or pumpernickel bread	95	Barley-flour bread
		68	Oat-bran bread	95	Gnocchi
		69	Multigrain bread	96	Muesli
		74	Buckwheat	100	Whole-meal wheat bread
		75	Bulgur bread	103	Millet
		79	Brown rice		
Dairy Products/Substitutes					
46	Skim milk	52	Yogurt		
43	Soy milk				
Simple Sugars					
31	Fructose	65	Lactos	92	Sucrose
				138	Glucose
				152	Maltose

Low GI (less than 50)		Medium GI (from 50–79)		High GI (greater than 80)	

Vegetables

Low GI		Medium GI		High GI	
12	Bengal gram dal	50	Green peas, dried	80	Potato, new, boiled
20	Soybeans	50	Lima beans	80	Sweet corn
32	Dried peas	54	Brown beans	88	Beet
37	Red lentils	55	Pinto beans	99	Rutabaga
43	Black beans	57	Haricot (navy) beans	100	Potato, mashed
45	Kidney beans, dried	59	Black-eyed beans	107	Pumpkin
46	Blackeyed peas	60	Baked beans (canned)	108	Broad beans (fava)
46	Butter beans	65	Green peas, frozen	117	Cooked carrots
46	Baby lima beans	65	Romano beans	118	Potato, instant
47	Rye kernels	68	Green peas	128	Potato, russet, baked
49	Chickpeas (garbanzo beans)	70	Potato, sweet	139	Cooked parsnips
	Most green vegetables	74	Yam		
		74	Kidney beans (canned)		

Fruits

Low GI		Medium GI		High GI	
10	Nopal (prickly pear)	53	Apple	80	Mango
32	Cherries	55	Plum	84	Banana
34	Plum	58	Pear	91	Raisins
36	Grapefruit	59	Apple juice	91	Apricots, canned
40	Peach	60	Fresh peach	93	Cantaloupe
44	Apricot	63	Orange	94	Pineapple
49	Strawberries	63	Pears, canned	103	Watermelon
		66	Pineapple juice		
		66	Grapes		
		69	Grapefruit juice		
		74	Orange juice		
		74	Peaches, canned		
		75	Kiwi		
		79	Fruit cocktail		

The Optimal Diet for an Athlete

Nutrition can be the toughest part of the performance equation. It involves a total dedication to eating only the best foods at the right times. Cutting back too much on total calories doesn't work because this approach compromises recovery and immune-system function. Further, a diet that is light on calories, particularly protein, can cause you to lose valuable lean-muscle mass. So we each need to learn the right balance based on our genetics, body size, and training load.

There is no magical formula for diet. Once you find a nutrition strategy that gives you plenty of energy and leaves your weight stable, you are there. At that stage, you can slightly trim your energy intake for a slow, safe weight loss. The ideal formula will vary from athlete to athlete.

Our personal experience, research, and the experience of the athletes that we coach have shown that the optimal diet for an athlete incorporates the principles contained in *The Paleo Diet* by Loren Cordain, Ph.D. The concepts of the paleo diet are quite simple:

◆ Eat lots of fruits and vegetables.
◆ Eat lean protein with every meal.
◆ Use high-GI carbohydrates during and after training for recovery.
◆ Avoid foods that contain saturated and hydrogenated fats.
◆ Eat moderate amounts of good fats.
◆ Eat a larger number of smaller meals.

For most people, it comes down to eating a lot more fruits and veggies and knocking cheese, butter, cream, and fast food out of their diets.

You will find that you need to eat constantly and eat more. If you are following a traditional Western diet, then you may be "starch addicted." If this is the case, you will experience a withdrawal period (from the blood-sugar spikes that typify a high-starch, high-sugar diet). The length of the transition period varies from person to person. Normally you are looking at a period of two to four weeks.

When on this plan, it is essential to eat high-GI carbohydrates (with protein) immediately after every training session or race lasting 90 to 180 minutes or longer. The reason for a wide range in our guideline is that more experienced athletes will have greater fat-burning ability and therefore less need to use high-GI carbohydrates. If your recovery starts to suffer or energy levels dip, then you might not be refueling quickly enough.

This plan makes the most sense for light training days. When you are training long and/or hard, you will need to eat substantial amounts of food. For example, elite athletes training 25 to 30 hours per week and doing multiple sessions every day will be eating constantly. The typical age-group athlete will find that higher-GI carbohydrates are required after his or her longest sessions but not so much after short, intense sessions.

Research coming out of the United States shows that intense training depresses the immune system. Maintaining a stable blood-sugar level, which can be accomplished by appropriate timing of carbohydrate intake, has been shown to reduce the impact of this stress. A traditional athletic diet that is based on highly processed carbohydrate food sources not only increases the stress on the body but is nearly nutritionally void in terms of the nutrients essential for recovery. No wonder so many athletes find themselves sick in the 10 to 14 days after their most intense training periods.

Athletes who frequently get sick after hard BT workouts should look at increasing their carbohydrate intake for the 3 to 72 hours postexercise. However, be careful that this increase does not cut into your protein intake. Low protein will contribute to frequent illness, loss of muscle mass, and lethargy.

Many athletes who eat a high-fiber diet can find it difficult to get in enough calories, as the fiber and grains leave them quite full. This is a good point for people who are chronically skinny to consider; a huge fruit intake could be counterproductive for an athlete who has trouble maintaining lean body mass.

Tips for Making the Change

◆ Make small and gradual changes —this is the only way to ensure long-term success.

◆ Try to reduce your saturated and partially hydrogenated (trans) fats—cheese, crackers, snack foods, etc.

◆ Ensure that you get enough protein. Tuna and other fish are good sources, as are meats from free-ranging cattle and poultry. It is important, particularly for female athletes, to eat protein with every meal.

◆ Don't watch your calories, but do watch your "bad" fats (saturated and hydrogenated). Also be aware of your omega-6 polyunsaturated (mostly vegetable oils and snack foods) intake because these fats, while beneficial in some ways, may increase your risk of inflammation. If you eat plenty of fruits, veggies, lean protein, and "good" fats such as mono-unsaturated and omega-3 polyunsaturated (olive, flaxseed, and canola oils; nut butters; fish oils), you will be fine.

◆ Eat more fruits and veggies. Whole fruits are superior to juices because the fiber in the fruit keeps them lower on the GI scale.

Timing Meals

Athletes should eat low-to-moderate-GI carbohydrates about two hours prior to a hard or long workout or race. There should also be some fat and protein in this meal.

During your BT workouts and races, you will need to take in high-GI carbohydrates, mostly in the form of fluids. Sports drinks are fine for this. Find one that you like the taste of and will drink willingly. Realize that sessions lasting less than about an hour (including warm-up) don't require any carbohydrates. Water will suffice. Fruit juices aren't as quickly available to the muscle as sports drinks. Other products that may be necessary, especially as the sessions get longer (in excess of two hours), are gels and sports bars.

A starting point for deciding how much to take in is based on 350 calories per hour. Larger and smaller athletes may vary this range considerably. How your gut handles food during exercise will also determine your unique intake needs. Also, the more anaerobic efforts your session demands, the fewer calories you will probably want to take in. It appears that the digestive processes slow down during anaerobic effort, which may cause a feeling of bloating or nausea if you are taking in greater amounts of food.

Some points to make clear for the more focused athletes:

◆ Carbohydrates are an essential part of our nutrition strategy. In working on your diet, it is imperative to eat the right foods at the right times. There is an important role for all types of healthy food.

◆ When volume is high, you may need to continue eating moderate amounts of moderate-GI carbohydrates for an extended period after training. Give your nutrition the same flexibility that you give to your training.

◆ If you are seeking to improve body composition, remember that you must eat to have the energy to train—to have the energy to burn fat. This is a virtuous circle and a healthy routine.

◆ In general, most athletes who are seeking to improve their body composition exercise control at the wrong time of the training/recovery cycle. The right choices are most important when training volume is low.

Periodization

The optimal diet for peak performance must vary with the athlete, just as the optimal training protocol must vary from person to person. We can't all eat the same things in the same relative amounts and reap the same benefits. Where your ancestors originated on the planet, and what they ate for the last thirty thousand years or so, are the most important determinant of what you should eat now.

The bottom line is that you must discover what mix of foods works best for you. If you have never experimented with this mix, don't automatically assume you have found it already. You may be surprised at what happens when changes are made at the training table. A word of caution: Make changes gradually, and allow at least three weeks for your body to adapt to a new diet before passing judgment based on how you feel and your performance in training. It usually takes two weeks of adaptation to change before seeing any results. During the adaptation period, you may feel "strange" and train poorly. For this reason, changes in diet are best done early in the season.

Not only seasonal changes have a bearing on the dietary mix you follow; age is also a concern. As you age, changes may occur in body chemistry, requiring further shifts in diet. Recent research has shown that aging athletes need a considerable amount of vegetables and fruits in their diets to maintain calcium and nitrogen balances.

An optimal diet to enhance training, racing, and recovery involves not only eating moderate amounts of the macronutrients—including carbohydrates, protein, fat, and water—but also varying the mix of these foods throughout the year. In other words, diet should cycle just as training cycles within a periodization plan. Protein serves as the anchor for the diet and stays relatively constant throughout the year as fat and carbohydrates rise and fall alternately.

In the Base period, when training volume is relatively high and intensity is low, eating a diet rich in "good" fats is beneficial to improving your ability to burn fat for fuel while conserving glycogen stores—a physiological goal of training at this time of the season. Such fats include mono-unsaturated oils with some polyunsaturated oils while avoiding saturated and partially hydrogenated fats. Simply emphasizing these foods, along with plenty of lean protein, fruits, and vegetables, puts you on the right track for this time of year.

In the Build period, when the intensity of training increases as you prepare for the first A-priority race of the season, the fat-carbohydrate balance should shift toward carbohydrate. But be careful here—this doesn't mean that you should pig out on starch and sugar. Treat these two types of carbohydrates strictly as recovery foods. They may be eaten in considerable quantities in the two to four hours immediately after a hard or long workout to restore glycogen levels but should otherwise be avoided. Instead, get your carbohydrates primarily from fruits and nonstarchy vegetables. The density of vitamin and mineral micronutrients in these foods far exceeds that of the starches and simple sugars. You'll recover faster, control weight, and be healthier by concentrating your diet around fruits and nonstarchy veggies.

Throughout the season, keep your intake of lean protein high by including such foods in every meal. The best sources of such foods are free-ranging cattle, chicken, turkey, and eggs (go easy on eggs—perhaps six per week). Do not buy products from animals that are feedlot-raised. Their body compositions are not suitable for good health—either theirs or ours.

Good snacks in the Base period, and year-round, are nuts and seeds. If you find that you need additional energy, then dried fruit may be mixed in with the nuts in the Build period to boost your carbohydrate intake. Go light on snack foods and remember the "Key Three."

If the "Key Three" are applied against perhaps 80 percent of everything you eat, while including good fats, then you will not have to be concerned with ratios or counting calories. You'll also recover better and race faster.

Diet, Aging, and Muscle

Popeye was right: Eating spinach can make you stronger and more muscular, especially if you're over fifty years of age. Here's why.

It's apparent that as we grow older, we lose muscle mass. Although this loss is slowed somewhat by weight lifting and vigorous aerobic exercise, it still happens. Even athletes in their sixties typically demonstrate considerably less muscle than they had in their forties.

Now there is research by T. Remer and F. Manz that shows why. Nitrogen, which is an essential component of muscle protein, is given up by the body at a faster rate than it can be taken in as we get older. This change is due to a gradual change in kidney function that comes with aging, producing an acidic state in the blood. Essentially, we are peeing off our muscles as we pass the half-century mark in life.

With a net loss of nitrogen, new muscle cannot be formed. This acidic state of the blood also explains why calcium is lost with aging, resulting in osteoporosis for many, especially women, with advanced age.

The key to reducing, or even avoiding, this situation is to lower the blood's acid level by increasing its alkalinity. There are studies demonstrating that taking a supplement called potassium bicarbonate daily for as few as eighteen days increases the blood's alkaline level by balancing nitrogen in the body. Although it can be purchased relatively inexpensively in laboratory supply shops, potassium bicarbonate is not currently available as an over-the-counter supplement, and there are no long-term studies of its effects on health. There is some evidence that it contributes to irregular ECG readings.

However, there is a natural way of achieving this same result through diet by eating foods that increase the blood's alkalinity—fruits and vegetables. Fats and oils have a neutral effect on blood acid. All other foods, including grains, meats, nuts, beans, dairy, fish, and eggs, increase the blood's acidity. If your diet is high in these foods but low in fruits and vegetables, you can expect to lose muscle mass and bone calcium as you age.

Remer and Manz's study ranks foods in terms of their effect on blood acidity and alkalinity. For example, the food that has the most acidic effect, therefore contributing to a loss of nitrogen and ultimately muscle, is parmesan cheese. The food they found to have the greatest alkaline effect, thus reducing nitrogen and muscle loss, is raisins. Among vegetables, spinach was the most alkaline food. So, you see? Popeye was right.

Table 12.1 is a ranking of common foods and their effect on alkalinity and acidity taken from Remer and Manz's study. The higher a food's positive acidic ranking, the more likely it is to contribute to a loss of muscle mass and bone-mineral levels. The more negative the food's alkaline ranking, the more beneficial is the effect on these measures.

Table 12.1 Acidic versus Alkaline Foods

Acid Foods (+)		Alkaline Foods (−)	
Grains		**Fruits**	
Brown rice	+12.5	Raisins	−21.0
Rolled oats	+10.7	Black currants	−6.5
Whole-wheat bread	+8.2	Bananas	−5.5
Spaghetti	+7.3	Apricots	−4.8
Corn flakes	+6.0	**Vegetables**	
White rice	+4.6	Spinach	−14.0
Dairy		Celery	−5.2
Parmesan cheese	+34.2	Carrots	−4.9
Processed cheese	+28.7	Lettuce	−2.5
Hard cheese	+19.2		
Cottage cheese	+8.7		
Whole milk	+0.7		
Legumes			
Peanuts	+8.3		
Meats, Fish, Eggs			
Trout	+10.8		
Turkey	+9.9		
Chicken	+8.7		
Eggs	+8.1		
Beef	+7.8		

Sports Drinks, Bars, Gels, and More

In the last three decades there has been a revolution in sports nutrition supplements. It all started in the 1970s with a sports drink developed at the University of Florida—Gatorade. There are now more products on the market than can be sampled in a four-hour workout.

The field has expanded well beyond drinks consumed during exercise. Now there are carbohydrate-loading drinks, recovery drinks, sports bars, and energy gels. Newer products include glycerol and choline. Glycerol is an additive that purportedly turns the body into a water-absorbing sponge. Choline is promoted as a nervous-system enhancer. Latest on the scene is a "supersugar" called galactose. To help clear the confusion, here is a quick primer in sports nutrition products.

Sports Drinks

Besides Gatorade, a few other products are PowerAde, Hydra Fuel, Cytomax, AllSport, XLR-8, GPush, Ultima Replenisher, Accelerade, GU2O, and Shaklee Performance. What all of these drinks have in common is carbohydrate content and the inclusion of sodium. Both have been found to speed fluid's movement from the stomach into the small intestine, where it can be absorbed.

Sports drinks should be used during exercise lasting an hour or more. Generally, an athlete should take in 16 to 32 ounces (480–960 ml) per hour, depending on body size, known rate of fluid loss, and heat. A few big gulps every hour have been shown to work better than frequent small sips. Cool liquids are also more effective than warm drinks.

Carbohydrate-loading drinks appeared in the early 1980s as carbohydrate loading came into general practice before long events such as marathons, and companies began marketing drinks that would help with loading with less bulk than solid foods such as pasta. Examples of these drinks are Accelerade, Champion Revenge, Prolab Carb Pro, Cytosport CytoMax, Sports Quest Carbo Pro, Twinlab Carbo Fuel, and Spiz. Such products are sometimes used on the last day before an event lasting 90 minutes or more. They help the body store more carbohydrates, thus pushing fatigue farther away from the start line. Besides carbohydrates, they usually contain some fat and protein to mimic a meal. Some athletes have started using them during events lasting longer than four hours, such as the ironman triathlons, since it's difficult to get in enough calories otherwise. Care must be taken in doing this because loading drinks containing more than 3 grams of fat per serving could delay absorption and lead to dehydration.

Recovery Drinks

There is a lot of crossover between loading and recovery drinks. The common element of products intended to speed recovery following long or intense exercise is the inclusion of protein along with carbohydrate.

Much of the fuel used during exhausting exercise comes from protein. If it is not replaced soon afterward, there may be a loss of muscle mass and a delay in recovery. Protein also speeds carbohydrate absorption.

Drinks in this category are Endurox R4, Shaklee Physique, Ultra Fuel, Metabolol Endurance, GPush G4, Sustained Energy, and Boost. They should be used immediately following exercise and up to two hours later for best results.

Sports Bars

In the mid-1980s PowerBar launched a new category into the fray—sports bars. Although they look much like a candy bar, the primary ingredient is usually carbohydrates, and all contain some fat and protein. Most have fewer than 3 grams of fat, although some have twice that amount.

Examples are PowerBar, Clif Bar, PR Bar, Twinlab Ironman Triathlon Bar, Sports Pharma, Xterra Q3, and Balance Bar.

Bars should be used in exercise lasting longer than about 90 minutes—three to four hours or longer is probably more appropriate. The major limiter for these products is their absorption rate. You must drink 8 to 16 ounces of fluid with every bar eaten, yet it still may take 30 minutes or more for the fuel to get to your working muscles.

Gels

The newest entry is energy gels—gooey liquids that come in ketchup-sized pouches to be torn open and sucked out. Their main attraction is the convenience of a small package, yet a high-energy yield—about 100 calories per packet.

In this category are PowerGel, GU, Carb-BOOM, Hammer Gel, Clif Shot, Jogmate, Ultra Gel, and Leppin Squeezy. During exercise lasting an hour or more, take one every 30 minutes, drinking eight to 10 ounces (240–300 ml) of fluid with each. During four-hour or longer events, consume a packet every 15 minutes, especially later in the contest.

Drink enough water when using sports bars and gels. If you don't, your gut will pull fluid from the blood to help in the digestive process, which causes dehydration.

Glycerol

Glycerol is a sweet, syrupy liquid found in fats. Several studies have demonstrated that using it with water prior to a race causes the body to store more water, thus helping to prevent dehydration and, as a possible result, cramping and bonking. The problem is that recent studies have not always been able to produce the same beneficial results, and many athletes (including Gordo) experience negative side effects from glycerol loading.

Glycerol is one of those products that should definitely be tested before an important race, as there are many possible side effects, including nausea, headache, lightheadedness, and bloating. If you decide to try it, be sure to carefully follow the instructions printed on the label.

Examples of glycerol-based products are Glycerate and Pro Hydrator. There have been no long-term studies on the effects of glycerol on health, but it is generally considered safe because it's present in dietary sources of fat.

Choline

Choline is a vitamin-like compound found in egg yolks, organ meats, spinach, cauliflower, nuts, soybeans, spinach, lettuce, and wheat germ. Some sports nutrition manufacturers have recently begun including it in their products because it has been shown to improve nervous-system function. About a half to a full gram of choline a day in the diet is all that most active people need. This quantity may be obtained through a normally healthy diet. But in races or training sessions lasting two hours or more, dietary choline may be on the low side, increasing perceptions of fatigue. Some studies have demonstrated that supplementing with 2.5 grams of choline before and again during long endurance exercise reduces feelings of fatigue and improves endurance performances.

As with glycerol, there are no known side effects from long-term use of choline, and it is generally considered safe to use. There are possible side effects, however, including diarrhea and flatulence.

Sports drink products containing choline and carbohydrates are Boston Sports Supplement, Pro Enhancer, Race Day, Prolyte, and TwinLab Choline Cocktail.

If you are taking any medications, including ibuprofen or aspirin, it's a good idea to check with your doctor before using a product such as choline or glycerol.

Galactose

The benefits of galactose were discovered through research at the University of Leeds in the United Kingdom in the mid-1990s and are just now being introduced to the market. Galactose is a "supersugar" with no existing specific usage in any food products but with enormous benefits over other sugars in the sports area. Galactose has the following advantages:

◆ noninsulogenic (does not initiate a primary insulin response) and hence reduces the likelihood of unwanted hypoglycemia
◆ naturally occurring monosaccharide that needs no digestion
◆ rapidly absorbed by sodium cotransport (the fastest sugar-transfer mechanism)
◆ integrates well into energy metabolism (liver pathway)
◆ low GI—0.20 versus 1 for glucose

GPush is a sports drinks containing galactose. Again, there are no long-term studies of the effects of galactose.

Update on Supplements

The nutritional supplement market is virtually unregulated so athletes should be aware that taking any supplements carries a risk of cross-contamination from banned and prohibited substances. For this reason, many athletes subject to drug testing have made a personal decision to move away from all forms of nutritional supplementation. The most difficult aspect of assessing the value of any nutritional supplement, dietary strategy, recovery technique, or training tool is that we have so much going on in our lives that it is tough to single out one aspect.

Quite often many of us are looking for a magic pill, session, or piece of equipment that will offer breakthrough success. Athletes should be very skeptical of any supplement appearing to offer huge benefits. One thing for sure is that most working athletes would go faster if they managed to get an extra hour of sleep every night. Sleep is a natural performance enhancer, and a lack of sleep is probably the single greatest challenge facing most working athletes.

Following is a review of some of the most common supplements. This is not an exhaustive review of all the supplements on the market. We have evaluated those supplements that we believe are beneficial as well as certain others that are widely used by athletes.

Antioxidants, Iron, and Calcium

It's an interesting observation that medical treatments and lifestyle practices that slow the aging process are often beneficial to athletic performance. A good example is antioxidants. They have been shown to prevent the damage that advances the aging of cells while helping to ward off such diseases as cancer and heart disease.

Antioxidants are part of an elaborate defense system the body employs to check cellular damage caused by free radicals—highly reactive atoms formed when oxygen interacts with certain molecules. The damage that free radicals cause to cellular components such as DNA or the cell membrane may be equated with what happens when rust forms on metal.

If you were to do only one thing in the way of supplements, antioxidants should be it. Take daily 400 to 800 IU of vitamin E (d-alpha tocopherols, not dL-alpha), 1 gram of vitamin C, and 2 to 5 grams of fish oil high in omega-3 DHA and EPA. When choosing vitamin E, d-alpha (a natural source) is superior to dL-alpha (a synthetic source), as it is more readily absorbed by the body. Although flaxseed oil is a source of omega-3 oils, studies have shown that fish oils are better absorbed by the body.

Omega-3 fats are powerful antioxidants, antiaging aids, and cancer fighters. They bind to free radicals (waste from exercise) and help remove them from the body. They lower bad serum cholesterol and are precursors to sex hormones that lead to normal body function and faster recovery. They also support the immune system, as do vitamins C and E.

Certain athletes may need to supplement their diet with iron. Never take iron supplements unless under the specific guidance of a physician. Unmonitored supplementation of iron can be very dangerous to your health.

Many athletes wonder about the need to supplement calcium. A basic concept of the paleo diet (see *The Paleo Diet*) is that calcium supplementation is not necessary when eating according to the guidelines expressed in this chapter. Eating alkaline foods (vegetables and fruits) in abundance will also prevent this from happening, as we explained earlier. After all, our ancestors for the better part of four and a half million years did not eat dairy and did not suffer from osteoporosis. Finally, the large amount of weight-bearing exercise done by triathletes makes a very positive contribution to overall bone health.

Increased fitness from regular exercise also means greater resistance to free-radical damage. Although regular and consistent exercise is effective for boosting the body's natural resistance to free-radical breakdown, "weekend warriors" create significant stresses on their bodies. Infrequent and excessive exercise overwhelms the body with free radicals and is too inconsistent to promote our natural defense system. This is one reason why sedentary people are urged to keep their periodic episodes of exercise brief and low intensity.

The human body contains several enzymes that prevent or reduce the severity of this damage by interacting with free radicals to render them harmless. This is the body's natural antioxidant system. There are also certain nutrients found in food that bolster this defense system. The principal dietary antioxidants are vitamins E and C. It has been well established that a deficiency of these vitamins greatly reduces endurance capacity. Other nutrients, especially beta-carotene, and to a lesser extent selenium and coenzyme Q10 (CoQ10), have also been shown to be effective at combining with free radicals.

Vitamin E (d-alpha tocopherol) is present in nuts, seeds, vegetable oils, fish-liver oils, and wheat germ. Vitamin C (ascorbic acid) is in citrus fruits and juices, sweet peppers, raw cabbage, berries, kiwifruit, cantaloupe, and green leafy vegetables. Such foods as carrots, sweet potatoes, spinach, cantaloupe, broccoli, dark green leafy vegetables, and orange vegetables and fruits are rich in beta-carotene, which is a precursor of vitamin A.

Some studies have shown that supplementing the diet with antioxidants well in excess of the recommended daily allowance (RDA) reduces free-radical damage in athletes. Although we recommend eating a diet rich in antioxidants, it is difficult to consume enough food to achieve the levels used in some of these studies, especially for vitamin E. Although somewhat controversial, supplementation is recommended for serious athletes.

The RDA for vitamin E is 15 IU per day for men and 12 for women. This amount may be well below what is necessary for serious endurance athletes. Recent studies have successfully supplemented with amounts as high as 200 to 800 IU daily. The RDA for vitamin C is 60 mg per day, but once again, dosages as high as 250 to 1,000 mg per day have typically been used by athletes. With a diet very high in plant foods, the lower end of these vitamin C dosages may be attained without supplementation.

Antioxidants are generally believed to play no direct role in performance enhancement. In other words, you won't be faster because of taking vitamin E and C supplements. On the other hand, at least one study, as reported by O. Anderson in *Running Research*

News, has shown a direct relationship between performance at high altitude and vitamin E supplementation.

So, should you supplement your diet with antioxidants? Although not overwhelming, the evidence at this time seems to indicate that there is good reason to do so. However, this advice applies only if you are not on certain medications such as blood thinners or pain relievers; if you are, vitamin E supplementation may cause complications. If you are on any medications at all, check with your physician before supplementing.

Caffeine

Many athletes use caffeine to "boost" their race-day performance or to get a "jump" before a BT workout. If you aren't used to caffeine, it is best to start with a single cup of coffee. Caffeine works best in low to moderate doses and at high levels is detrimental to performance. If you start to shake, you'll know you have gone too far. There are, however, many side effects to the use of caffeine.

- ◆ It is easy to become habituated to the response. Some research indicates less of a beneficial effect in habitual drinkers.
- ◆ You will sleep better if you have had no caffeine during the day. Many athletes experience disrupted sleep patterns from caffeine. Given the recovery benefits of sleep, caffeine use is likely counterproductive for these athletes.
- ◆ Caffeine is easy for some athletes to get hooked on.
- ◆ Stomach upset is common. Experiment with dosages in race-simulation training and B- and C-priority races. Use less caffeine in an A-priority race because of the additional stresses associated with a race situation.
- ◆ It is possible to test positive for excessive caffeine—besides the fact that it works best in moderation, this is another reason to be reasonable in its application. If you are considering using caffeine in any drug-tested race, then you should make yourself aware of the limits and ensure that you stay well below the maximum limit.

Creatine

Some athletes supplement with creatine to aid recovery and enhance strength. However, this substance is useful only for people who have power (not muscular endurance) as a limiter, and it is not recommended for endurance athletes. For endurance athletes, there is still quite a bit to be learned about this ergogenic aid, and there is likely to be a downside. Probably the greatest risk that you face in using any strength-oriented supplement is the risk of inadvertent doping owing to poor quality control by the manufacturer. In recent years there have been a number of studies that have shown a lack of purity in dietary supplements generally.

Glutamine and Branch-Chain Amino Acids

One study has shown that taking 8 grams of the amino acid glutamine immediately after stressful exercise improved the capacity to recover by improving the glucose absorption rate. Such research is still in the preliminary stages.

This amino acid was once considered "nonessential." It is now thought of as "conditionally essential." There is evidence that under traumatic conditions (heavy periods of training, stage racing, or bodily injury), the body is unable to produce enough glutamine. Glutamine is essential to muscle growth, has positive effects on the immune system, and may improve insulin metabolism. It has the ability to preserve skeletal muscle mass in times of stress, which is one of the reasons it is added to IV bags for hospital patients.

Should you decide to supplement L-glutamine, consider starting on the low end, 2 grams per day.

Branch-chain amino acids (BCAAs) may also enhance recovery during heavy periods of training. All of the amino acids can be found in meats, and a nutritional analysis will provide information about adequate protein. However, if it is unclear whether the quantity of amino acids in an athlete's diet is sufficient, then consuming 35 mg of BCAA for each pound of body weight each day during periods of high stress may be beneficial.

In the cases of both BCAAs and glutamine, supplement half the dose after training (or a race) with a recovery drink and the other half with a snack before bed. Food slows the absorption rate and helps the body utilize more of the supplement. If you decide to use any supplements, record the dose taken, the time, and any other particulars in a training journal. Also comment on whether you believe the supplementation helps compared with past seasons of heavy racing or training. We do not recommend taking these supplements daily, year-round.

Sodium

Those at the greatest risk for electrolyte problems are the 13-hour-plus ironman-distance athletes because their pace is slow enough that they can drink large quantities of fluid all day. Combine that rate of consumption with a high sweat rate, and you risk seriously diluting your electrolytes.

For longer, hot races the use of salt/electrolyte tablets has proven successful. A common rate of sodium loss is in the range of 1.8 grams (not mg) to 3.5 grams of sodium per liter of sweat. The low figure is for a fit, acclimatized athlete, and the high figure is for an unfit, nonacclimatized athlete.

The average person has about 80 grams of sodium in his or her body and consumes 5 to 20 grams of sodium per day. As you can see, you would have to sweat an awful lot of end up salt depleted. However, the issue is more complicated because sodium balance affects your ability to move fluid from the stomach to the bloodstream. For this reason, many athletes view sodium supplementation as a source of insurance while racing. They may not need the additional electrolytes, but they feel better taking them.

Many middle-of-the-pack and back-of-the-pack athletes overhydrate, thus diluting the sodium content of their blood. Two ways to avoid this result are to drink less or supplement.

Once again, it is a case of needing to experiment during training in order to recognize what works for you. If you have hypertension or are on a low-sodium diet, then you should consult your physician before starting any sodium supplementation. Indeed, as we mentioned earlier, you should discuss any potential supplementation with your physician.

Sodium Phosphate

Note: Do not supplement with sodium phosphate to get electrolytes.

For the novice endurance athlete, there's no reason to use pharmacological ergogenic aids. Training to develop basic levels of fitness must come first. For experienced athletes who are approaching their physical potential, however, safe and legal ergogenic aids are a viable option for attaining peak fitness for A-priority races. One of the more common ergogenic aids is sodium phosphate.

There is only a handful of research that has shown direct benefits of sodium phosphate for endurance performance, but the results of some of these studies are quite impressive. For example, R. B. Kreider and associates at Old Dominion University in Norfolk, Virginia, tested six trained male cyclists and triathletes for VO_2max, lactate threshold, power, and performance in a 40K time trial. The subjects took either sodium phosphate or a dummy placebo for three days before the testing. With sodium phosphate there was a 10 percent increase in VO_2max, a 10 percent jump in lactate threshold, and a 9 percent boost in power at lactate threshold when compared with the placebo results. As a result of these benefits, their 40K time trial was completed at a 17 percent higher average power output and the 40K times were 3.5 minutes faster using sodium phosphate.

One of the first studies to show a benefit for endurance events was conducted in the early 1980s. Ten well-trained runners loaded with sodium phosphate or a placebo for three days before a max treadmill test and a run to exhaustion. The results were similar to the previously mentioned research. VO_2max rose 6 to 12 percent, and the run to exhaustion was 3 to 9 minutes longer with sodium phosphate. Other research has shown similar results.

Sodium phosphate offers two major benefits among the several it provides. The first is that it causes the blood to "unload" more oxygen at the muscle (not all of the circulating oxygen is uncoupled from the blood hemoglobin when it is needed). The more oxygen consumed, the higher your VO_2max. Second, it buffers the hydrogen ions given off when lactate enters the blood (hydrogen inhibits energy production and reduces muscle force). This essentially means that you can go faster before becoming anaerobic.

Best of all, there have been good race results for many athletes over the past few years when they've used sodium phosphate. Unfortunately, not everyone has reported a noticeable performance enhancement. But since there are so many variables that go into final preparation for an important competition—not the least of which is rest—it's sometimes difficult to determine what may have resulted in a particularly good race.

Should you decide to load with sodium phosphate for important races this season, follow these guidelines:

◆ Use sodium phosphate only two or three times a year, as it is believed to leach calcium from bones with continuous, high-dosage use.

◆ Try it once before a C-priority race or a hard rest-and-recovery-week workout to see how it affects you before using it for an A-priority race.

◆ Take 1 gram three or four times a day, with meals, for three to five days leading up to the race. Take 1 or 2 grams on race day with the pre-race meal.

◆ If while experimenting you experience an upset stomach or diarrhea, reduce the daily dosage and spread the same total amount over more days. Even 1 gram a day for nineteen days with some days off is effective.

Recommended Reading

Anderson, O. Antioxidants: Do They Really Speed Your Recovery from Strenuous Training? *Running Research News* 13 (4) (1997): 1–5.

Cade, R., et al. Effects of Phosphate Loading on 2,3-diphosphoglycerate and Maximal Oxygen Uptake. *Medicine and Science in Sport and Exercise* 16 (3) (1984): 263–268.

Clarkson, P. M. Antioxidants and Physical Performance. *Critical Reviews in Food Science and Nutrition* 35 (1–2) (1995): 131–141.

Cordain, Loren. *The Paleo Diet*. New York: Wiley & Sons, 2002.

Frassetto, L. A., et al. Effect of Age on Blood Acid-Base Composition in Adult Humans: Role of Age-Related Renal Function Decline. *American Journal of Physiology* 271 (6–2) (1996): F1114–1122.

———. Potassium Bicarbonate Reduces Urinary Nitrogen Excretion in Postmenopausal Women. *Journal of Endocrinology and Metabolism* 82 (1) (1997): 254–259.

Ji, L. L. Oxidative Stress during Exercise: Implication of Antioxidant Nutrients. *Free Radicals in Biology and Medicine* 18 (6) (1995): 1079–1086.

Kleiner, S. M., and M. Greenwood-Robinson. *High-Performance Nutrition*. New York: John Wiley and Sons, 1996.

Kreider, R. B., et al. Effects of Phosphate Loading on Metabolic and Myocardial Responses to Maximal and Endurance Exercise. *International Journal of Sports Nutrition* 2 (1) (1992): 20–47.

——. Effects of Phosphate Loading on Oxygen Uptake, Ventilatory Anaerobic Threshold, and Run Performance. *Medicine and Science in Sport and Exercise* 22 (2) (1990): 250–256.

Noakes, Tim. The Low Figure Is for a Fit Acclimatized Athlete and the High Figure Is for an Unfit Non-acclimatized Athlete. *Lore of Running*, 4th ed. Champaign, IL: Human Kinetics, 2002.

Remer, T., and F. Manz. Potential Renal Acid Load of Foods and Its Influence on Urine pH. *Journal of the American Dietetic Association* 95 (7) (1995): 791–797.

Robertson, J. D., R. J. Maughan, G. G. Duthie, and P. C. Morrice. Increased Blood Antioxidant Systems of Runners in Response to Training Load. *Clinical Science* 80 (6) (1991): 611–618.

Rokitzki, L., E. Logemann, G. Huber, et al. Alpha-tocopherol Supplementation in Racing Cyclists during Extreme Endurance Training. *International Journal of Sport Nutrition* 4 (3) (1994): 253–264.

Sebastian, A., et al. Improved Mineral Balance and Skeletal Metabolism in Postmenopausal Women Treated with Potassium Bicarbonate. *New England Journal of Medicine* 330 (25) (1994): 1776–1781.

Stewart, I., et al. Phosphate Loading and the Effects on VO_2max in Trained Cyclists. *Research Quarterly for Exercise and Sport* 61 (1) (1990): 80–84.

Witt, E. H., E. Z. Reznick, C. A. Viguie, et al. Exercise, Oxidative Damage and Effects of Antioxidant Manipulation. *Journal of Nutrition* 122 (3) (1992): 766–773.

Chapter 13

Damage-Limitation Strategies

"Call the doctor, I think
I'm gonna crash."
—The Eagles,
"Life in the Fast Lane"

Training for, and racing in, an Ironman® triathlon is a large undertaking. The training involves long hours laced with numerous trials and tribulations. Race day is the icing on the cake, but even the icing runs from time to time. It's a long day out there, and anything can happen at any time.

In order to prevent some of the more common errors in training, do your best to learn from the common mistakes of others. The best way to overcome race-day mishaps is to prevent them from the beginning and remain calm while dealing with them if they come up.

Common Race-Day Errors

The number-one rule on race day is "nothing new." You've spent many months training and preparing for this one day. Waking up on race morning and deciding you're going to try this new sports drink your friends swear by, or throwing on a brand-new pair of running shoes, is not the wisest choice. Always go with what you've used in training and what works for you—from nutrition to equipment to clothing. Here are the classic errors that many athletes make in a race situation (we've both made them all).

Going too hard in the swim. Many athletes get caught up in the mass energy at the race start and hit the water full speed ahead. The start can be crazy with so many people so close, and you can easily find yourself 300 meters from the start blown up, heart rate over the top, and gasping for breath. You aren't going to win the race by winning the swim, but you can certainly lose it.

Aim for a pace that is somewhere between easy and steady. After a full taper and pumped with adrenaline, you might feel as if you are taking it easy when in fact you are swimming moderately hard to hard. Pick up a draft and ride a set of feet through the swim. You can easily take 5 minutes off your swim time without any extra effort. The key thing to remember during the swim is to stay relaxed with a smooth stroke. If you stay aerobic, draft well, and maintain your stroke mechanics, a pleasant surprise will likely await you at the swim exit.

Hammering the bike. We keep repeating this one, so it must be important. At the start of the bike, ride easy and let your body and, specifically, your heart rate settle. When you come out of the water, your heart can be racing. Early on, you may feel fantastic and can easily push the pace too hard too early. It will be tough to let a few people drop you, but you must let your system settle and start to take in the nutrition that you lost on the swim. Pushing too hard too soon can leave you with nothing in the tank late in the day.

The race will feel easy for the first 3 to 4 hours. Don't be fooled. It will get tough later. By conserving on the bike, you will put yourself in a position to run the marathon. The mental benefit of passing people on the run far outweighs the 10 to 15 minutes that you might save by pushing on the bike. A solid pacing strategy will see you to T2 in good shape.

Stick to your pre-race plan during the run. Avoid taking it out too hard if you are feeling good in the first 12 miles. The marathon is a test of how much patience you're prepared to exercise so that you don't expire or explode before the second half of the marathon—which is where the real race begins.

Misjudging Mother Nature. You may have had a top taper. Nutrition and pacing may be spot-on. You may be feeling unstoppable. However, the one formidable force you forgot to prepare for was the elements. The race goes on, rain or shine. Being unprepared for heat and glaring sun or rain and cold can ruin what would otherwise be a perfect day out. In hot races, don't forget the sunscreen and reflective clothing. If there is a chance of rain, pack more clothing than you think you need—arm warmers, leggings, gloves, and socks.

Preventing Common Aches and Pains

For endurance athletes, there are a variety of common issues that can develop due to the nature of our training and racing. Although many are easily prevented, left unattended they can develop into serious problems or injuries. The following are some of the most common issues faced in training and racing long. We offer some simple advice on how to prevent them and care for them when they do occur.

Abdominal pain: Abdominal pain is very common among endurance athletes—more often during running than swimming or cycling. Aside from stitches, which are discussed later in this chapter, stressed gastrointestinal (GI) symptoms appear in such forms as belching, flatulence, nausea, vomiting, diarrhea, bloating, intestinal cramps, and stomachache. A major contributor to GI problems is dehydration. This becomes even more of an issue when an athlete loses more than 4 percent of his or her body weight during a race. Pre-race meals are another contributor to GI stress. Meals within 30 minutes of a race start and meals high in fat or protein content have been shown to cause vomiting, and meals high in fiber have been shown to cause intestinal cramps. Pre-race and race diet are discussed in detail in Chapter 10.

Many GI problems can be prevented by ensuring proper hydration. This is best done by drinking ample quantities of a 6 to 8 percent carbohydrate solution. Cooler beverages have been shown to empty from the stomach at a faster rate. If you are using bars or gels, consume them with plenty of water because gastric emptying slows once the fluids in your gut have a greater than 10 percent carbohydrate content.

If you experience severe or progressive GI symptoms, we recommend a visit to your doctor because there may be a more serious underlying problem. If you experience GI problems in a race, remember the golden rule of digestive distress: "Slow down." Quite often a seemingly insurmountable issue will sort itself out during a 10- to 15-minute "stand-down," or a period of lower-intensity racing.

Back pain: Low-back pain is common when logging long hours on the bike, especially when down in the aero position. The majority of lower-back problems begin with poor posture; however, they are more significant when cycling. Many athletes tend to round up the lower back, stressing ligaments along the spine that provide support and stability. This stress causes irritation and inflammation of the ligaments, which leads to lower-back pain. Rotating your pelvis forward on the saddle and dropping your stomach toward the top tube to maintain a flat back can alleviate these stresses. More important is ensuring that your bike is correctly set up.

If you are susceptible to lower-back pain, avoid standing when climbing, as this position places additional strain on the lower back. In addition, be very careful with the effort level of all climbs, particularly those early in the race.

A regular stretching and strengthening routine, including supporting muscles of the back (abs, hamstrings, hip flexors, shoulders) as well as the lower back itself, will improve flexibility and posture, thereby reducing lower-back pain. Many of these exercises are discussed in Chapter 16.

Ibuprofen and Other NSAIDs

Ibuprofen and other nonsteroidal anti-inflammatory drugs (NSAIDs), such as Naprosyn, Aleve, and Motrin, are risky during any training or races because they have been shown to negatively affect kidney and liver function by restricting blood flow and filtration rates. This effect has the potential to promote hyponatremia (low sodium levels) and dehydration. In sustained exercise, these problems can not only reduce performance but even threaten health.

Some authorities implicated these drugs in numerous cases of symptomatic hyponatremia several years ago at Ironman® Canada. Many athletes were hospitalized after this event, and in review, it was discovered that most of them had been using NSAIDs for several days prior to the race or were using them during the race. NSAID-induced hyponatremia is related to impairment in antidiuretic hormone release. Additionally, NSAIDs can cause acute renal failure in dehydrated athletes, NSAID toxicity, and rhabdomyolysis (skeletal muscle breakdown after repetitive muscle trauma, for example, pavement pounding).

Acetaminophen, such as Tylenol, has a less dramatic effect on these functions and may relieve the discomfort just as well as ibuprofen. Acetaminophen, however, is not an anti-inflammatory. There are also concerns about its long-term health consequences for those who use it regularly.

Another reason not to use NSAIDs during race situations is their effect on the gut. Many endurance athletes and weekend warriors find themselves being treated for gastrointestinal bleeding. The decreased blood supply to the gut during endurance events may increase the risk of bleeding, and anyone who has experienced side stitches after ingesting food or carbohydrate-replacement solutions during exertion can be sure that their blood supply to the gut is less than optimal.

If you are taking any NSAIDs for pain, avoid taking any for at least forty-eight hours prior to and also during the race. It is best not to use any medications at all, including over-the-counter drugs, unless under a doctor's direction.

Black toenails: Black toenails are very common among long-distance runners. They are caused by your toes repeatedly hitting the front of your running shoe, causing bruising and bleeding beneath the toenail. This happens when your shoes are too tight, fit poorly, or have a toe box that is the wrong shape for your foot. The bruised toenail will turn black and eventually fall off as a new nail grows underneath.

To prevent black toenails, choose running shoes for racing that are a half size too large and the correct shape for your foot. This will leave enough room for your toes to slide without hitting the front of the toe box. Another solution for some is to wear extra-thin socks with their normal-sized running shoes. Keeping your toenails trimmed evenly and straight across the tops of the toes will also help.

If you feel pain or excessive pressure beneath the toenail, we recommend a visit to your doctor, who can alleviate the pressure by making a small hole in the nail.

Blisters: Blisters are a common problem for long-distance runners and are generally caused by poorly fitting shoes, swollen feet, running in wet shoes and socks, and friction from poor sock choices.

Small blisters are best left alone, but large blisters should be drained to relieve pressure. This can be done with a safety pin or sewing needle after heating it over a flame until it is glowing red. Once it cools, puncture and gently drain the blister. Apply an antibiotic ointment such as Polysporin or Neosporin to the area and cover with a bandage.

To prevent blisters, ensure that your shoes are the right size and shape for your foot. Choose socks made from synthetic blends, and avoid socks with thick stitch seams. Applying petroleum jelly or talcum powder to your feet can aid in reducing friction. Do your best to avoid getting your shoes and socks wet during races.

Bloating: Along the same lines as stomach cramping is stomach bloating. Generally common in races, this effect is often the result of going too hard, which forces your stomach to "shut down," meaning your stomach stops clearing liquids and foods. This throws your electrolytes out of balance, causing further problems. The best method of repair is to slow down, relax, and move to water only. To prevent bloating from happening, know your sodium needs from training and previous racing, and remember to stick with what worked on your long workouts and previous races.

Calluses: Another ailment of long-distance running is calluses—areas of thick, hard skin caused by pressure or friction from running, poorly fitting shoes, flat and high arched feet, or a bony prominence in the foot.

Calluses can be removed by gently filing them with a pumice stone or other gentle abrasive surface after either a bath or soaking the feet in a bucket of warm water and Epsom salts. Avoid letting calluses get too large, as the skin can crack, which may lead to infection.

To prevent calluses, regularly apply moisturizers to keep the skin supple. Choose shoes with good arch support and shock absorption. When running, wear thicker socks to reduce friction, apply moleskin to friction areas, or use an insole that absorbs shock inside the shoe.

Chafing: Chafing is another common problem owing to friction that can affect triathletes during swimming, cycling, and running. Chafing can occur during the swim if your wetsuit rubs against the back of your neck. A sleeveless wetsuit may cause chafing under the arms. Inner thighs may become chafed on the bike by shorts that are too short, allowing your skin to rub against the nose of your bike seat. On the run, you may experience chafing in the inner thighs if your legs rub against each other or under the arms from your racing singlet.

The best way to prevent chafing is to apply a lubricant, such as Body Glide or petroleum jelly, to the skin in areas where friction is common.

Muscle cramps: Very common among endurance athletes are muscle cramps. Although they can affect any muscle, calves, hamstrings, and quadriceps are most commonly affected. Pain from muscle cramps can vary in intensity and duration.

Although the precise causes of cramps are unknown, the common theories are exercising or racing in heat, dehydration and overexertion leading to electrolyte depletion or imbalance, poor stretching routines, muscle fatigue, poor posture, poor conditioning, and inefficient biomechanics.

Measures to prevent or reduce the frequency of muscle cramps include regular stretching and flexibility exercises before and after workouts, strengthening of muscles prone to cramping along with their antagonistic muscles, improving biomechanics, hydrating regularly and before you get thirsty, and consuming a sports drink while training or racing in heat for longer than one hour.

The day before and the morning of a long race, it may be a good idea to use table salt more liberally on your food to increase the body's sodium levels. On race day, the sports drink used for the race should also provide adequate levels of sodium, and eating salty foods may also help prevent cramping. Race-day nutrition is discussed in more detail in Chapter 10.

Neck pain: Athletes often suffer from stiff, sore necks and shoulders on long rides. If there is no actual pathology in the neck or shoulders, time in the saddle goes a long way toward strengthening these areas. Ensuring correct bike setup can help prevent this problem, and so can flattening your back and relaxing more on the aerobars. Some athletes may find that they are doing a "crunch" for the whole ride.

Nothing may be wrong with your bike setup, but many people have a tendency to ride with a death grip on the bars. Once you learn to relax your upper body, the pain will likely disappear. Upper-body relaxation starts with your face and jaw. Making sure that your face and jaw are always relaxed will reduce upper-body tension and increase your economy in all sports.

Numb feet and hands: Two common problems for cyclists are numbness in their hands and feet. Pedals with small platforms, shoes that are too small or narrow, and shoes that allow too much flex in the sole often cause numb feet. Shoes that are too small or narrow squeeze the toes together, thereby putting pressure on the nerves in your feet. Platforms that are too small combined with shoes that are too flexible can produce uneven pressure on the feet, thereby causing numbness.

To prevent foot numbness, ensure that your shoes are properly fitted to your feet, that the soles are strong, and that your platforms are suitable. Shift your feet and roll your toes regularly while riding to help keep the blood moving.

Cyclists often experience numbness or tingling sensations in their hands. This is called "cyclist's palsy" and is generally caused by compression of the ulnar nerve. Although not a serious problem, it can lead to carpal-tunnel problems if not addressed.

Hand numbness can be prevented by correct bike setup, adjusting the aerobars, wearing cycling gloves with gel padding, using aero pads with gel padding, switching hand positions often during a ride, and stretching your wrists after all rides.

Saddle sores: More common than numbness while cycling are saddle sores. Irritated skin, blocked pores, and friction from pressure points on the saddle are the common causes. Heat and moisture within cycling shorts also allow increased bacteria into the pores, causing pimples and blisters.

Saddle sores need to be cleaned, and an antibiotic ointment, such as Polysporin or Neosporin, should be applied. The area should then be kept dry when not riding by applying a talcum powder daily after showers. This will help prevent a bacteria-friendly environment.

Using a lubricant such as Body Glide or Chamois Butter directly on the shorts will help to prevent saddle sores caused by friction. Be sure that your shorts are cleaned after every ride and replaced when they become worn, and choose shorts with padding that doesn't have excessive stitching. Avoid wearing anything under your shorts, as seams from cotton or nylon underwear can cause friction and irritate the skin. Clean the area immediately following every ride, using a gentle soap. Don't use alcohol, as it will dry out and irritate your skin more. If you are unable to clean the area right away, change into a pair of loose-fitting, dry shorts to allow the skin to breathe.

Choice of saddle will also help in preventing saddle sores. There are many ergonomic saddles on the market. Find one that fits your anatomy and is comfortable for long periods of time.

Standing out of the saddle frequently on long rides will also help to relieve pressure.

Side stitches: Almost every athlete has experienced side-stitches—a sharp pain just under the rib cage. As with muscle cramps, what actually causes side stitches is unknown. However, it is commonly believed that stitches are caused by a cramp in the diaphragm muscle, exercising too soon after eating, or training at too high an intensity without a proper warm-up. Some research has shown fewer side stitches in athletes with better aerobic fitness.

The frequency of side stitches can be reduced by not eating closer than one to two hours prior to a workout or two to three hours prior to a race, including side stretches in your warm-up routine, and ensuring that you are properly hydrated. To relieve a side stitch, breathe rhythmically and deeply, exhaling forcefully when the foot opposite the stitched side strikes the ground. For example, with a right-side stitch while running, you may find that exhaling when your left foot strikes the ground and inhaling on your right-foot strike may cause it to go away. If you ease up the pace a little, stitches will generally subside.

Side stitches are particularly common for runners; it is unusual to get a side stitch on the bike unless the course is quite rough for an extended time and there is some sort of jostling. Cyclists are more likely to experience intestinal angina—pain from too intense an effort while food is being absorbed.

Swim vertigo: Many athletes experience swim vertigo, or dizziness, when swimming in open water. One cause may be the chop and bump from waves (seasickness); however, most often athletes become dizzy when colder water gets into their ears, affecting their equilibrium.

To prevent this problem, try swimming with earplugs and increasing your open-water swimming workouts. The more experienced and comfortable you get in open water, the less likely you are to suffer swim vertigo.

Case Studies

If you are done talking,
can we ride now?
—Clas "the Baron" Bjorling,
Swedish champion duathlete

This chapter gives training period examples for the three most common athlete types: the novice, the runner, and the experienced athlete. We will explain the profile of each athlete type, cover each type's key limiters, and detail the goals and structure of three training periods: Base, Build, and Peak.

Weekly training volumes are not shown in the annual training plans (ATPs); instead period goals and period tactics are outlined. For best results in scheduling workouts, we recommend that you build the entire training period at one time. Place your workouts in your weekly schedule using this priority system:

- Note your races and nontraining commitments (travel, business trips, family commitments).
- Schedule the workouts that address your period goals—in other words, your BT workouts.
- Block out appropriate recovery time (passive or active) following your BT workouts.
- Add workouts to ensure appropriate frequency in each sport (workout frequency can vary between weeks and throughout the year).
- Note the session details for each of your scheduled workouts, refer back to your period goals, and ensure that your training focus is appropriate for the time of year.

Chapter 14

- ◆ If you are a novice or time-constrained athlete, then you should stop at this stage. Extra volume will merely reduce the quality of your training and slow your BT workout recovery.

If you think you can handle greater volume, then schedule additional sessions in line with your period goals and tactics. Remember that it is the quality of your training, not the volume, that will determine your ultimate success. Here are some tips for considering appropriate levels of weekly volume:

- ◆ In the Prep and early Base periods, keep the volume comfortable in all weeks.
- ◆ In the middle of the Base period, it is OK to have one "stretch," or challenging week per period.
- ◆ In the late Base period, experienced athletes may be able to handle two "stretch" weeks per period.
- ◆ If scheduling a Build period is appropriate, then you should "stretch" by way of race-specific intensity rather than volume.

If you make a scheduling mistake, err on the side of too little volume and too much base training. If you are aiming for a late-season peak, then ensure that you schedule a midseason break from structured training.

The Novice

Nick the Novice has been in the sport of triathlon for three years. He's done a few triathlons and at the end of last summer completed his first half-ironman-distance race. His main goal for this coming season is to complete an end-of-season ironman-distance race. Although he'd like to post a solid time, his overriding goal is to have a good experience. Nick works full-time and has two kids. Sunday is family day, and therefore he likes to limit his volume on this day.

In his half-ironman-distance race, Nick swam 40 minutes; his key swim limiter is technique. He's never swum more than 2,800 meters in any workout and is concerned about his overall endurance. He has access to a masters' squad, but they tend to swim pretty hard, and he struggles to keep up.

In preparing for his goal race last summer, Nick's longest ride was 4 hours. His bike split in the race was 3:25 on a moderately difficult course. He has access to all kinds of training terrain. Nick has a tough time in the hills and is concerned about some long climbs that are a feature of his goal race. Darkness and weather limit his weekday riding time in the winter.

Nick has never run a marathon and expects that he will use a run/walk strategy for his first ironman-distance race. In recent half-ironman race, he used a run/walk strategy for a run split of 2:20.

Nick's season will be structured around building his overall endurance to complete his goal race. His training will start with a frequency and technique focus, then move toward building endurance. He will target a late-spring half-ironman-distance race and have a midseason break to ensure that he remains fresh through the summer. Heading into his goal race, he will cut back on his racing to better enable him to focus on (and recover from) his key endurance BTs. In order to build his confidence, two century rides and a long open-water swim have been scheduled.

Table 14.1 Novice Nick's ATP

Week of	Races	Priority	Weeks to Race	Period	Weights
Oct. 28			27	Prep 1	AA1
Nov. 4			26	Prep 1	AA1
Nov. 11			25	Prep 1	AA1
Nov. 18			24	Prep 1	AA1
Nov. 25			23	Prep 2	AA2
Dec. 2			22	Prep 2	AA2
Dec. 9			21	Prep 2	AA2
Dec. 16			20	Prep 2	AA2
Dec. 23			19	Prep 3	AA3
Dec. 30			18	Prep 3	AA3
Jan. 6			17	Prep 3	AA3
Jan. 13	Half-Marathon	B	16	Prep 3	AA3
Jan. 20			15	Base 1	MS▲
Jan. 27			14	Base 1	MS
Feb. 3			13	Base 1	MS
Feb. 10			12	Base 1	MS
Feb. 17			11	Base 1	SM■
Feb. 24			10	Base 1	SM
Mar. 3	Spring Duathlon	C	9	Base 1	SM
Mar. 10			8	Base 1	SM
Mar. 17		C	7	Base 2	SM
Mar. 24	Century Ride	C	6	Base 2	SM
Mar. 31			5	Base 2	SM
Apr. 7			4	Base 2	SM

Table 14.1 continued

Week of	Races	Priority	Weeks to Race	Period	Weights
Apr. 14		C	3	Peak	SM
Apr. 21			2	Peak	SM
Apr. 28	Half-Ironman	A	1	Race	
May 5			16	Trans	
May 12			15	Base 1	AA1
May 19			14	Base 1	AA1
May 26	2-mile Open-Water	C	13	Base 1	AA1
June 2			12	Base 1	AA1
June 9	Century Ride	C	11	Base 2	AA2
June 16			10	Base 2	AA2
June 23			9	Base 2	AA2
June 30	Olympic	B	8	Base 2	AA2
July 7			7	Base 3	AA3
July 14			6	Base 3	AA3
July 21	Sprint	C	5	Base 3	AA3
July 28			4	Base 3	AA3
Aug. 4			3	Peak	SM
Aug. 11			2	Peak	SM
Aug. 18	Ironman	AAA	1	Race	
Aug. 25				OFF	
Sept. 1				OFF	
Sept. 8				OFF	
Sept. 15				OFF	

▲ MS = maximum strength ■ SM = strength maintenance

Table 14.2 Novice Nick's ATP Period Goals and Tactics

Period	Week of	Period Goals	Period Tactics
Prep 1	Oct. 28	Reestablish structured training	Workout frequency
Prep 1	Nov. 4	Improve strength-training technique	Two sessions with personal trainer to review program
Prep 1	Nov. 11	Improve technical skills	No masters' swimming, solo technique-oriented sessions
Prep 1	Nov. 18		
Prep 2	Nov. 25	Improve swimming balance	No masters' swimming, solo technique-oriented sessions
Prep 2	Dec. 2	Extend overall endurance	Three out of four Saturdays are long, low-intensity aerobic training
Prep 2	Dec. 9	Improve flexibility	Start yoga, continue 2x per week until end March
Prep 2	Dec. 16	Prepare body for longer runs	Two out of four weeks have increased run frequency
Prep 3	Dec. 23	Increase strength	Lower reps, increase intensity in the gym
Prep 3	Dec. 30	Improve swimming stroke mechanics	Start swim cords, continue twice per week until end of March
Prep 3	Jan. 6	Increase running endurance	Two out of four weeks have one long and one moderately long endurance run
Prep 3	Jan. 13		
Base 1	Jan. 20	Increase strength	Max-strength lifting phase
Base 1	Jan. 27	Improve swimming body position	Continue as per previous block
Base 1	Feb. 3	Increase cycling endurance	Target two long rides; if poor weather then substitute winter cross-training
Base 1	Feb. 10		

Table 14.2 continued

Period	Week of	Period Goals	Period Tactics
Base 1	Feb. 17	Increase cycling endurance	Target three long rides; if poor weather then substitute winter cross-training
Base 1	Feb. 24	Increase running endurance	Three out of four weeks have long run; one weekend BT is all-day hike
Base 1	Mar. 3	Increase swimming endurance	One endurance workout and one masters' session added to swim program
Base 1	Mar. 10		
Base 2	Mar. 17	Increase cycling endurance	Century is key long ride; weeks before and after are moderate rides
Base 2	Mar. 24	Increase running endurance	Complete two trail runs of 1:45 and 2:00 duration
Base 2	Mar. 31	Start with moderate ME training	Add weekly indoor-trainer ME session
Base 2	Apr. 7	Maintain swimming endurance	Continue as per previous block
Peak	Apr. 14	Specific race preparation	One race simulation brick per week
Peak	Apr. 21		Add one ME swim per week
Race	Apr. 28		
Trans	May 5	Race recovery	Total rest
Base 1	May 12	Ensure race recovery	First week very easy, second week moderate, third week "normal," followed by recovery week
Base 1	May 19	Start to rebuild strength	Start very light with single set of each exercise, build from there to AA1 levels

Period	Week of	Period Goals	Period Tactics
Base 1	May 26	Maintain aerobic pathways	Focus on workout frequency; resist urge to add lots of endurance
Base 1	June 2	Maintain skills	Weekly skills session in each sport
Base 2	June 9	Increase cycling endurance	Weekly long rides; focus is extending comfortable aerobar ride time
Base 2	June 16	Increase running endurance	Weekly long run
Base 2	June 23	Maintain swimming endurance	One masters' session; one endurance swim per week—other swimming technique oriented
Base 2	June 30		
Base 3	July 7	Race-specific cycling endurance work	Weekly moderate-intensity hill ride
Base 3	July 14	Maintain running endurance	Weekly long run
Base 3	July 21	Increase strength	AA3 strength training
Base 3	July 28		
Peak	Aug. 4	Specific race preparation	One race simulation brick per week
Peak	Aug. 11		Add weekly open-water swim
Race	Aug. 18		
OFF	Aug. 25	Rejuvenation	
OFF	Sept. 1		
OFF	Sept. 8		
OFF	Sept. 15		

Table 14.3 Novice Nick's Training Period, Early Base

	Mon.	Tues.	Wed.	Thurs.	Fri.	Sat.	Sun.	Weekly Total
Mar. 17–23								
Swim	60		60		90			3.5
Bike	90	30	75	75		45		5.3
Run		30		45		105		3.0
Strength		60						1.0
Total	2.5	2.0	2.3	2.0	1.5	2.5	0.0	12.8
Mar 24–30								
Swim	60		60		90			3.5
Bike	60	30	75			340		8.4
Run	30	30		90		20		2.8
Strength		60						1.0
Total	2.5	2.0	2.3	1.5	1.5	6.0	0.0	15.8

Note: Workout details are in minutes; totals are in hours. Boxes indicate bricks.

Table 14.4 Novice Nick's Training Period Notes

Mar. 17	A.M. session is aerobic ride, P.M. session is technique swim
Mar. 18	Run speed skills, strength maintenance, then easy spin
Mar. 19	A.M session is ME bike on trainer, P.M. session is masters' swim
Mar. 20	Aerobic maintenance brick that includes cycling speed skills
Mar. 21	Endurance swim
Mar. 22	A.M session is endurance trail run, P.M. session is easy spin
Mar. 23	Day off
Mar. 24	A.M session is aerobic maintenance brick, P.M. session is technique swim
Mar. 25	Run speed skills, strength maintenance, then easy spin
Mar. 26	A.M session is ME bike on trainer, P.M. session is masters' swim
Mar. 27	Endurance run in rolling terrain
Mar. 28	Endurance swim
Mar. 29	Century ride with easy transition run
Mar. 30	Day off

Table 14.5 Novice Nick's Training Period, Late Base

	Mon.	Tues.	Wed.	Thurs.	Fri.	Sat.	Sun.	Weekly Total
July 7–13								
Swim	60		60		90			3.5
Bike	60	15	90			180		5.8
Run	30	30		105		30		3.3
Strength		60						1.0
Total	2.5	1.8	2.5	1.8	1.5	3.5	0.0	13.5
July 14–20								
Swim	60		60		90			3.5
Bike		15	90	90		240		7.3
Run	90	30		30		30		3.0
Strength		60						1.0
Total	2.5	1.8	2.5	2.0	1.5	4.5	0.0	14.8

Note: Workout details are in minutes; totals are in hours. Boxes indicate bricks.

Table 14.6 Novice Nick's Training Period Notes

July 7	A.M. session is aerobic maintenance brick, P.M. session is masters' swim
July 8	Run speed skills, strength maintenance, then easy spin
July 9	A.M. session is hill oriented ride, P.M. session is technique swim
July 10	Endurance run, 45 minutes easy pace, 60 minutes steady pace
July 11	Endurance swim
July 12	Steady ride BT with easy transition run
July 13	Day off
July 14	A.M. session is endurance run, P.M. session is masters' swim
July 15	Run speed skills, strength maintenance, then easy spin
July 16	A.M. session is hill-oriented ride, P.M. session is technique swim
July 17	Brick, insert speed skills into an easy ride, run steady pace off the bike
July 18	Endurance swim
July 19	Steady ride BT with easy transition run
July 20	Day off

Table 14.7 Novice Nick's Training Period, Peak

		Mon.	Tues.	Wed.	Thurs.	Fri.	Sat.	Sun.	Weekly Total
Aug. 4–10									
Swim		60		75		90			3.8
Bike		60	15		105		150		5.5
Run			30		45		60		2.3
Strength			60						1.0
	Total	2.0	1.8	1.3	2.5	1.5	3.5	0.0	12.5
Aug. 11–17									
Swim		60		75		90			3.8
Bike		45	15		75		90		3.8
Run			30		30		30		1.5
Strength			60						1.0
	Total	1.75	1.8	1.3	1.8	1.5	2.0	0.0	10.0

Note: Workout details are in minutes; totals are in hours. Boxes indicate bricks.

Table 14.8 Novice Nick's Training Period Notes

Aug. 4	A.M. session is steady ride, P.M. session is open-water swim
Aug. 5	Run speed skills, strength maintenance, then easy spin
Aug. 6	ME swim
Aug. 7	Aerobic maintenance brick
Aug. 8	Endurance swim
Aug. 9	Race-simulation brick
Aug. 10	Day off
Aug. 11	A.M. session is steady ride, P.M. session is open water swim
Aug. 12	Run speed skills, strength maintenance, then easy spin
Aug. 13	ME swim
Aug. 14	Aerobic maintenance brick
Aug. 15	Endurance swim
Aug. 16	Race-simulation brick
Aug. 17	Day off

The Runner

Rachel the Runner has been running for most of her adult life. She has done a number of marathons and has qualified for the Boston Marathon. Her running endurance is excellent. She has done a few triathlons, including a half-ironman-distance race last season. She managed to get through her half-ironman-distance race, but it hurt! Her legs were completely dead coming off the bike, and she ran 30 minutes slower than she expected.

Over the years, Rachel has had a wide range of overuse injuries, but she is proud of her ability to train through anything. Her swimming results have been solid, but she has noticed that her average heart rate by sport tends to decline as the race progresses. She has a good cycling endurance base but lacks the power to push a big gear or to do anything other than spin up hills. This is a major concern for her because she has heard that the bike course on her goal race is tough!

Rachel's season will be built around the bike. Her key limiter is muscular endurance on the bike. Given her injury history, Rachel is going to be very cautious with her run volume and frequency.

Running races will be used to ensure that she maintains her subthreshold speed. To train her legs to run off the bike, frequent bricks will be scheduled throughout the year. Rachel is very goal oriented and will purchase a powermeter so that her progress can be tracked by regular power testing.

Rachel has experience with strength training, but when she's honest with herself, she realizes that she has tended to focus more on cosmetic lifting than sport-specific work. Given her limited experience with lower-body strength training, she will skip the max strength phase this season. Tables 14.9–14.16 detail Rachel's ATP.

Table 14.9 Runner Rachel's ATP

Week of	Races	Priority	Weeks to Race	Period	Weights
Dec. 30			31	Prep 1	AA1
Jan. 6			30	Prep 1	AA1
Jan. 13			29	Prep 1	AA1
Jan. 20			28	Prep 1	AA1
Jan. 27			27	Prep 2	AA2
Feb. 3			26	Prep 2	AA2
Feb. 10			25	Prep 2	AA2
Feb. 17	Half-Marathon	C	24	Prep 2	AA2

Table 14.9 continued

Week of	Races	Priority	Weeks to Race	Period	Weights
Feb. 24			23	Prep3	AA3
Mar. 3			22	Prep 3	AA3
Mar. 10			21	Prep 3	AA3
Mar. 17			20	Prep 3	AA3
Mar. 24			19	Base 1	AA1
Mar. 31	Century Ride	C	18	Base 1	AA1
Apr. 7			17	Base 1	AA1
Apr. 14	Half-Marathon	C	16	Base 1	AA1
Apr. 21			15	Base 2	AA2
Apr. 28			14	Base 2	AA2
May 5	Olympic	C	13	Base 2	AA2
May 12			12	Base 2	AA2
May 19			11	Base 3	AA3
May 26	10K	C	10	Base 3	AA3
June 2	Half-Ironman	B	9	Base 3	AA3
June 9			8	Trans	
June 16			7	EZ	
June 23			6	Build	SM∎
June 30			5	Build	SM
July 7	Century Ride	B	4	Build	SM
July 14			3	Peak	SM
July 21			2	Peak	SM
July 28	Ironman	AAA	1	Race	
Aug. 4				OFF	
Aug. 11				OFF	
Aug. 18				OFF	
Aug. 25				OFF	

∎ *SM = Strength maintenance*

Table 14.10 Runner Rachel's ATP Period Goals and Tactics

Period	Week of	Period Goals	Period Tactics
Prep 1	Dec. 30	Reestablish structured training	Workout frequency
Prep1	Jan. 6	Improve strength-training technique	One session per week with personal trainer to learn proper technique
Prep 1	Jan. 13	Improve technical skills	Twice-weekly swim and bike skills training
Prep 1	Jan. 20		
Prep 2	Jan. 27	Improve swim technique	Attend weekend swim clinic
Prep 2	Feb. 3	Improve ability to run off the bike	Four rides per week, short run following every ride
Prep 2	Feb. 10	Build overall endurance	Use bike-run-bike-run sessions to build endurance and improve transitions
Prep 2	Feb. 17		
Prep 3	Feb. 24	Stay healthy and injury free	Reduce running, no racing, increase long ride duration
Prep 3	Mar. 3	Improve cycling-specific strength	Steady increases in cycling-specific gym work
Prep 3	Mar. 10	Build run endurance	Gradually extend endurance workout toward 1:40 workout duration
Prep 3	Mar. 17		
Base 1	Mar. 24	Start building bike ME	Start eight-week protocol for early season bike ME
Base 1	Mar. 31	Extend overall endurance	Ride long three out of four weeks
Base 1	Apr. 7	Maintain run strength	Weekly long run includes cruise intervals to maintain leg speed
Base 1	Apr. 14		
Base 2	Apr. 21	Continue to build bike ME	Use moderate ME training, save the toughest sessions for later in the season
Base 2	Apr. 28	Build subthreshold run speed	Weekly tempo run session used to complement endurance running

Table 14.10 continued

Period	Week of	Period Goals	Period Tactics
Base 2	May 5	Maintain swim endurance	Regular attendance at masters' swimming
Base 2	May 12		
Base 3	May 19	Maximize cycling specific gym strength	Two strength sessions per week, early-week session tough, later-week session moderate
Base 3	May 26	Prepare for half-ironman race	Two weeks out, do a 4.5-hour race-simulation brick, thereafter very cautious with running
Base 3	June 2		
Trans	June 9	Rejuvenation	Week of unstructured training
EZ	June 16	Avoid temptation to return too soon	Week of easy training
Build	June 23	Build race-specific ME	Race-simulation bricks in weeks 1 and 2, focus on TT strength through rolling hills
Build	June 30		Midweek bike ME session
Build	July 7		Target large negative split on century ride, maximize time on the aerobars
Peak	July 14	Specific race preparation	Two race-simulation bricks per week
Peak	July 21		Add weekly open-water swim
Race	July 28		
OFF	Aug. 4		
OFF	Aug. 11		
OFF	Aug. 18		
OFF	Aug. 25		

Table 14.11 Runner Rachel's Training Period, Base

	Mon.	Tues.	Wed.	Thurs.	Fri.	Sat.	Sun.	Weekly Total
Apr. 28–May 4								
Swim		75		45		90		3.5
Bike	15		90		45		300	7.5
Run	30	75	60				30	3.3
Strength	60				60			2.0
Total	1.8	2.5	2.5	0.8	1.8	1.5	5.5	16.3
May 5–11								
Swim		75		75		45	???	3.3
Bike	15	105	90	45		30	???	4.8
Run	30		60			15	???	1.8
Strength	60			60				2.0
Total	1.8	3.0	2.5	3.0	0.0	1.5	0.0	11.8

Note: Workout details are in minutes; totals are in hours. Boxes indicate bricks.

Table 14.12 Runner Rachel's Training Period Notes

Apr. 28	Run speed skills, strength maintenance then easy spin
Apr. 29	A.M. session is masters' swim, P.M. session is aerobic run
Apr. 30	A.M. session is ME bike on trainer, P.M. session is tempo run
May 1	Technique swim
May 2	Bike speed skills, strength maintenance, then easy spin
May 3	Masters' swim
May 4	Endurance ride with easy transition run
May 5	Run speed skills, strength maintenance, then easy spin
May 6	A.M. session is masters' swim, P.M. session is aerobic ride
May 7	A.M. session is ME bike on trainer, P.M. session is tempo run
May 8	A.M. session is bike speed skills, strength maintenance, then easy spin, P.M. session is technique swim
May 9	Day off
May 10	Open-water swim, easy spin, easy run
May 11	Olympic-distance triathlon

Table 14.13 Runner Rachel's Training Period, Build

		Mon.	Tues.	Wed.	Thurs.	Fri.	Sat.	Sun.	Weekly Total
June 23–29									
Swim			75		75		90		4.0
Bike		15	90	150	90		45	180	9.5
Run		30		30				90	2.5
Strength		60							1.0
	Total	1.8	2.8	3.0	2.8	0.0	2.3	4.5	17.0
June 30–July 6									
Swim			75		75		90		4.0
Bike		30		120	90			240	8.0
Run				60		75		60	3.3
Strength		60							1.0
	Total	1.5	1.3	3.0	2.8	1.3	1.5	5.0	16.3

Note: Workout details are in minutes; totals are in hours. Boxes indicate bricks.

Table 14.14 Runner Rachel's Training Period Notes

June 23	Run speed skills, strength maintenance, then easy spin
June 24	A.M. session is masters' swim, P.M. session is steady ride
June 25	Steady brick
June 26	A.M. session is masters' swim, P.M. session is ME bike
June 27	Day off
June 28	A.M. session is masters' swim, P.M. session is bike speed skills
June 29	Race-simulation brick
June 30	Easy spin to warm-up, strength maintenance, then easy spin
July 1	Masters' swim
July 2	Steady brick
July 3	A.M. session is masters' swim, P.M. session is ME bike
July 4	Tempo run
July 5	Masters' swim
July 6	Race-simulation brick

Table 14.15 Runner Rachel's Training Period, Peak

	Mon.	Tues.	Wed.	Thurs.	Fri.	Sat.	Sun.	Weekly Total
Aug. 4–10								
Swim	75		45		75		45	4.0
Bike		30	90		90	180		6.5
Run	60		45			60		2.8
Strength		45						0.8
Total	2.3	1.3	3.0	0.0	2.8	4.0	0.8	14.0
Aug. 11–17								
Swim	75		60		75		60	4.5
Bike		30	90		60	75		4.3
Run	45		30			45		2.0
Strength		45						0.8
Total	2.0	1.3	3.0	0.0	2.3	2.0	1.0	11.5

Note: Workout details are in minutes; totals are in hours. Boxes indicate bricks.

Table 14.16 Runner Rachel's Training Period Notes

Aug. 4	A.M. session is masters' swim, P.M. session is run speed skills
Aug. 5	Easy spin to warm-up, strength maintenance, then easy spin
Aug. 6	A.M. session is technique swim, P.M. session is race-simulation brick
Aug. 7	Day off
Aug. 8	A.M. session is masters' swim, P.M. session is aerobic maintenance ride
Aug. 9	Race-simulation brick
Aug. 10	Open-water swim
Aug. 11	A.M. session is masters' swim, P.M. session is run speed skills
Aug. 12	Easy spin to warm-up, strength maintenance, then easy spin
Aug. 13	A.M. session is technique swim, P.M. session is race-simulation brick
Aug. 14	Day off
Aug. 15	A.M. session is masters' swim, P.M. session is aerobic maintenance ride
Aug. 16	Race-simulation brick
Aug. 17	Open-water swim

The Veteran

Kona Ken has been in the sport of triathlon for a number of years. His sole focus for the upcoming season is to qualify for Ironman® Hawaii . He came painfully close to a roll-down slot this past season, missing by less than 15 minutes. He is a well-balanced athlete, and his times are consistently in the top 25 percent for all three sports. He loves to ride and has excellent overall endurance. He works full-time but has significant flexibility with his schedule.

Ken has read a number of training guides and has a good understanding of all aspects of training. He's had a few minor injuries over the years but is biomechanically sound. His work ethic is well-known in the local triathlon community, and he prides himself on his ability to train hard year-round. Last season he had excellent performance in his early races but was disappointed when his early results didn't translate to late-season ironman-distance performance. In reviewing his past season, Ken realizes that he was likely tired for most of the summer.

Ken's race season is geared toward giving him the maximum opportunity to qualify. Ken lives in a climate that enables him to ride outdoors year-round, and he has plenty of tribuddies who are up for a tough session at any time. Ken's season is built around two ironman-distance races. If he manages to qualify at his first ironman-distance race of the year, then he plans on skipping the second to focus on Ironman® Hawaii.

In order to ensure freshness through the season, Ken is going to limit his group training until he is in the Build period for his first ironman-distance race. Following that race, he has scheduled two weeks completely off, followed by two transition weeks. When he returns to training after his midseason break, he is going to repeat Base 1 and Base 2 but shorten them to three-week periods. To ensure that he maintains his overall strength, he is going to repeat the Prep phase of his strength program.

Ken's qualification strategy is to use specific race-simulation workouts to better guide his race-day pacing. Improved pacing, better recovery, and avoiding last year's burnout should give him the boost that he wants to get to the Big Show. If he makes it to Kona, then he's promised himself to enjoy the day and celebrate the hard work that it took to get there.

Table 14.17 Kona Ken's ATP

Week of	Races	Priority	Weeks to Race	Period	Weights
Sept. 30			27	Prep 1	AA1
Oct. 7			26	Prep 1	AA1
Oct. 14			25	Prep 1	AA1
Oct. 21			24	Prep 1	AA1
Oct. 28			23	Prep 2	AA2
Nov. 4			22	Prep 2	AA2
Nov. 11			21	Prep 2	AA2
Nov. 18			20	Prep 2	AA2
Nov. 25			19	Base 1	AA3
Dec. 2			18	Base 1	AA3
Dec. 9			17	Base 1	AA3
Dec. 16			16	Base 1	AA3
Dec. 23			15	Base 2	MS ▲
Dec. 30			14	Base 2	MS
Jan. 6			13	Base 2	MS
Jan. 13			12	Base 2	MS
Jan. 20			11	Base 3	SM ■
Jan. 27			10	Base 3	SM
Feb. 3			9	Base 3	SM
Feb. 10	Half-Marathon	B	8	Base 3	SM
Feb. 17			7	Build	SM
Feb. 24			6	Build	SM
Mar. 3			5	Build	SM
Mar. 10	Olympic	C	4	Build	SM
Mar. 17			3	Peak	SM
Mar. 24			2	Peak	SM
Mar. 31	Ironman	A	1	Race	
Apr. 7			21	OFF	
Apr. 14			20	OFF	
Apr. 21			19	Trans	AA1
Apr. 28			18	Trans	AA1

Table 14.17 continued

Week of	Races	Priority	Weeks to Race	Period	Weights
May 5			17	Base 1	AA1
May 12	Olympic	C	16	Base 1	AA1
May 19			15	Base 1	AA1
May 26			14	Base 2	AA2
June 2			13	Base 2	AA2
June 9	Olympic	C	12	Base 2	AA2
June 16			11	Base 3	AA3
June 23			10	Base 3	AA3
June 30			9	Base 3	AA3
July 7	Half-Ironman	B	8	Base 3	AA3
July 14			7	Trans	
July 21			6	Build	SM
July 28			5	Build	SM
Aug. 4			4	Build	SM
Aug. 11			3	Peak	SM
Aug. 18			2	Peak	SM
Aug. 25	Ironman	AAA	1	Race	
Sept. 1			6	Trans	
Sept. 8			5	Trans	
Sept. 15			4	Trans	SM
Sept. 22			3	Peak	SM
Sept. 29			2	Peak	SM
Oct. 6	Ironman	Fun	1	Race	
Oct. 13				OFF	
Oct. 20				OFF	
Oct. 27				OFF	
Nov. 3				OFF	

▲ MS = maximum strength   ■ SM = strength maintenance

Table 14.18 Kona Ken's ATP Period Goals and Tactics

Period	Week of	Period Goals	Period Tactics
Prep 1	Sept. 30	Reestablish structured training	Workout frequency
Prep 1	Oct. 7	Improve strength training technique	One session per week with personal trainer to learn proper technique
Prep 1	Oct. 14	Improve technical skills	Twice-weekly swim and bike skills training
Prep 1	Oct. 21		
Prep 2	Oct. 28	Build swim endurance	Swim a lane down in masters', focus on perfect subthreshold technique
Prep 2	Nov. 4	Stay fresh	Avoid group training, limit riding to small chain ring only
Prep 2	Nov. 11	Increase functional strength	Learn new strength-training techniques (Swiss ball and medicine ball)
Prep 2	Nov. 18		
Base 1	Nov. 25	Build run endurance prior to MS lifting	Weekly endurance run session
Base 1	Dec. 2	Stay fresh	Continue to avoid group training
Base 1	Dec. 9	Build bike endurance	Weekly long ride and cycling frequency focus
Base 1	Dec. 16		
Base 2	Dec. 23	Get strong	Achieve life-best strength in key lifts
Base 2	Dec. 30	Stay healthy	Show caution with run volume
Base 2	Jan. 6	Build bike endurance	Build long ride volume and focus on cycling frequency
Base 2	Jan. 13		
Base 3	Jan. 20	Start ME bike training	First four weeks of eight-week bike ME program
Base 3	Jan. 27	Increase bike endurance	One stretch week with cycling volume focus
Base 3	Feb. 3	Test subthreshold run speed	Half-marathon race at end of recovery week
Base 3	Feb. 10		

Table 14.18 continued

Period	Week of	Period Goals	Period Tactics
Build	Feb. 17	Specific race preparation	Run-pacing BT to determine appropriate run speed
Build	Feb. 24		Use steady ride BT to determine appropriate bike effort
Build	Mar. 3		Use race-specific ME BTs to prepare for specific race terrain
Build	Mar. 10		Strength training takes backseat to sport-specific work
Peak	Mar. 17	Specific race preparation	Two race-simulation bricks per week
Peak	Mar. 24		Add weekly open-water swim
Race	Mar. 31		
OFF	Apr. 7	Rejuvenation	No training at all
OFF	Apr. 14		
Trans	Apr. 21	Rejuvenation	Skills and light aerobic training only
Trans	Apr. 28		Return to gym for high-repetition, low-intensity training
Base 1	May 5	Stimulate aerobic systems	Focus on workout frequency
Base 1	May 12	Target a late-season peak	Limited use of ME training, interval duration kept short
Base 1	May 19	Maintain quickness in all sports	Weekly speed skill sessions
Base 2	May 26	Reestablish race-specific endurance	Increase steady-state training in all sports
Base 2	June 2	Stay fresh	Show caution with group training
Base 2	June 9		

Period	Week of	Period Goals	Period Tactics
Base 3	June 16	Build race-specific ME	Steady-state endurance training with moderate ME inserts
Base 3	June 23	Complete overall endurance focus	Two stretch weeks with bike volume focus
Base 3	June 30	Check overall fitness	Use half-ironman race to test fitness and guide final preps
Base 3	July 7		
Trans	July 14		
Build	July 21	Specific race preparation	No racing to focus on race-simulation training
Build	July 28		Same tactics as previous Build period
Build	Aug. 4		Apply lessons from training and racing to date
Peak	Aug. 11	Specific race preparation	Two race simulation bricks per week
Peak	Aug. 18		Add weekly open-water swim
Race	Aug. 25		
Trans	Sept. 1	Rejuvenation	
Trans	Sept. 8		
Trans	Sept. 15		
Peak	Sept. 22	Ensure freshness on race day	Repeat previous Peak period but eliminate all high-intensity work
Peak	Sept. 29		
Race	Oct. 6		
OFF	Oct. 13		
OFF	Oct. 20		
OFF	Oct. 27		
OFF	Nov. 3		

Table 14.19 Kona Ken's Training Period, Base

	Mon.	Tues.	Wed.	Thurs.	Fri.	Sat.	Sun.	Weekly Total
June 16–22								
Swim	75		75		90			4.0
Bike	15	180	150	105		300		12.5
Run	30		30	90		30		3.0
Strength	60							1.0
Total	3.0	3.0	4.3	3.3	1.5	5.5	0.0	20.5
June 23–29								
Swim	75		75		90			4.0
Bike	15	120		45		300		8.0
Run	30		120			30		3.0
Strength	60			60				2.0
Total	3.0	2.0	3.3	1.8	1.5	5.5	0.0	17.0

Note: Workout details are in minutes; totals are in hours. Boxes indicate bricks.

Table 14.20 Kona Ken's Training Period Notes

June 16	A.M. session is run speed skills, strength maintenance, and easy spin; P.M. session is masters' swim
June 17	Easy ride
June 18	A.M. session is steady-paced brick with short ME inserts; P.M. session is masters' swim
June 19	A.M. session is easy to steady ride, P.M. session is endurance run
June 20	Endurance swim
June 21	Endurance ride with easy transition run
June 22	Day off
June 23	A.M. session is run speed skills, strength maintenance, and easy spin; P.M. session is masters' swim
June 24	Easy ride
June 25	A.M. session is endurance run; P.M. session is masters' swim
June 26	Easy spin to warm-up, strength maintenance, and easy spin
June 27	Endurance swim
June 28	Endurance ride with easy transition run
June 29	Day off

Table 14.21 Kona Ken's Training Period, Build

	Mon.	Tues.	Wed.	Thurs.	Fri.	Sat.	Sun.	Weekly Total
July 21–27								
Swim			90		60		90	4.0
Bike	180		30	240		30		8.0
Run	90			30		45	120	4.8
Strength			45			45		1.5
Total	4.5	0.0	2.8	4.5	1.0	2.0	3.5	18.3
July 28–Aug. 3								
Swim		90			90		45	3.8
Bike		90	240		30	150		8.5
Run			60			90		2.5
Strength					45			0.8
Total	0.0	3.0	5.0	0.0	2.8	4.0	0.8	15.5

Note: Workout details are in minutes; totals are in hours. Boxes indicate bricks.

Table 14.22 Kona Ken's Training Period Notes

July 21	Race-simulation brick
July 22	Day off
July 23	A.M. session is easy spin, strength maintenance, and easy spin; P.M. session is endurance swim
July 24	Steady-ride BT with easy run
July 25	Technique swim
July 26	Run speed skills, strength maintenance, and easy spin
July 27	A.M. session is ME swim; P.M. session is run-pacing BT
July 28	Day off
July 29	A.M. session is endurance ride; P.M. session is endurance swim
July 30	Race-simulation brick
July 31	Day off
Aug. 1	A.M. session is easy spin, strength maintenance, and easy spin; P.M. session is ME swim
Aug. 2	Race-simulation brick
Aug. 3	Technique swim

Table 14.23 Kona Ken's Training Period, Peak

		Mon.	Tues.	Wed.	Thurs.	Fri.	Sat.	Sun.	Weekly Total
Aug 11–17									
Swim		75		45		90		75	4.8
Bike			30	135		75	150		6.5
Run			30	75		15	60		3.0
Strength			45						0.8
	Total	1.3	1.8	4.3	0.0	3.0	3.5	1.3	15.0
Aug 18–24									
Swim			75			75		60	3.5
Bike		15	45	105		75	105		5.8
Run		30		45		15	30		2.0
Strength		45							0.8
	Total	1.5	2.0	2.5	0.0	2.8	2.3	1.0	12.0

Note: Workout details are in minutes; totals are in hours. Boxes indicate bricks.

Table 14.24 Kona Ken's Training Period Notes

Aug. 11	Technique swim
Aug. 12	Run speed skills, strength maintenance, and easy spin
Aug. 13	A.M. session is technique swim; P.M. session is race-simulation brick
Aug. 14	Day off
Aug. 15	A.M. session is aerobic-maintenance brick; P.M. session is ME swim
Aug. 16	Race-simulation brick
Aug. 17	Open-water swim
Aug. 18	Run speed skills, strength maintenance, and easy spin
Aug. 19	A.M. session is easy spin; P.M. session is endurance swim
Aug. 20	Race-simulation brick
Aug. 21	Day off
Aug. 22	A.M. session is aerobic maintenance brick; P.M. session is ME swim
Aug. 23	Race-simulation brick
Aug. 24	Open-water swim

Chapter 15

Common Injuries: Identification, Treatment, and Prevention

> Over the years, I learned when to back off.
> — Mark Allen,
> world champion triathlete

For an athlete, nothing is worse than an overuse injury. Not only is there discomfort, but there is also a feeling of frustration as hard-earned fitness erodes. Among the worst injuries are stress fractures, patellar tendonitis, chondromalacia patella, plantar fasciitis, and iliotibial band syndrome.

Poor technique or improper equipment selection and setup may cause some of these injuries. Others can result from inherited biomechanical traits, such as flat feet. An improper balance between training workloads and rest is often the final straw that produces the injury. It's worth remembering that nearly every injury exhibits early warning signs; it is only when these signals are ignored that a full-blown injury develops. By staying in tune with your body, focusing on your recovery, and backing off when required, you can stay injury free.

Of course it is always better to prevent injuries than to deal with them after they occur. Proper technique, good equipment, ample flexibility, and sound muscular strength provide the best safeguards. Adequate recovery time following long or hard workouts is also necessary to stay injury free. Experience will tell you how much downtime you need after a stressful workout.

There are many different kinds of pain that you will encounter through your athletic career. Part of your role is to learn the difference between normal training discomfort and a signal that an injury could be developing. Given the fitness losses that occur when an athlete is faced with forced downtime, you would be well advised to take a conservative course of action when assessing any sort of pain.

If you are faced with muscle or connective tissue tenderness, take immediate action. At the first sign of a potential injury, cut back your workout immediately and head for home at a leisurely pace. Don't push through unusual discomfort thinking it will go away by itself. Pain is your body's way of telling you "too much."

Should you suspect an injury, here are the immediate steps to take (also known as the RICE method):

Rest the injured area immediately to minimize hemorrhage, protracted injury, and swelling. Stay off it as much as you can. Don't try to stretch it for the first twenty-four hours or test it with even limited activity. Let it rest.

Ice it. Apply ice at the first sign of an injury. Use an ice pack (ice-chest coolers or bags of frozen corn make great ice packs) or water frozen in a Styrofoam or paper cup. With a frozen cup, massage the area gently. In either case, apply the ice for 8 to 20 minutes at a time. The appropriate length of icing will depend on the tissue thickness. For most areas of the body, 12 to 15 minutes is an appropriate duration. Ice no more frequently than every 90 minutes; prolonged application of ice can be counterproductive.

Compress it. With some types of injury, such as a sprained ankle, wrapping an elastic bandage snugly around the area will help to control swelling and limit edema. Be careful to ensure full blood circulation.

Elevate it. Keep the injured extremity elevated so that gravity is working for you rather than against you. This also helps to control swelling and limit edema.

If you are not sensitive to aspirin or ibuprofen (Advil, Nuprin), take them according to the directions on the label to help control inflammation. Use anti-inflammatory drugs conservatively (see the sidebar "Ibuprofen and Other NSAIDs" in Chapter 13). You might also try topical treatments such as Aspercreme, Rub A-535, or Icy Hot. Research has shown the active ingredient in these products to be effective in delivering anti-inflammatory medication to soft-tissue injuries such as tendonitis and pulled muscles.

If the injured area doesn't respond to such treatment in the first five days, then it's time to see your doctor. For some injuries you may be referred to a specialist, such as a podiatrist, orthopedist, or physical therapist. In the rehabilitation period, it is essential that athletes avoid all activities that may cause further irritation and resist the urge to "test" their recovery. Athletes who seem to be doing everything right but are slow to heal should see a sports nutritionist to ensure that their nutrition strategy is appropriate.

Following are some of the more common injuries to which endurance athletes are susceptible. This list is not exhaustive. With any potential injury, it is best to seek the advice of your general physician or sports medicine doctor.

Achilles Tendonitis

Achilles tendonitis is common among runners and cyclists and may even be caused by pushing off of the wall when swimming. It can also begin in the weight room with increased loads.

The Achilles tendon is the common tendon of the triceps surae. The triceps surae is the name applied collectively to the gastrocnemius and soleus muscles (the main muscles of the calf). The gastrocnemius originates on the lower (distal) end of the femur, or above the knee, and the soleus originates on the top, or proximal, end of the tibia. The gastrocnemius is the outer calf muscle, and the soleus is a bit deeper and more medial. They eventually join to form the powerful Achilles tendon. This tendon is under extreme loads and warrants attention when painful.

Pain is usually felt in the lower calf or as discomfort at the back of the heel and is worsened by running or other use of the lower leg, especially on hills, where loads are increased. This injury is prevalent in women who wear high heels because these shoes seem to shorten the tendon so that wearing flat shoes may stretch the tendon to a point of injury. In cyclists, the injury commonly appears as a result of excessive volume, particularly from long, multiday rides.

The most common factors that contribute to Achilles tendonitis are too much volume, duration, or intensity too quickly; excessive hill running; poor recovery practices; a brittle tendon; and leg-length discrepancies. Additional contributors are shoes that are too stiff at the ball of the foot, forcing your calf muscles to work harder to lift the heel off the ground and increasing tension on the Achilles tendon. Shoes with excessive heel cushioning also stretch the Achilles tendon, as the heel sinks lower in the shoe while absorbing shock as the body continues in a forward motion.

Treatment: For a mild strain, the RICE method is the first option. Following that, physical therapy such as ultrasound and microcurrent may be required. Partial tears are sometimes treated with a night splint or boot to hold the foot dorsi-flexed (toe pointing upward) overnight. This allows the muscle fibers to heal in a lengthened position. Complete tears or ruptures normally require surgical intervention followed by up to twelve weeks in a cast. The rehabilitation process begins with the use of a heel lift for as long as one year as well as flexibility and strength exercises.

For ongoing management of an irritated tendon, body-weight calf extensions (done on a stair or ledge) are very effective. Athletes who are susceptible to Achilles irritation should consider a protocol of light calf stretching combined with one or two sets of calf raises (15 to 30 repetitions) done twice per day (morning and night). This simple protocol has proven highly effective for a number of athletes. For best results, the treatment must be done every day, even after symptoms have disappeared.

Be aware that although strains and partial tears can be very painful, they may disappear once you are warmed up and moving. This phenomenon causes many to keep training long after rest and treatment should have started. Don't be fooled. The absence of pain when training followed by limping the next morning can be a sign of serious irritation or tear.

Prevention: Keep the muscles of the calf and hamstrings stretched and relaxed through gentle stretching, as muscular tightness not only increases the chance of injury but can prolong the tendonitis. Avoid the common training error of too much volume or intensity too fast, and choose appropriate running shoes.

Ankle Sprains

The most common injury to the ankle is a sprain—the stretching and tearing of ligaments surrounding the ankle. Sprains most commonly occur when running on an uneven surface where the weight-bearing foot "rolls in" as force is applied. This action causes stress to the ligaments stabilizing the lateral area of the ankle. Often there is a "popping" sound as the injury occurs—pain and swelling follow shortly thereafter.

Ankle sprains are graded by three degrees of severity. Stretched ligaments or minor tears of the ligament are Grade I. A Grade II sprain is a tear of the ligament with some minor laxity in the ankle. A complete tear of the ligament and a very lax ankle is a Grade III sprain.

Your doctor will need to determine the severity of the sprain and whether or not X-rays are necessary. Occasionally the bones of the leg or ankle may fracture, and so an X-ray examination may at least help to rule out this possibility.

Treatment: The most important and immediate form of treatment for Grade I and Grade II sprains is the RICE method. Stay off the ankle completely for the first twenty-four hours (or longer depending on severity) while keeping it elevated and iced. Also during the first twenty-four hours, avoid hot showers, heat-rub creams, hot packs, alcohol, and aspirin, as these may increase swelling. Tylenol or ibuprofen may help alleviate pain.

Although most sprains heal completely within a few weeks, severe sprains may need rehabilitation for up to two months. Grade I sprain swelling usually subsides within a few days. Grade II sprains require more time to heal and may need to be placed in a splint.

Grade III sprains may require a short leg cast or brace for up to three weeks, as there is a risk of permanent ankle instability. Surgery is rarely needed in athletes; however, those suffering from chronic ankle sprains may require surgery to tighten the ligaments.

Prevention: Sprains can happen anytime and anywhere—stepping out of a car, for example—and not specifically because of training errors. However, attention to running terrain and shoes with lateral support can help prevent them. Exercises to increase your flexibility, balance, and coordination are also helpful.

Chondromalacia Patella (Runner's Knee)

Chondromalacia patella, often called runner's knee, is one of the most common causes of knee pain in runners and cyclists under load as well as one of the most difficult to treat. It is a wearing of the soft cartilage on the underside of the kneecap, or patella. The patella is a sesamoid bone, meaning it is floating or embedded in the common tendon of the quadriceps. It acts as a pulley while moving back and forth over the femur under great loads. If excessive pressure on the cartilage occurs, or if your kneecap tracks incorrectly over the femur owing to biomechanical issues, the kneecap can soften and wear the cartilage.

Knee pain ranging from dull to sharp is usually felt in the front part of the knee. Pain may also be felt on the inside or outside of the knee and is sometimes difficult to pinpoint. In general, the pain will not radiate beyond the knee area.

Causes for this injury may include training errors. Excessive hill work while either running or cycling, too much volume or distance, or allowing the legs to flex to near 90 degrees during squats or while lowering weight during leg-extension exercises can irritate the cartilage. Riding hills during high-intensity strength training phases is another common mistake. Tight or weak calf muscles, hamstrings, gluteus, vastus medialis, iliotibial band, or vastus lateralis can be contributors. Biomechanical abnormalities such as overpronation, knock knees, wide hips (women), and poor pelvic control are also factors.

Treatment: Use the RICE method initially. Running should be decreased and downhill running avoided. Hill cycling and cycling intensity should be decreased, and exercises with the knee bent should be avoided because they increase forces under the kneecap. Taping the knee can aid in correcting any abnormal positioning of the patella.

Prevention: A focused stretching routine, including calf and hamstring muscles, and a focused strength-training program that includes leg extensions, concentrating on the last 15 degrees, are ways to prevent and relieve runner's knee. Refer to Chapter 16 for guidance on proper leg extension form, as improper form can lead to further damage. Choosing running shoes with extra support and using orthotics, if required, will help prevent this injury. Review your training schedule to ensure that training stresses such as maximum-strength weight lifting and hill cycling are performed at complementary, not contradictory, phases of your training periodization.

Compartment Syndrome

The muscle groups in the legs, arms, feet, and buttocks are encased within a tough inelastic fascia. When the pressure within a muscular compartment increases through overuse or traumatic injury, blood supply to the affected area is decreased. This restriction in blood supply can cause blood-vessel, nerve, and muscle-cell damage—even tissue death. This condition is referred to as compartment syndrome.

Compartment syndrome is a painful and generally chronic overuse injury in athletes—most commonly in runners. Pain is normally felt in the lower extremities, beginning during activity, progressively worsening, and then dissipating during rest. Occasionally there is numbness in the affected compartment as well.

This injury must be diagnosed and treated immediately after symptoms appear; otherwise, irreversible damage can occur. Your doctor must diagnose it by conducting a pressure test of the compartment. Other overuse injuries such as stress fractures and tendonitis must also be ruled out.

Treatment: A conservative approach is generally the first course of treatment: rest, ice therapy, and elevation as well as anti-inflammatory medications to reduce swelling. Compression is not recommended, as it may increase the pressure, causing further damage. Soft-tissue massage therapy can also be effective. Severe cases may require surgery to release the fascia.

Prevention: A running program with gradual increases in volume and duration can prevent compartment syndrome, as can choosing correct shoes that address any biomechanical issues. Additionally, regular sports massage can be beneficial.

Hamstring Strain

The hamstring muscles run down the back of the thigh, helping to extend the leg at the hip and bend at the knee. These muscles can tear when subjected to high-tension loads, such as when sprinting without a full warm-up or when muscles are not fully recovered from a previous hard workout.

Mild strains are caused by tight, fatigued, or weakened muscles that are then strained by overuse, overtraining, and repetitive movements, such as long-distance running or long hill climbs when cycling.

Acute injuries are caused by an inadequate warm-up or stretching routine, poor hamstring flexibility, muscular-strength imbalances in the quadriceps, poor lower-back flexibility, or weak abdominal muscles that cause a forward pelvic tilt.

A mild strain may feel like no more than a tight muscle. A sharp pain in the hamstring during full stride generally indicates a more severe tear. A rupture, or complete tear, can be a painful and debilitating injury that leaves you unable to walk or straighten your leg.

Treatment: A complete tear of the muscle may require surgery to reattach it; however, most strains and partial tears can be effectively treated with the RICE method. Following that protocol, a gentle stretching and strengthening routine should be implemented. Soft-tissue massage therapy can be useful to break down any scar tissue.

Return to activity gradually to prevent reinjury, and include an extended and complete warm-up routine. Coming back too quickly can lead to chronic hamstring problems.

Prevention: The best way to prevent a hamstring injury is through a focused stretching routine, both before and after exercise, and a full warm-up. Attention should also be paid to an overall flexibility and strength program, including eccentric exercises (the muscle lengthens as it exerts force, for example, lowering a weight) such as hamstring curls, where an athlete focuses on lowering in a smooth, controlled manner.

Heel Spurs and Plantar Fasciitis

The plantar fascia is a thin layer of tough, fibrous tissue that supports the arch of the foot. Microscopic tears in the fascia lead to inflammation, which causes pain in the arch toward the heel. This is referred to as plantar fasciitis. In situations where the tear is severe enough to pull the fascia away from the heelbone, the bone will try to heal itself by growing new bone. This excess bone growth is referred to as a heel spur.

Pain from both injuries can be felt when "toeing off" while running or walking and is normally worse when first stepping out of bed.

Overpronation is the most common cause of these injuries; however, other factors such as a sudden increase in running volume or intensity, tight calf muscles, poor ankle flexibility, shoes too worn or with too much flex in the arch, and flat feet or weak and high arches can also contribute.

Treatment: Treatment should begin at the first sign of symptoms. Left too long, healing becomes difficult and could take as much as eighteen months or more. The first course of treatment is ice, relative rest, anti-inflammatory medications, and stretching the calf muscles and bottoms of the feet. Massaging the arch and heel before getting out of bed in the morning is also helpful. If these treatments fail, physical therapy such as ultrasound and electric stimulation can be applied. Additionally, heel cups, night arch taping, and orthotics should be considered. Final options are first cortisone injections and then surgery.

Prevention: A regular stretching and strength routine of the calf muscles and foot can prevent plantar fasciitis and heel spurs. Strength exercises for the foot include picking up small objects with your toes. Shoes should be chosen with good shock absorption and soft arch support. There should be no flex in the arch area of the shoe. Shoes should be replaced regularly, and orthotics may be required to correct overpronation.

Iliotibial Band Syndrome

The iliotibial band (ITB) is a large tendon that runs along the outside of the thigh from the knee to the hip. As the leg is flexed and extended, the ITB, which acts as a stabilizer while running, can become irritated from overuse. Pain can vary from slightly annoying to debilitating and is usually felt toward the end of a long run. Women are more prone to pain in the hip area, whereas men often feel pain around the knee.

Iliotibial band syndrome can be caused by abnormal biomechanics such as bowed legs, pronation of the foot, leg-length discrepancy, and lateral pelvic tilt. It is also caused by training errors such as running on crowned surfaces and running on tracks without frequent directional changes. A tight iliotibial band as well as tight gluteal or quadriceps muscles can aggravate these factors.

Treatment: Decrease training at the first sign of trouble. Rest, ice, massage, anti-inflammatory medications, and gentle stretching are the first methods of treatment. Be careful when icing this area, as the tissue is relatively thin and can literally be frozen. Failing these, physical therapy (pelvic leveling, ultrasound, and microcurrent) is effective. Gentle stretching of the ITB and gluteus and quadriceps muscles is also recommended.

Do not ignore or train through this injury. If it is caught early, treatment can be very successful. Left too long, it could take months, if not years, to fully heal.

Prevention: Run on level surfaces as much as possible, make sure to change direction often on roads and running tracks, and shorten your stride by increasing your cadence. Follow a regular stretching routine, and wear orthotics or motion-control shoes that limit pronation.

Cycling can sometimes worsen the effects of ITB syndrome, and it is important to ensure correct bike setup. When cycling, the most common contributor to ITB issues is a saddle that is too high. Athletes should always remember to make gradual changes in saddle height, particularly when moving the seat up.

Metatarsalgia and Morton's Neuroma

Metatarsalgia is a bruised feeling in the ball of the foot, where the long bones meet and join your toes. The capsule of the joint becomes inflamed as a result of repetitive trauma such as running or cycling. You may also experience numbness or burning.

Morton's Neuroma is a burning pain in the bottom of the foot, which typically radiates into the third and fourth toes. Symptoms may be as light as numbness or as debilitating as a burning pain that makes walking difficult. A neuroma is a cyst, a benign tumor, or a thickening of the nerve. In the case of Morton's Neuroma, the nerve is affected just before the point where it separates into the toes.

These two forefoot conditions may develop separately or at the same time and are both overuse injuries that can occur in both runners and cyclists. In running, athletes who overpronate are more likely to develop injuries of the forefoot. In cycling, lateral compression caused by too small a toe box can often impinge on the nerves of the foot that travel between the metatarsal heads and cause numbness and burning. Hot spots can result from a cleat position too far fore or aft, or pedals that do not suit the athlete.

Treatment: Prevention and quick action at the first signs of these injuries are important because they can be difficult to eliminate. In the early stages, reducing swelling and inflammation with rest, ice, anti-inflammatory medications, ultrasound, and other forms of physical therapy may be enough to alleviate your symptoms. Treatment should always be accompanied by preventative measures, such as proper equipment, training on appropriate surfaces, appropriate training volumes, and in some cases a change in running technique.

Prevention: Preventative measures include changing your running shoes often, wearing running shoes with ample forefoot cushion, running on trails and soft surfaces, and ensuring that your cycling shoes have ample room in the toe box.

Reducing trauma to the forefoot may involve altering running technique in some athletes, for example changing from a heel striker to a mid- or forefoot striker. As cadence quickens and strides soften, wear and tear on the foot is reduced. A quieter, more efficient gait results in less pounding absorbed from the road.

Piriformis Syndrome

Piriformis syndrome is both difficult to diagnose, owing to symptoms similar to those for several injuries, and difficult to eliminate because of its location deep in the gluteal region. When you are walking, running, or cycling, you can usually feel the pain in the buttocks, hips, or hamstrings; it is generally located in the back of the leg and in the lower back. The general cause of piriformis syndrome is the piriformis muscle passing over repeatedly and irritating the sciatic nerve, or a structural abnormality in the path of the sciatic nerve. This irritation may refer pain along the sciatic nerve—called sciatica. Pain is generally most acute when running. Piriformis syndrome cannot be accurately diagnosed with X-rays, MRI, or nerve conduction tests; it can be diagnosed only on the basis of symptoms and physical examination.

Treatment: The first course of treatment is rest and curtailment of all running, cycling, and other activities that cause you to bend at the hip while keeping your knees straight. Very easy swimming is acceptable as long as there is no pain (avoid kick sets and consider the use of a pull-buoy).

A stretching routine focusing on the piriformis, abductors, hip flexors, adductors, and hamstrings, along with physical therapy treatments such as ultrasound, can be effective. Any biomechanical issues, such as overpronation, should be identified and corrected.

Pain may disappear after a few days to several months of rest; however, it often does not. In this situation, your doctor may recommend cortisone injections into the piriformis muscle where it passes over the sciatic nerve. Failing these, surgical exploration may be required. Most athletes will find that rest and a focused program of flexibility and deep-tissue massage yield results.

Prevention: As with Achilles tendonitis, ITB syndrome, and iliopsoas tendonitis, prevention is important, as a piriformis issue is a very difficult problem to eliminate.

Avoid running downhill too fast or too often, running on crowned surfaces, and long strides. Shorten your stride by increasing your cadence. Focus on a complete stretching and strength program. Consider using orthotics to correct overpronation or any other biomechanical issues.

Shin Splints

Another common overuse injury in runners is shin splints—pain along the tibia. The pain from splints is vertically oriented in one of two locations—posterior (along the inside of the tibia) and anterior (along the outside of the shin). Generally developing over a few weeks or months, the pain is noticeable at the beginning of a run as the heel strikes the ground. As with most injuries, both forms of shin splints can occur from overtraining. Training errors and abnormal biomechanics also play a part in this type of injury.

Posterior shin splints are caused by overpronation of the foot, tight calf muscles, flat arches, and running on crowned surfaces. Excessive downhill running, running on concrete, shoes without adequate shock absorption, and sudden increases in volume or duration cause anterior shin splints. Novice athletes beginning a new running program too aggressively are often prone to shin splints.

Treatment: For both forms of shin splints, the first order of treatment is a substantial decrease in workout volume, frequency, and intensity along with post-workout icing of the area. In more acute cases, anti-inflammatory medication and physical therapy such as electrical stimulation and ultrasound can be used. For more severe shin splints, your doctor may recommend a bone scan to rule out stress fractures.

Deep-tissue massage is useful to break down any scar tissue and to gently stretch the calf and the hamstring muscles after running.

A heel lift may be used to reduce the pulling effect of tight calf and hamstring muscles, and orthotics may also be considered to address biomechanical issues.

Prevention: As with many overuse injuries, the best prevention is a regular stretching and flexibility routine—for shin splints specifically, the calf and hamstring muscles. Athletes prone to posterior shin splints should choose shoes with good arch support, and those prone to anterior shin splints should choose shoes with good shock absorption. Orthotics may be required to correct pronation. Be sure to replace your shoes on a regular basis.

As with any new running program, or return to running after injury, volume and duration should be increased gradually. Attention to terrain will also aid in preventing shin splints. Avoid excessive downhill running and running on concrete. We highly recommend that you choose routes with softer surfaces, for example trails, bark chips, or hard-packed dirt.

Stress Fractures

Like most common sports injuries, stress fractures are an overuse injury. Repetitive stresses, such as those from long-distance running, fatigue and overload the muscles, which then transfer added shock to the bone. This shock causes small, nearly invisible cracks in the bone—called stress fractures. According to the American Academy of Orthopedic Surgeons, more than 50 percent of all stress fractures occur in the lower leg.

Factors leading to this type of injury are too quickly increasing training volume, duration, or intensity; lack of proper recovery time between workouts; poor conditioning; sudden changes in running surfaces; and worn or inflexible running shoes.

Female athletes are more prone to stress fractures than male athletes as a result of a condition referred to as "the female-athlete triad"—eating disorders, amenorrhea, and osteoporosis. This condition leads to decreases in the female athlete's bone mass, which then increases her chances of stress fractures. Whenever a female athlete experiences stress fractures, a thorough nutritional review should be undertaken.

Treatment: Rest and a curtailment of running are the only treatment for a stress fracture. Most stress fractures can take six to eight weeks to heal. Returning to running should be done slowly, with gradual increases in volume and intensity. Too quick an increase can lead to chronic problems and permanently prevent proper healing.

Prevention: Increasing running volume and duration slowly, maintaining a healthy diet, and replacing your running shoes frequently, before they lose their shock absorption capabilities, can prevent stress fractures.

Swimmer's Shoulder

Swimmer's shoulder is a classic overuse injury in swimmers and commonly refers to soreness, inflammation, or tendonitis of the rotator cuff muscle. Pain is generally felt during or after swimming. In addition to increasing volume and intensity too quickly, the most common cause of swimmer's shoulder is poor stroke technique, particularly a lack of body roll. Lack of balanced upper-body strength also plays a role in causing this injury. Finally, excessive use of paddles or swim bands can also lead to irritation of the shoulder. Athletes who are new to paddle or band use should exercise significant caution when incorporating this type of work into their swim routines.

What is commonly referred to as "dropping the elbow" is a movement that severely limits the rotator cuff's movement, squeezing it within the structure of the shoulder. This impingement is repeated with every stroke, leading to irritation.

Treatment: As with all overuse injuries, the first course of treatment is relative rest, ice, and anti-inflammatory medications. Once inflammation and swelling have been eliminated, athletes should continue to swim. Backstroke and fly should be avoided, but most athletes will benefit from low-intensity, biomechnically correct freestyle swimming. Do not use swim paddles or bands, as these increase the load on the shoulder joint. In order to further reduce the shoulder load, you can use a pull-buoy or fins.

During the rehabilitation period, a focus on technical improvement as well as a stretching and strength routine are recommended. Most athletes will benefit from a program of deep-tissue work on the shoulder joint. This treatment can be quite painful but is effective in speeding the recovery process.

You should have your stroke reviewed by an experienced coach or swimmer to develop better stroke mechanics. This training will help alleviate your problem and result in a more efficient stroke.

Should the problem persist, your doctor may consider cortisone injections. In rare severe instances, surgery may be required. Finally, athletes should have a muscle balance assessment done. Quite often a relative weakness in the muscles that externally rotate the shoulder can lead to impingement.

Prevention: It is much easier to prevent swimmer's shoulder than to treat it. Gradually increase swim volume and intensity and focus on correct technique, good balance, and developing a deeper shoulder roll. A good on-deck coach can help with your technique, and bilateral breathing is beneficial in learning proper body rotation. A focused stretching and strength routine that includes stretch-cord exercises (discussed in Chapter 5) and weight-room exercises such as triceps dips, bent-arm pulldown, and seated row (discussed in Chapter 16) can help prevent this injury.

Tendonitis and Bursitis

Tendonitis (inflammation or irritation of a tendon—thick, fibrous cords that attach muscles to bone) and bursitis (inflammation or irritation of a bursa—small sacs between moving parts) are common overuse injuries that, although they can affect any tendon or bursa in the body, usually affect those located around joints. These are normally temporary and can be quite responsive to conservative treatment. However, if not treated at the first sign of symptoms, they may develop into hard-to-heal, chronic problems.

Classic symptoms of bursitis and tendonitis are pain and stiffness aggravated by movement. There is pain when warming up that may go away during exercise and return after cool-down and again the next morning. Both tendonitis and bursitis are most commonly caused by overuse, particularly if the athlete is poorly conditioned, has bad posture, or uses incorrect technique. Diagnosis by your doctor is recommended in order to rule out diseases such as rheumatoid arthritis and diabetes that may present similar symptoms.

Treatment: The first order of treatment is the curtailment or reduction of the exercise that caused the injury, followed by heat or ice therapy and a focused stretching routine. If these approaches fail, physical therapy such as night splints, ultrasound, and electric stimulation are helpful.

Prevention: It is very important to prevent recurrences of these injuries to avoid a chronic problem. Proper conditioning, focus on correct technique, ensuring a complete pre-workout warm-up, and a regular stretching and flexibility routine will aid in preventing these types of injuries.

Recommended Reading

Achilles Tendonitis. About.com Sports Medicine,
  http://sportsmedicine.about.com/library/injury/bl_ankle3.htm.

Ankle Sprains. Rice University. SportsMed Web,
  http://www.rice.edu/~jenky/sports/ankle.sprain.html.

Compartment Syndrome. American Academy of Orthopaedic Surgeons. http://
  orthoinfo.aaos.org/fact/thr_report.cfm?Thread_ID=287&topcategory=About%20
  Orthopaedics, June 2001.

Hamstring Injuries. Rice University. SportsMed Web,
  http://www.rice.edu/~jenky/sports/ham.inj.html.

Hamstring Muscle Strain. American Academy of Orthopaedic Surgeons. http://
  orthoinfo.aaos.org/fact/thr_report.cfm?thread_id=137&topcategory=wellness,
  February 2002.

Iliotibial Band Friction Syndrome. Rice University. SportsMed Web,
  http://www.rice.edu/~jenky/sports/itband.v2.html.

Jenkins, M. The Compartment Syndrome. Rice University. SportsMed Web,
  http://www.rice.edu/~jenky/sports/cmpt.html.

———. Swimmer's Shoulder. Sports Med Web, http://www.rice.edu/~jenky/sports/
  swim_shoulder.html.

Johnson, J. Swimmer's Shoulder. http://swimheat.com/swimmersshoulder.htm.

Koehler, S., and D. Thorson. Swimmer's Shoulder: Targeting Treatment. *The Physician
  and Sports Medicine* 24 (11) (1996),
  http://www.physsportsmed.com/issues/1996/11_96/koehler.htm.

Luebbers, M. Swimmer's Shoulder. Resources for Prevention and Rehabilitation.
  About.com Swimming Guide,
  http://swimming.about.com/library/weekly/aa010601a.htm?terms=injury.

Mirkin, G. Piriformis Syndrome. http://www.drmirkin.com/fitness/F230.html.

Patello-Femoral Syndrome. Rice University. SportsMed Web,
  http://www.rice.edu/~jenky/sports/pfs.html.

The Piriformis Syndrome. Rice University. SportsMed Web,
  http://www.rice.edu/~jenky/sports/piri.html, 1997.

Plantar Fasciitis. Rice University. SportsMed Web,
http://www.rice.edu/~jenky/sports/plantar.fasc.html.

Pribut, S. Achilles Tendonitis and Achilles Tendon Ruptures.
http://www.drpribut.com/sports/spinjur.html#achilten, 1998.

———. Hamstring Pulls: Prevention and Treatment. http://www.drpribut.com/sports/hamstring.html, 2002.

———. Heel Spurs and Plantar Fasciitis. http://www.drpribut.com/sports/heelhtm.html, 2001.

———. Iliotibial Band Syndrome. http://www.drpribut.com/sports/spinjur.html#itbs, 1998.

———. Shin Splints—A Simplified Clinical Classification.
http://www.drpribut.com/sports/spshin.html, 1998.

Pribut, S., and A. Perri-Pribut. Piriformis Syndrome: The Big Mystery or a Pain in the Behind. http://www.drpribut.com/sports/piriformis.html, 2001.

Purcell, K. Achilles Tendonitis. E-Tips 5 (1) (2002), http://www.ultrafit.com/etips.asp.

Shin Splints. Rice University. SportsMed Web,
http://www.rice.edu/~jenky/sports/shin.html.

The Shoulder. American Academy of Orthopaedic Surgeons,
http://orthoinfo.aaos.org/fact/thr_report.cfm?Thread_ID=121&topcategory=Shoulder&searentry=t he%20shoulder, March 2000.

Sprained Ankle. American Academy of Orthopaedic Surgeons. Co-developed by the American Orthopaedic Foot and Ankle Society,
http://orthoinfo.aaos.org/fact/thr_report.cfm?thread_id=152&topcategory=foot, April 2001.

Stress Fractures. American Academy of Orthopaedic Surgeons.
http://orthoinfo.aaos.org/fact/thr_report.cfm?Thread_ID=46&topcategory=Sports&searentry=stress%20fractures, March 2000.

Tendonitis/Bursitis. American College of Rheumatology, 2000.

Chapter 16

Strength Training for Triathletes

You never fail, you
simply produce results.
Learn from these.

—Anonymous

G iven the endurance focus of triathlon, many athletes wonder if they stand to benefit from strength training. Even
among leading coaches, there is a wide range of views on
the benefits of traditional strength training. This chapter covers
our views on strength training.

Who Benefits?

Of the three sports in triathlon, strength training appears to
have the greatest impact on cycling. However, running and
swimming will also benefit from the gains associated with a
properly constructed strength program.

Many male athletes, particularly those under thirty, have the
ability to hold their strength through the season. For these athletes, it can make sense to strength train a few months a year
or avoid lifting altogether. Building their general endurance
rather than spending time in the gym will also better serve
many time-constrained novice athletes.

Given their physiology, female and masters' athletes have
much to gain from year-round strength training. Because these
athletes are prone to lose strength over time, a maintenance
program of at least one session per week is recommended
even when sport-specific intensity is high.

Athletes who are seeking to improve cycling performance
will see benefits from increasing their lower-body strength.

Traditional strength training can provide a suitable platform upon which the athlete can launch the higher-intensity work associated with the late Base and Build periods.

Athletes who are prone to injuries will benefit from including a strength regime in their Prep and Base periods. Once biomechanical and equipment causes are ruled out, many aches and pains (particularly in the knee and back) are actually caused by either structural weaknesses or muscular imbalance.

Structuring Your Plan

Before starting any training plan, it is worth spending a little time deciding on the goals of your program. The first step of this planning process is to consider your key triathlon limiters. In thinking about these limiters, consider which can be specifically addressed through the strength program.

In deciding the best exercises to include in the plan, remember that many athletes have an imbalance toward the front of their bodies—that is, the muscles of the chest, biceps, abdominals, and quadriceps dominate the muscles of the back, triceps, glutes, and hamstrings. In triathlon, the major posterior muscle groups are very important.

After you decide on the key areas of the plan, you need to decide on the duration of the strength plan. In general, you should start strength training four weeks after your last A-priority race and switch to strength maintenance no less than seven weeks before your first A-priority race of the upcoming season. These guidelines give most athletes four to six months for their focused strength training. Table 16.1 shows guidelines for strength-training periodization.

Within your strength plan, you should include a solid focus on core muscles, as well as hip flexors, once or twice per week. A strong core is key to racing the ironman distance comfortably, as it keeps the pelvis in a neutral position on the run, keeps the legs and hips up while swimming, and enables you to generate more force on the bike. A strong lower back also means a more comfortable aero position on the bike. The advantages of strong hip flexors are numerous. The main hip flexor (the iliopsoas) is not only the primary mover to get good knee lift and drive you forward, it is also the major trunk stabilizer, keeping your lower spine stable when running and cycling.

Each phase is assumed to last four weeks (note that the Anatomical Adaptation phase consists of three phases). Owing to scheduling issues, some athletes may have to reduce some of the phases to three weeks' duration. This reduction makes sense when you are trying to have an early-season race fall at the end of a recovery week.

You should start each block at the top end of the repetition range. As the block progresses, weight can be gradually increased and repetitions reduced, except in strength maintenance (SM). In the AA phase, it is very important to avoid repetition failure.

Table 16.1 Strength Training Periodization

Stage	Goal	Types of Exercises	Intensity	Sets & Repetitions
AA1	Help muscles and connective tissues become used to regular strength training	Wide range of whole-body exercises	Low, never to strain, never to failure	One or two sets of 25 repetitions with 30–45 seconds rest between sets
AA2	Continue to build a muscular base with increasing intensity	Wide range of lower-body and core exercises, upper-body exercises become more focused	Moderate, some strain on final repetitions of last set, never to failure	Two sets of 15–20 repetitions with 30–45 seconds' rest between sets
AA3	Specifically prepare body for the rigors of the MS phase	Specific range of lower- and upper-body exercises, continue core exercises with a wide range	Moderately high, final repetitions of both sets require focus, never to failure	Two sets of 12–15 repetitions with 60–90 seconds' rest between sets
Maximum Strength (MS)	Increase maximal strength for all key lifts	Specific range of lower- and upper-body exercises, core exercises continue with a wide range	High, final repetitions of last two sets require heavy focus, possible assistance of spotter required on final rep of final set	Four sets of 6–10 repetitions with 2–3 minutes' rest between sets
Strength Maintenance (SM)	Maintain strength, sport-specific and functional strength training dominates	Limited number of exercises, selected in light of athlete's limiters	Low to moderate, inversely related to the intensity of sport-specific and functional training	One warm-up set and one set of 6–10 repetitions with 30–60 seconds' rest between sets

The repetition and intensity protocol for core exercises is different from the guidelines for other exercises. You should start with a core session that lasts for 5 minutes and builds to a session of 15 to 20 minutes' duration.

In all exercises, emphasize perfect technique at all times. The absolute amount of weight lifted is of limited importance. Focus your energies on gradual, consistent improvement. The greatest increases in strength will happen during the AA 3 and maximum strength (MS) phases. Give your body adequate time to prepare for the increased stress associated with these phases of the program. Rushing the body's natural speed of adaptation can lead to injury.

If you are uncomfortable with the intensity of the MS phase, you should consider skipping the MS phase and moving directly to the SM phase.

Assuming that each phase lasts four weeks, it will take four blocks to move through to SM. Many athletes assume that additional benefits will result from extending the MS phase. It is worth emphasizing that we recommend that the MS phase last for a maximum of four weeks. Athletes will show superior gains from moving to sport-specific strength work rather than repeating the MS phase. Those living in a climate conducive to year-round training will find sport-specific work much more valuable than gym-based ME work. This comment applies to both cycling and running.

Exercises

For AA1, we recommend a wide range of full-body exercises. For AA2 and beyond, we recommend the following exercises. MS exercises are in bold; athletes who are short on time should focus on these primary lifts.

- **Squats or leg press** (always do a set of very light or no weight to warm up)
- Lat pulldowns (to front)
- **Knee extension**
- **Hamstring curl**
- **Bent-arm pulldown**
- **Core**
- Calf raise
- **Seated row**
- Dips (use dip machine)
- Tricep extension

We recommend that these lifts be done in the order that they are listed.

Ten to 15 minutes of light aerobic activity should always precede strength training. As a cool-down, many athletes enjoy a brief swim or cycle. Stretching should follow.

Technique Tips

Weight: With all lifts, you should start lighter than the weight you think you need. Avoid the natural urge to rush. Focus on quality because good form yields the most benefits. However, good form means that you will not be able to use as much weight. You will be well served by leaving your ego in the locker room and remembering that you want to impress only yourself on race day.

Stretching: Post-lifting is the ideal time for an extended full-body stretch and a perfect time to improve flexibility. Gyms are warm, dry environments where you can focus on your limiters. You should also stretch briefly after each set to help maintain range of motion and ensure an adequate recovery after each set.

Squats/leg press: The goal of this exercise is to improve force delivery to the pedal in cycling. The squat is one of the most dangerous options for the novice athlete, and great care is necessary to protect the back and knees; therefore, the leg press is recommended. For both squats and leg press, correct technique is essential to avoid injury or muscular imbalances.

Squats: Never descend past 90 degrees—100 to 110 degrees is fine for the strength gains required for triathlon. Show control on the speed of repetition, and never "bounce" off the bottom. Breathing should be controlled and deep; exhale in a controlled fashion when extending. The pelvis should rotate forward and down as the weight is lowered. The squat bar should move vertically without any forward or backward movement. It is best to have your feet rotated 5 to 10 degrees outward, as this position promotes the correct firing of the muscles.

Leg press: Never push on your knees, and maintain your back perfectly flat against the backrest. As with squats, breathing should be controlled and deep; exhale in a controlled fashion when extending.

Knee extension: This exercise improves the balance between the lateral and medial quadriceps. You need to move only in the range of 120 to 180 degrees (knee slightly bent to fully straight). The key is the final 20 to 30 degrees, where you should focus on achieving maximum extension. A 90-degree or greater range of motion has been shown to irritate the patella tendon. A common phenomenon in cyclists is knee trouble because their quadriceps are not firing properly. The best way to promote correct firing of the quadriceps is to really focus on the final 15 degrees of the extension and a solid contraction of the inner quadriceps. You can actually make things worse if you fail to do the full extension.

Hamstring curls: This exercise improves the strength ratio between the quadriceps and hamstrings. It is best done one leg at a time in a controlled fashion (stable core, slow repetition speed). Rocking the hips and using a rapid lift speed can cause injury.

Calf raise: This exercise aids in improving force delivery to the pedal in cycling as well as improving running strength. Feet should be aligned or heels turned slightly inward. Legs, hip, back, and shoulders should be aligned at all times.

Core: The key for working the core is to use 100 percent correct technique, slow repetition speed, and a wide variety of exercises. As the majority of athletes have an imbalance, with greater strength in their upper abdominal region, focus should be placed on the lower abdominals, obliques, lower back, and glutes. The training objective should be slow, high-quality repetitions that utilize a wide range of motion. Core exercise examples appear later in this chapter.

Hip drive: As with core exercises, the key for improving hip flexors is 100 percent correct technique and stable core support. See hip-drive exercises later in this chapter.

Seated row: The seated row strengthens your core and lower back. Your back should be vertically aligned. Grasp the bar so that your thumbs are pointing up and elbows are drawn backward and in toward the body. The chest remains out in a "proud" position, and the back should not rock. Use less weight if you find yourself rocking.

Lat pulldowns: This exercise stabilizes the shoulder. Shoulder blades are pulled down and in, and the bar is pulled to a "proud" chest. You should always pull to the front and focus on both phases of the lift (pulldown and return).

Tricep dips: Elbows should point backward at all times. Hands should grip at slightly wider-than-shoulder width. Avoid superdeep or superwide dips, as they are not required for the targeted strength gains.

Tricep extensions: Elbows should remain locked in place at sides. Pause at full extension and keep tension on the muscle at the top of the cycle. Feel free to alternate between rope extensions and bar extensions (attachments are available in most gyms).

Standing bent-arm pulldown: The goal of this exercise is to simulate the catch and pull of swim stroke. Many athletes will achieve a higher-quality exercise by using stretch cords. As in swimming, you should focus on maintaining a high elbow. Maintain correct swimming form in both directions (pulldown and return). Exercises using stretch cords are discussed in more detail in Chapter 5.

Common Concerns

Many athletes have a concern that weight training will result in bulking up. For the vast majority of the population, it is extremely difficult to add muscle mass. For triathletes, endurance training makes it even tougher. Indeed, though some athletes will add some muscle mass during the winter, it tends to "burn away" in the spring once the longer endurance sessions begin.

Some athletes respond very quickly to weight training, and these athletes should keep the MS phase specifically focused on the areas that they are seeking to improve. Male athletes who carry a lot of upper-body muscle will often find that focusing primarily on the lower body and core region makes the most sense.

Another concern common among athletes is that strength training will reduce their quickness and agility. An easy way to address this concern is to maintain speed-skills sessions in all sports. However, slowing down is normal in the MS phase. In fact, if you don't slow down, you may not be working hard enough (assuming you have the appropriate strength and technique base for pushing MS). You will also find that your hill-climbing ability and power generation declines. This is normal, and your power will return once you ease off the weights.

A reduction in range of motion can also be a concern. The 10- to 20-minute period after strength training is an ideal time to undertake a full-body stretching program.

Timing

In order to get the full benefit from your strength session, you should be fresh. For all AA and MS sessions, it is best if strength training is the first workout of the day. If this timing is not possible, you should try to get as much rest as possible between your morning aerobic session and your evening strength session.

In the AA1 phase, the intensity is low enough for some athletes to include some light aerobic work before lifting. However, in AA2 and beyond, it is best for the strength work to come first. In the AA3 and MS phases, the goal is to increase maximal strength, so it is essential that you be fresh.

Many athletes wonder about the risk of injury by training after lifting. The risk varies tremendously by athlete as well as by the intensity of the lifting. You should be very cautious about scheduling any activity after intense strength training; running in particular should be avoided. Keep all sessions light in the 24 to 48 hours after strength training. Athletes in the SM phase have more scheduling flexibility.

Table 16.2 shows strength targets. Stronger athletes should never exceed these weight targets. Rather than increasing weight beyond these points, you should increase the number of repetitions.

Table 16.2 Strength Targets

Squat	1.3–1.7 x BW
Leg press (sled)	2.5–2.9 x BW
Step up	0.7–0.9 x BW
Seated row	0.5–0.8 x BW
Standing, bent-arm lat pull	0.3–0.5 x BW

General Tips

Change is the key to making progress. The body adapts to the training stress, and by varying that stress, you are able to achieve constant adaptation (i.e., progress).

Heavy weights will affect the quality of sport-specific sessions. For this reason, it is best to complete the MS phase no later than the middle of the Base period. During that time of the year, you are training in endurance and technique. Therefore, the strength gains outweigh the negative impact on the sport-specific work.

Start out easy, as muscles adapt more quickly than connective tissue. Many athletes have injured themselves seriously by rushing the natural pace of their bodies. This is a powerful argument for avoiding all supplements that are designed to speed muscular adaptation, regardless of the ethical and legal reasons.

Be especially conservative with increasing intensity until you are six to eight weeks into your program (twelve weeks for novices). Relax about the amount that is being lifted, and remember your program goals. Quite often novices will find themselves becoming numbers-driven. The safest and most effective approach is to establish excellent technique, prepare the connective tissues, and then increase intensity. Training with consistency and patience will ensure the best results. You will get significant gains in the first eight weeks of any strength program because of the "recruitment" of your muscles. Initially, the training teaches your body to use the muscles it already has. By the time you have tapped much of these gains, your muscles will also be stronger from the training.

Four weeks of MS lifting is plenty for triathletes. The goal of this strength program is to build sport-specific strength. Once the majority of the gains have been made, it is time to switch to sport-specific work.

Core Strength Exercises

For those with strong cores, meaning you have been doing fifty-plus crunches in a traditional manner, it is time to shake things up a little. The following are advanced core workouts. Remember to exercise caution when beginning a new routine.

Aside from incline twisting sit-ups, no equipment is required. If you feel like your current routine is becoming easy, or if the number of repetitions required for your routine is high, try this out.

Supermans: Body is in push-up position, except your elbows are together directly under your shoulders. Your elbows and forearms are on the ground at a 90-degree angle with your shoulder, elbows about 6 inches apart as if you are praying (Figure 16.1). Keep shoulder blades together (no curve in shoulders). Keep hips a little higher than a push-up, back perfectly straight, on your toes with legs straight. Hold for 15 seconds, move elbows forward 2 inches and hold for 15 seconds, move elbows forward another 2 inches and hold 15 seconds. Your hips may be falling now; keep them up—no bow in the back. Keep extending until you really feel it. If you aren't shaking after 45 seconds, the technique needs modification (if body is straight, then make sure hips aren't too low). Flip over and do twenty slow crunches, then repeat the Superman. You will feel this one in your back and abs.

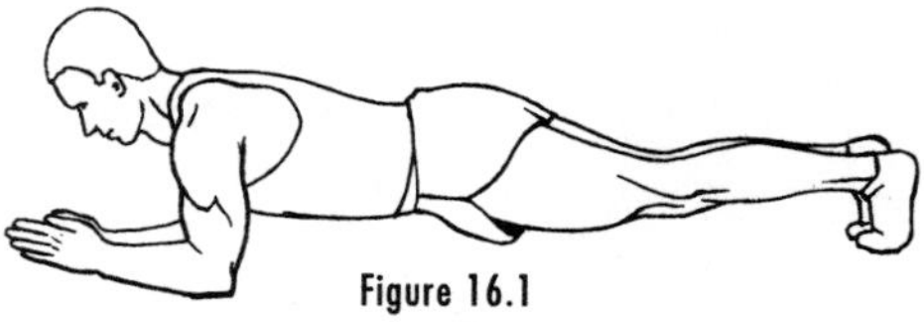

Figure 16.1

Rear Supermans: Lie flat on your belly with arms and legs extended. Lift right arm (thumb pointing up) and left leg (Figure 16.2). Tighten glutes hard, crunch, and hold for 10 to 15 seconds. Lift left arm (thumb up) and right leg. Alternate four to six times on each side, keeping tension in the glutes, both thumbs pointing up and no rotation of the core.

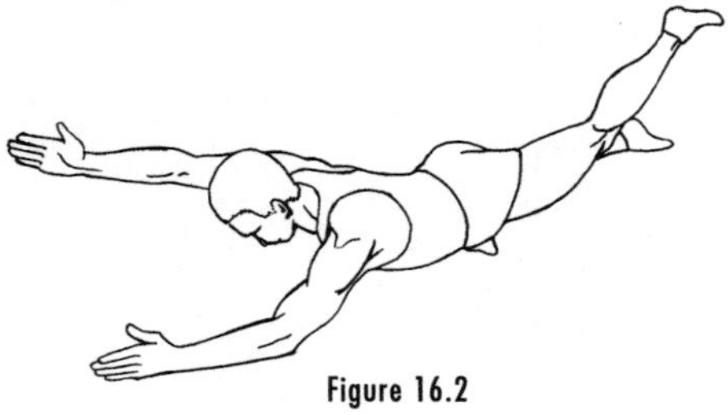

Figure 16.2

Pikes: Place your hands together on the ground, keeping your arms straight and directly under your shoulders (Figure 16.3). Make a triangle. The points of the triangle are your hands, shoulders, and feet. On your toes, keep your body perfectly straight. Slowly open upward by rotating torso outward (Figure 16.4). Keep both arms straight (one will be coming off the ground). Continue to rotate until you have gone 90 degrees and you are in a "cross" position, arms fully extended, one still on the ground (Figure 16.5). Hold, return, rotate in the other direction, repeat as desired. Keep the movement slow.

Figure 16.3

Figure 16.4
Figure 16.5

Obliques: Neck remains neutral, no "pull" on the head. Lift comes solely from oblique (Figures 16.6 and 16.7).

Figure 16.6
Figure 16.7

Advanced obliques: Lie on your side and support your upper body with your elbow. Keep your higher arm flat against your side. Body is straight, chest and hips perpendicular to the ground. Lift your hips so your waist is about 8 to 12 inches off the ground, and hold for 10 seconds (Figures 16.8 and 16.9). Lower slowly for a 5-second count, then lift back to ready position. Five repetitions on each side are suggested for beginners. Work yourself up to ten reps.

Lower abdominal/oblique combo: Lying on your back with your knees bent, perform a twisting crunch and touch your elbow to the opposite knee. The outside of your right elbow should touch the outside of your left knee.

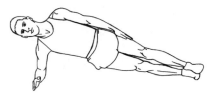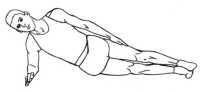

Figure 16.8
Figure 16.9

Swiss Ball Core Strength Exercises

Before beginning these exercises, open your hips and stretch your back by lying backward over the ball. Work through the exercises in a "bottom-up" order. The last thing you raise is your head. Upper abdominal exercises should be done last, as they are generally the strongest core muscle for most athletes. Begin with exercises requiring balance.

Key points:

◆ The goal is the *work*, not the reps.

◆ Move slowly, and stay in control.

◆ Breathe.

Swiss ball bridges: Lie on your back with arms extended at your sides. Place your feet on the ball about shoulder-width apart, and lift your hips so your torso is straight. Bend your knees so your lower legs are perpendicular with the ground (Figure 16.10). Hold for 1 to 3 seconds, relax, and repeat.

Figure 16.10

Swiss ball back: *Alternating leg lift*—Lie on your belly over the ball and roll so that your arms are resting on the ground. Lift and extend one leg at a time. Move slowly and smoothly through the full range of motion (Figure 16.11). *Dual leg lift*—Same as alternating leg lift, only this time lift and extend both legs. Hold for 10 seconds. *Traditional back extension*—Lie on your belly over the ball with your right leg extended behind and your right arm extended forward (Figure 16.12). Move slowly and smoothly through the full range of motion. Increase the degree of difficulty by crossing your arms on your chest.

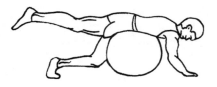

Figure 16.11
Figure 16.12

Lower abdominals: *Over and around*—Lie on your back on the floor, and place a water bottle at your feet. Keeping the small of your back pressed against the ground and your legs extended, lift your legs up and over the bottle (Figure 16.13). Repeat side to side. *In and up*—Lie on your back with legs extended. The first movement is to lift your legs just off the

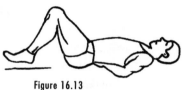

Figure 16.13
Figure 16.14

ground and pull your heels back to your buttocks (Figure 16.14), then extend back to the starting position. The second movement is to lift your legs straight up and perpendicular to the ground. Keep movement speed slow and controlled.

Swiss ball obliques: *Oblique crunch*—Lie on your side across the ball with your inside leg bent against the ball and your outside leg extended. Place your upper hand on the ball and rest your head on your bottom hand. Laterally lower and raise your torso slowly, keeping your hips and shoulders aligned (Figure 16.15). *Russian twist*—Lie on your back, placing the ball under your shoulders. Move your feet about shoulder-width apart and lift your hips up so your body is parallel to the ground (Figure 16.16 and 16.17). Extend your arms and roll back and forth, twisting at the abdominals. The key to this exercise is to roll the *ball*, not the body.

Figure 16.15

Figure 16.16
Figure 16.17

Swiss ball crunches: Lie with the small of your back against the ball and feet shoulder-width apart. Place your hands across your chest or at your temples. Slowly crunch, lifting your shoulders and upper back off the ball (Figure 16.18).

Figure 16.18

Medicine Ball Core Strength Exercises

Key points:

◆ Start with a light ball

◆ Learn the movement pattern, then

◆ Add speed, then

◆ Add resistance

Chop to ankle, knee, and waist: To the ankle, start with the ball held overhead and off to one side. Chop down and across to the opposite-side ankle. Be sure to bend, flexing at the ankle, knee, and hip. Stand up fully and reach as high as possible after each repetition. Repeat five times to each side. To the knee, start with the ball overhead and off to one side, then chop down to the opposite-side knee. Repeat ten times to each side. To the waist, start with the ball overhead and off to one side, then chop down to the opposite-side hip. Repeat ten times to each side.

Lunges: Move the ball across the front of your body as you lunge forward in a controlled manner. The ball will end up outside the lunging leg. Return the ball to the starting position as you return to the "ready" position. For an advanced exercise, use the same starting position. Swing the ball as if you are chopping wood. The ball will travel in an arc, from over your head to the same finishing position. Return the ball to the "ready" position by swinging it back. Lunges should always be done in a controlled manner. Maintain alignment between your third toe, knee, and ankle. Ensure that your leading knee stays behind your leading toes when lunging.

Twisting "throws": Start with the ball between your knees and your butt down (as if you are doing a squat). As you extend upward, twist your body as if you were throwing the ball over one shoulder. Move in a controlled manner and perform ten repetitions to each side. This exercise places a dynamic load on the back, so use caution when learning it. Always bend at the ankles, knees, and hip when performing this exercise (as well as the chops listed in the preceding section).

Exercise Tips

◆ Be very careful with new exercises. They are a different form of muscular contraction from crunches and traditional sit-ups. You can easily strain yourself for days if you overdo it.

◆ Remember to breathe!

◆ Use slow, controlled movements in all core exercises.

◆ If possible, do these exercises at a track where you can run easy (and tall) for 100 meters between sets. If you are at the gym, stand and do some torso stretching in between sets. Don't rush these exercises because they are tough.

◆ Go easy when you start. This point can't be emphasized too much. You don't want to be "crunched" for four days afterward.

◆ Quality over quantity.

Hip-Drive Exercises

There are three levels of exercise to strengthen your hip flexors (iliopsoas). Ensure good posture and body position when doing these exercises. If all your muscle groups are stable around the hips, then you will get the most out of the exercises, recover more quickly, and achieve better stability.

For all these exercises, you will need a 2-meter piece of bungee cord, or you can use swim cords. Most gyms will have a good selection of stretch cords. Begin with a light-resistance cord and move to heavier resistance as you get stronger.

After a session of hip-flexor work, it is important to loosen up with an easy jog or high-cadence (90 rpm) easy cycle and a good stretching of your hip muscles.

Base-leg drive: Attach the bungee cord around the bottom of a solid table leg. Lie on your back far enough out from the table that there is some resistance on the cord around your foot (Figure 16.19). Place your hands under your lower back. Bring your knee to your chest with a fast, controlled movement. Slowly lower your leg back to the floor on a 5-second count. On the backward movement, make sure that your back is flat and the pressure remains on your hands. You can have your nonbungee leg slightly bent to make this easier. Repeat until fatigued—fifteen to thirty repetitions—or until you lose the ability to control your lower spine.

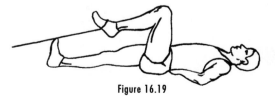

Figure 16.19

Figure 16.20

Figure 16.21

Standing hip drive: Stand with your right hand against the wall, and place your left hand behind your back so you can touch your right buttock muscle. Before beginning the movement, squeeze your buttocks together. Stand tall in an upright position and drive your left knee forward (Figure 16.20). Ensure that your upper body remains stable and your right buttock muscle is tight. There should be no lateral movement. Slowly lower the leg back to the starting position. Repeat until fatigued—twenty to thirty repetitions.

Dynamic hip drive: Free-standing with the bungee cord in the same position as in the standing hip drive (Figure 16.21). The purpose of this exercise is to mimic the movement pattern of uphill running. After you drive your knee forward, hold your body position at the top of the movement for a moment. This requires the constant activation of not only your hip flexors but also the buttock, calf, and abdominal muscles. Drive your knee forward using a running-style motion with your arms. Just before the top of the movement, come up onto your toes and extend your hip. This requires good stability and strength, and you will initially be unstable. Repeat until fatigued—thirty to forty repetitions.

Recommended Reading

Aaberg, Everett. *Resistance Training Instruction.*
Champaign, IL: Human Kinetics, 1999.
American Council on Exercises Personal Trainers Manual.
San Diego, CA: American Council on Exercise.
Friel, Joe. *The Triathlete's Training Bible*. Boulder, CO:
VeloPress.
Gambetta, Vern, and Steve Odgers. *The Complete Guide to
Medicine Ball Training*. Sarasota, FL: Optimum Sports
Training.

Epilogue

Gordo's Epilogue

Though the basics of long-course success have been unchanged for years, we are constantly learning more about the most effective training techniques. Rapidly developing fields, such as sports nutrition and power-based training, mean that the most effective protocol today may become dated over time. This book represents our view on current best practice for long-course training. As we learn and become more experienced, our views will continue to develop and grow. These changes will likely be reflected in later editions as well as on my personal website, http://www.gordoworld.com.

Joe's Epilogue

Triathlon is a challenging and fulfilling sport made all the more enjoyable when success accompanies participation. Going long is the biggest challenge in triathlon. I hope you have found this book to be helpful as you prepare for your next ironman-distance race. Please let us know what you discovered, as we are always interested in hearing from real athletes like you. To contact Gordo or me, go to our website at www.Ultrafit.com. We look forward to hearing of your success in long-distance triathlon racing.

Key Training Sessions

The following workouts cover the most important physiological aspects of ironman-distance racing. Use caution with these workouts, as they are the absolute toughest ones required in your training. To get the most out of these sessions, you must allow adequate recovery time.

These workouts are the best time to work on race focus, technique under pressure, and keeping your face, jaw, and shoulders relaxed at all times. The six workouts that follow cover all the key attributes required for ironman-distance success.

Workout 1—The Steady Ride

The purpose of this workout is to give you an idea about what it takes to ride 4 to 6 hours at a steady pace. The harder efforts within the workout are designed to promote muscular endurance. The overall intensity of this ride is likely to be greater than what you will use on race day, and therefore, your observations through the ride will be educational in forming an appropriate race strategy.

◆ Start with 60 to 90 minutes of easy-paced riding, then ride 2 to 5 cycles of 40 minutes steady, then 20 minutes moderately hard (mod-hard).

◆ Steady pace should be your view of ironman-distance race pace; mod-hard should be your view of half-ironman-distance race pace.

◆ Try to keep this ride in flat to rolling terrain and use your aerobars as much as possible. If you are riding up a grade and can stay down on the bars, then do it.

◆ Focus on your effort for this entire ride. There may be wind, and the wind will affect your pace. Stay mentally focused and control effort rather than riding to a set speed.

◆ If a transition run is scheduled, then run easy off the bike, no more than 3 miles.

◆ Be sure to save plenty of energy for the final 2 hours. Eat and drink at race levels.

◆ Note your heart rate and RPE changes through the session.

Workout 2—Race-Specific ME

This workout is designed to target a number of different aspects of TT fitness within an endurance training session.

◆ Start with 60 minutes of easy-paced riding, then ride 2 to 5 cycles of 40 minutes steady, then 20 minutes of "main set."

◆ Main-set options

Threshold intervals: 5 x 3 minutes on 1 minute rest interval (RI), interval intensity builds to hard pace.

Strength intervals: 5 x 3 minutes on 1 minute RI, focus on low-cadence, large-gear work.

◆ Subthreshold power—20 minutes mod-hard.

◆ If you keep the total ride time under 4 hours, then you can add the following run.

◆ Quick transition to a 60- to 90-minute run. Split the run into thirds. During the first third, focus on a relaxed, comfortable cadence. The middle third should be steady pace. The final third should build to a tempo finish (mod-hard pace).

Workout 3—TT Strength

This workout is designed to build subthreshold power. It is quite useful for athletes who have excellent endurance but find that they lack the strength (mental or physical) to fully tap their TT potential.

◆ Warm up for 45 to 75 minutes as if you were going to do an LT test.

◆ Option A: Ride 30 km where you build to mod-hard pace in the first 3–4 km, then mod-hard to hard pace for the rest of the TT. Note that this is not an all-out TT, simply solid tempo work.

◆ Option B: Ride 2 x 20 km. Build to mod-hard to hard pace over the first 5 km and hold until the end. During the final 5 km of the second TT, build to hard pace. First TT should be about 85 to 90 percent effort, second TT should be about 90 to 95 percent effort. Spin for at least 30 minutes between TT efforts.

◆ Following the second TT ride, for 30 to 60 minutes easy to steady pace.

◆ Transition to a 30-minute steady-pace run.

Workout 4—Climbs

This workout is designed to build climbing strength in experienced cyclists. Novice and less experienced cyclists should consider building strength in rolling terrain before attempting a ride of this nature.

◆ Start with 60 to 90 minutes of easy-paced riding, then ride a series of long climbs. Each climb should last 15 to 40 minutes.

◆ Early in the season, ride steady to mod-hard on the climbs. As your key race approaches, climbs can build to near-threshold efforts.

◆ Aim to have your highest power output at the tops of the climbs; build your effort as you climb.

◆ Include some lower-heart-rate strength work where you ride with a low cadence.

◆ Distance traveled and average pace are not important for this workout. Your aim should be to complete some solid climbs.

Workout 5—Run Pacing Test

This workout can be a useful way to estimate a reasonable pace to target for your run leg. If you are able to hold a steady pace to the end of this workout without significant increases in heart rate or RPE, then it is a reasonable starting point for calculating your target pace for your run leg.

◆ The total run duration should be 2:00 to 2:15. Split the run into thirds.

◆ First third, run easy pace and pay little attention to mile splits.

◆ Second third, run steady pace and note average mile split pacing.

◆ Final third, hold the same average pace as the middle third and notice changes in RPE and average heart rate (they will both rise).

Workout 6—Triple Brick

Another race pacing session that helps train appropriate pacing.

◆ Three 90-minute cycles of bike 60 minutes, then run 30 minutes.

◆ All transitions should be quick.

◆ The first brick should be slower than goal race effort, the second brick should be at goal race effort, and the final brick should be faster than goal race effort.

◆ Watch your pace, particularly on the second run, to be able to finish strong.

Testing and Warm-up Protocols

Although laboratory tests can provide interesting data, we train in the field, and therefore our experience is that the most useful tests are completed in the field. The tests below have been proven to provide a wide range of athletes with accurate intensity zones for their training and racing.

Run and Bike Lactate Threshold Heart Rate (LTHR) Test

Following a deep warm-up, perform a 30-minute TT, going at your fastest maintainable pace. After 10 minutes, hit the lap button on your heart-rate receiver. Your average heart rate for the last 20 minutes of the time trial will roughly be your LTHR—or the bottom of heart-rate Zone 5a.

Most people go too hard the first time and therefore end up with a lower average heart-rate reading for the last 20 minutes. This is okay because when you are starting, a little low is better than a little high. With time and experience, you will become more accurate.

LTHR testing should be done separately for running and cycling to determine heart-rate training zones for each of those sports. These tests are demanding, so you should treat them as BT workouts and ensure proper recovery between tests (allowing at least forty-eight hours between any two tests is a good rule of thumb).

Swim Lactate Threshold Pace Test

Swimming is better tested on pace rather than heart rate. In order to determine lactate threshold (LT) pace, start with a deep warm-up and then swim a 1,000-meter time trial at the fastest pace you can maintain for the distance. For best results, hold back at the start and build your effort through the test. Your average pace per 100 meters is referred to as your T(1) per 100 pace.

Sample Swim Test Warm-up

◆ 10–20 minutes of easy bilateral swimming
◆ 5–10 minutes of steady swimming
◆ 6 x 50 done as 25 build and 25 easy
◆ 4 x 50 done as 12.5 sprint and 37.5 easy

RI between each of the above and after each 50 should be 10 to 20 seconds.

Shorter Race Warm-up

This warm-up is good for short races up to Olympic distance and for athletes who are endurance limited across their race distance.

Ride 15 to 30 minutes easy to warm up your legs. Then do some lower-body stretching for 5 to 10 minutes. Following the stretching, walk around, keep your legs warm, and continue to do some light stretching. As close to the race start as possible, do a short skills run consisting of five Strides with walk-backs.

Deeper Race Warm-up

This warm-up can be used up to the Olympic distance for most age-group athletes and up to the half-ironman distance for elite and experience athletes. Strong swimmers (those who can swim an ironman-distance swim in 60 minutes or less) can use the swim portion of this warm-up for all distances.

Start your warm-up about 75 to 90 minutes pre-race with a 10- to 15- minute spin on the bike to check gearing and wake up the legs. Return to the transition area, set up, then jog 10 to 15 minutes, stretch and do four to five Strides. Start swim warm-up at least 35 minutes prior to race start with the following:

◆ 10 minutes easy/steady, including 25 backstroke every 100 meters. Swim steady to get the arms going, approximately 600 meters. Do a few arm stretches.
◆ 5 x 100 meters on 10-second rest intervals as: 25 hard stroke, 25 easy, 50 steady (25 stroke done as free, fly, back, fly, free—25 easy and 50 steady are always free).
◆ 200 steady including three pickups, good kick drive on the last pickups.
◆ Stretch arms while waiting for swim start.

With most ironman-distance races, you will not be able to get your bike out of the transition area. For this reason, a run-swim warm-up combination is recommended for elite and experienced athletes.

A Note on Maximum-Heart-Rate Tests

Maximum-heart-rate tests are not recommended, as they are generally inaccurate and extremely stressful on the body. In order to get a true maximum heart rate, you need to push yourself to your absolute limits. This effort can lead to tunnel vision, hearing loss, and near (or actual) collapse. The lactate threshold tests outlined in this appendix are much safer and more accurate for the purposes of long-distance training and racing.

Swim Workouts

Swimming Glossary

Refer to this glossary for definitions of terms and abbreviations used in the swim workouts.

3/4 Drill (3/4) Three strokes freestyle, then four strokes backstroke; goal is to keep hips high through transition. Do not start stroking until head and chin have made the transition. Three strokes free, rotate, chin up, four strokes back, rotate, chin down, three strokes free—using this pattern, you will work both rotation directions.

3/5 Alternate between three-stroke and five-stroke breathing unless otherwise noted.

bk Backstroke

b/l Bilateral, three strokes per breath unless otherwise noted

br Breaststroke

Build effort Increase your effort within the interval

DAB Double-arm backstroke

Descend effort Increase your effort by interval as the set progresses.

DPS Distance per stroke

dr Drill

fly Fly

free Freestyle

IM Individual medley—order is fly, backstroke, breaststroke, then freestyle—if fly is difficult, then you can use polo instead; if your fly or polo form goes, then switch to normal freestyle.

Polo Water-polo swimming, head-up freestyle, focus on high elbows

Pull f/g Pull with full gear (band, buoy, paddles)

Pull pads Pull with paddles

RI Rest interval

T(1) Average pace for a 1,000-meter TT

TT Time trial

Wave catch (w/c) One-arm drill where you breathe every two strokes. Staying mainly on your side, focus on recovery up the body line and high elbow on entry, catch, and pull.

Workouts
Technique 1—Freestyle Technique

This is a challenging session. Focus on duration for this type of swimming. Distance guidelines are for each component of the swim workout; you can mix and match different components to suit your time and swim limiters.

1. 4 x 50 of each of the following:

Side-Kick, arm at side

Side-Kick, arm extended

Side-Kick, one stroke, three breaths

Side-Kick, three strokes, three breaths

Three-stroke swim

- ◆ Fins can be used for all Side-Kick Drills, but no fins is a superior workout for experienced drillers.
- ◆ If swimming short course, then stop every 25 or 50, change at each 12.5.
- ◆ If swimming long course, then stop every 50, change at each 12.5 or 25.
- ◆ You must stay relaxed: Pace should be easy, rest interval is whatever is required to stay comfortable and relaxed.
- ◆ Beyond this point, if you feel fatigued or if your stroke starts to go, then you should stop and repeat the "Side-Kick, three strokes, three breaths" (SK33) for 200 meters of easy pace, pausing every 25 to 50.

2. 4–6 x 100 b/l free

Perfect form with 5 to 10 seconds RI at 50 and 15 to 20 seconds RI at 100.

- ◆ If technique starts to go, then jump back to SK33 Drill.
- ◆ Rest interval should be as long as is required to maintain perfect, relaxed form. You will speed up naturally over time; have patience.

3. 2–6 x 50 bk

Perfect form with 15 to 20 seconds RI at each 50.

First thing to focus on is quick arm action on recovery—stroke can be mellow, but recovery should be quick, straight-arm recovery.

Second thing to focus on is head remains perfectly still, with shoulder opposite to stroking arm coming out of water—this position is very similar to the Progression Drill, where you drop alternating shoulders while kicking on back/side—just as in freestyle, this stroke is done from side to side and requires comfortable balance with side-kicking.

4. 4–8 x 50 b/l 3

Count strokes on each 50, easy pace, 10 to 20 seconds RI.

- ◆ A good count would be 40 strokes when swimming long course meters (LCM) of 40 to 50 seconds.
- ◆ If your stroke count is above 50, then you want to focus on DPS—this can be achieved through better stroke finishing, improved balance, and comfort in the water.
- ◆ If your stroke count is below 40 strokes per LCM 50, and you are swimming >50s, then you may be gliding too long, and you may benefit from increasing your hip drive to generate more efficiency. Your stroke rate should climb only slightly, but you will get a lot more speed and power. The increase in stroke rate will feel very fatiguing, as your body will be used to lots of rest. This tip is appropriate only for well-balanced athletes who swim with a normal stroke that essentially looks like catch-up drill.

5. 2 x 600 swim limiter

Choose your personal technique limiter (stroke finish, balance through rotation, catch and pull straight back, enter in front of shoulder and pull straight back—all these are ideas for you).

Swim 25s or 50s, working exclusively on your personal limiter.

- ◆ If swimming short course, then stop every 25 or 50, change at each 12.5.
- ◆ If swimming long course, then stop every 50, change at each 12.5 or 25.
- ◆ You *must* stay relaxed: Pace should be easy, rest interval is whatever is required to stay comfortable and relaxed.
- ◆ Advanced athletes can swim 100s or 200s—however, you must be able to hold perfect form and work on limiter for entire time.

6. 2–6 x 50 3/4 Drill, 10 to 20 seconds RI

7. 2–1,200 Stroke Count

Swim either 50s, 100s, or 200s on 10 to 20 seconds RI.

- ◆ If you are swimming short course, then count your even-length strokes.
- ◆ If you are swimming long-course 100s, then count your return-length strokes.
- ◆ If you are swimming long-course 50s, then count all strokes.
- ◆ Pace should be comfortable at all times; if you feel winded at any time, then swim a shorter interval. If you require more than 20 seconds of recovery, slow down and swim a shorter interval.
- ◆ If balance and comfort in the water are your limiter, then interval distance and speed are not important. Rest a lot, and keep interval distance short. If you are a 70-minute-plus ironman-distance swimmer or if your T(1) pace is 1:50 per 100 meters LCM or slower, then you should assume that this is the case. Round numbers T(1) LCM of 1:50 per 100 would be about 1:40 per 100 yards short course yards (SCY).
- ◆ If stroke endurance is your limiter (the likely issue for 70-minute or faster ironman-distance swimmers), then your goal is to increase your interval distance while holding perfect form. For this type of swim, I don't believe it is necessary to go much beyond 200s—unless you are comfortably under an hour for an ironman-distance swim. Then some mod-hard stroke endurance work at distances up to 400 meters can be beneficial.
- ◆ Once you can swim 1,000 total with perfect form, increase your pace from easy to steady; note what happens to your stroke count. We only want to see a small increase in stroke count. What is small? A total stroke increase of 5 percent is reasonable. As a guide, until you are under 50 strokes per LCM length, it doesn't make sense to speed up.

Technique 2—Stroke Technique

Warm-up

500, mix of strokes

5 x 100 easy free on T+20 seconds RI

Kick Set with fins

4 x 50 IM order on 30 seconds RI

Pull Set

4 x 200 on 15 seconds RI, easy pace breathing pattern by 50 is 3, 5, 7, 9—if you have trouble with 9, then use 7; if you have trouble with 7, then use 3, 5, 7/3, 7/5

Main

5 IM swims—10 fly strokes, 20 bk strokes, 10 br strokes, and 20 free strokes
  ◆ Goal is max distance on each swim—take 45 seconds RI
3 x 100 IM, count strokes for each leg, try to hold good DPS—take 45 seconds RI
200 IM, aim for a relaxed and smooth swim

Cool Down

200 choice, with fins

Technique 3—Shorter Recovery Swim

This swim would be appropriate for an active-recovery day or following a strength-training session.

3–600 fr with every fourth length bk
3 x 200, breathe by 50 as 3, 5, 7, 7
400 straight b/l 5, focus on offside arm mechanics
3 x 100 b/l 3, focus on a limiter that you noticed during the previous 400
100 bk
100 br

Rest intervals are as required to keep heart rate well down.

Endurance 1

Warm up with 300 easy choice

Pull Set—Two times through

150, 3 x 50
10 seconds RI on each interval, 20 seconds RI at end of each set
150 is long and smooth, 50s are faster and smooth

Kick Set—Once through, fins okay

3 x 200 done as 100 kick with board, 100 kick/swim by 50
Descend effort on 30 seconds, then 45 seconds RI

Main Set—30 minutes of 100s

Swim T(1) + 5 seconds per 100 pace and take 10 seconds RI per interval
  ◆ Hold the same split the whole way through
  ◆ Key focus is maintaining stroke mechanics
  ◆ This is a pacing and stroke endurance set—swim exactly T(1)+5 seconds pace with perfect form

Cool-down

200 easy mix of strokes

Endurance 2

Warm-up

300 b/l 3, 400 IM (no fly, use b/l 3 to start), 100 kick—all on 10 seconds RI

4 x 50 w/c on 10 seconds RI

Distance Set—6 x [4–6 x 100]—Sets 1 and 2 b/l

Set 1—pull f/g on T(1) + 15 seconds per 100

Set 2—pads only on T(1) + 10 seconds per 100

Set 3—swim on T(1) + 10 seconds per 100

Set 4—fin kick on T(1) + 15 seconds per 100

1-minute break

Set 5—swim on T(1) + 10 seconds per 100

1-minute break

Set 6—swim on T(1) + 15 seconds per 100

Cool-down

200 choice

Endurance 3

Warm-up

800 DPS, easy to steady pace

4 x 100 alternate by 50 kick/dr

◆ All on 10 seconds RI

Main Set

3–5 x [300, 100]

◆ 300s are pull b/l steady (buoy, pads, band optional) on T(1) + 15 seconds per 100

◆ 100s are swim hard on T(1) + 10 seconds per 100

Fin Set

200 bk easy

2 x [2 x 50, 4 x 25]

◆ 25s are hard on 10 seconds RI

◆ 50s are hard on 10 seconds RI

Cool-down

200 choice, easy pace, fins optional

Endurance 4

Warm-up

400 free, every fourth length nonfree, easy

300 b/l 5, steady

200 bk kick, mod-hard

100 IM

- ◆ All on 15 seconds RI

Speed Set

Transition with 2 x 100 easy

5 x 100, take 20 seconds RI on first interval and hold split

- ◆ 100s are 25 polo, 25 easy free, 50 free
- ◆ Descend the final 50 to hard effort

Transition with 2 x 100 easy

Main Set

400 pull b/l 5, steady on T(1) + 10 seconds per 100 pace

2 x 200 swim b/l 3 mod-hard on T(1) + 10 seconds per 100 pace

4 x 100 swim b/l 3 hard on T(1) + 15 seconds per 100 pace

2 x 200 swim b/l 3 mod-hard on T(1) + 10 seconds per 100 pace

400 pull b/l 5, steady on T(1) + 10 seconds per 100 pace

Cool-down

200 easy, mix of strokes

Muscular Endurance 1

Warm-up

500 long and steady

Pull Set

1–2 x [200, 4 x 50]

- ◆ 200s are mod-hard on 30 to 40 seconds RI
- ◆ 50s are hard on 5 seconds RI (hold same split)
- ◆ 1 minute extra rest between sets—start on a convenient top or bottom

Kick Set with fins

3–4 x 200, descend on 40 seconds RI

- ◆ Done as 100 kick with board, 50 kick no board, 50 swim

Speed Set

2 x [3 x 50]

- ◆ All on greater of 1:20 and 20 seconds RI
- ◆ Sprint 1—first third, then easy, Sprint 2—middle third, then easy, Sprint 3—last third, then easy

Main Set

2–5 x [3 x 100]

- ◆ Each cycle, 1 and 2 are free, best average pace on 45 seconds RI
- ◆ 3 is either IM order (fly, bk, br, free) or IM
- ◆ 3 RI is 45 seconds, with 10 seconds extra rest at 50 mark
- ◆ 3 is hard effort

Cool-down

200 easy

Muscular Endurance 2

Warm-up

400 easy, every fourth bk

Pull Set

100, 200, 300, 400

- ◆ Split in half—first half is easy pace, second half is hard pace
- ◆ 30 seconds RI

Speed Set

10 x 50 on greater of 1 minute and 10 seconds RI

- ◆ Odds are easy, evens are hard

Main Set

Transition with 100 very easy choice

3–6 x 200 best average pace

- ◆ Leave on T(1) + 10 seconds per 100 pace

Cool-down

200 easy, mix of strokes, fins okay

Muscular Endurance 3

Warm-up

2 x 300 free (b/l 3 or 3/5), easy with 15 seconds RI

Kick Set

2 x [3 x 50], kick/swim by 25

- ◆ Descend 1–3 to hard pace, RI is 15 seconds
- ◆ No extra rest between sets

Main Set

6–12 x 150 on 15 seconds RI

◆ Hold same split

◆ Swim 150s as 50 build/50 hard/50 DPS (easy)

200 choice, very easy

15 minutes continuous with pull-buoy, 3/5 breathing, easy pace

Muscular Endurance 4

Warm-up

2 x 400 easy mix of strokes

Pull Set (no pads, no band)

2–3 x [4 x 50] Fists Drill on 10 seconds RI

2 x [3 x 50], kick/swim by 25

◆ Swim the 50s in cycles of four. First one is all fists; second one is 75 percent fists, then swim; third one is 50 percent fists, then swim; last one is 25 percent fists, then swim

◆ Focus on front end of stroke

Kick Set with fins

8 x 100 on 20 seconds RI

◆ Odds are kick with board

◆ Evens are kick/swim by 50

Descend in 2s (so 7 and 8 are fastest)

Main Set

1–2 x [6 x 200]

◆ Descend 1 to 6, no extra rest between sets

◆ Send-off is T(1) + 30 seconds per 100 to start, reduce total send-off by 10 seonds per interval; this implies T(1) + 5 seconds per 100 for 6 (and 12)

◆ The long rest will tempt you to go hard early, but show discipline; if you can swim T(1) pace the whole way, then you are doing very well!

Cool-down

200 easy, mix of strokes

Additional swims can be found on Gordo's Tips page, http://byrn.org/gtips.htm, and on the TrainingBible.Com website, http://www.trainingbible.com.

Indoor Bricks

The workouts below are intended to give you some training ideas for when weather or other factors force you indoors.

Session 1—Run 30, Bike 120, Run 45 (3.25 hours)

Strides to warm up

Bike 120 (60 minutes easy, then 60 minutes steady)

Run 45 minutes off bike (15 minutes cadence work, then 15 minutes steady, then 15 minutes cadence work)

End with a minimum of 15 minutes stretching

Session 2—Run 30, Bike 75, Run 30, Bike 75, Run 30 (4 hours)

Strides to warm up

Bike 75 (middle 15 minutes are mod-hard, rest is easy)

Run 30 minutes (focus on cadence, head up)

Bike 75 minutes (easy/steady/mod-hard—25 minutes of each zone)

Run 30 minutes (15 minutes of cadence focus, then last 15 minutes builds to mod-hard)

End with a minimum of 15 minutes stretching

Session 3—Run 30, Bike 45, Run 30, Bike 45, Run 30 (3 hours)

First and last run include Strides with walk-backs, otherwise easy

Middle run final 15 minutes should be mod-hard, all else steady pace

First bike is easy, include 5 x 20 seconds big-gear sprints on 4-minute easy recoveries

Second bike is 15 minutes of easy/steady/mod-hard (each)

End with a minimum of 15 minutes stretching

Session 4—Run 30, Bike 75, Run 30, Bike 75, Run 30 (4 hours)

First and last run include Strides with walk-backs, otherwise easy

Middle run is 10 minutes, focus on smooth cadence 85 to 90 rpm, then mod-hard for 10 minutes, final 10 minutes steady

First bike is 20 minutes easy, then 5 x 30 m seconds big-gear sprints on 4-minute easy recoveries, then hold steady

Second bike is 1/2/3 pyramid (easy/steady/mod-hard), using a 30/30/15-minute protocol

End with a minimum of 15 minutes stretching

Session 5—Run 30, Bike 75, Run 15 (2 hours)

First run includes Strides with walk-backs, otherwise easy

Bike is 20 minutes easy, then 4 x 30-second big-gear sprints on 4-minute easy recoveries, then 10 minutes steady, then 5 x 1-minute low cadence mod-hard on 1-minute steady recovery, then steady to finish

Second run is easy focus on a smooth cadence

End with a minimum of 15 minutes stretching

Session 6—Bike 45, Run 30, Bike 45, Run 30, Bike 30 (3 hours)

Ride 1, include 5 x One-Leg Drills to fatigue with 2-minute spin RI

Ride 2, include 5 x spin-ups, spin-ups 30 seconds' duration with 2:30 spin RI

Ride 3, include 5 x 20-second big-gear sprints (seated), with 2:40 light spinning RI

Runs are steady, rides are easy to steady pace

End with a minimum of 15 minutes stretching

Hip Progression

These stretches are best done in order, for one complete side of the body before working the other side (please note that the figures show a mix of left- and right-side stretching). Stretch only as far as you can comfortably breathe, and remember that quality of stretch is more important than range of stretch.

- Lying on your back, slowly roll one leg at a time from side to side. When rolling, your hips remain stable and your foot moves from 3 to 9 o'clock. Repeat eight times.
- Bend one knee and clasp your hands together over your knee, pulling it back toward your chest (Figure E.1). Hold and relax eight times. To reduce the intensity of the stretch, slightly bend your other leg. As your flexibility increases, your goal is to keep your nonstretching leg straight, your foot flexed upward, and your knee on the ground.

Figure E.1

- Still holding your knee, slowly rotate your leg in small semicircles, working in both directions and with a variety of circle sizes.

◆ Place a belt or band under (or slightly behind) the ball of your foot. Keeping both legs straight, gently lift your leg toward your head. Stretch only as far as is comfortable. In most cases, your knee should remain locked, and you should have the sensation that you are extending through both legs. If you are unable to achieve a 45-degree angle, then bend the leg that is against the ground—you should always keep the stretching leg fully extended (Figure E.2).

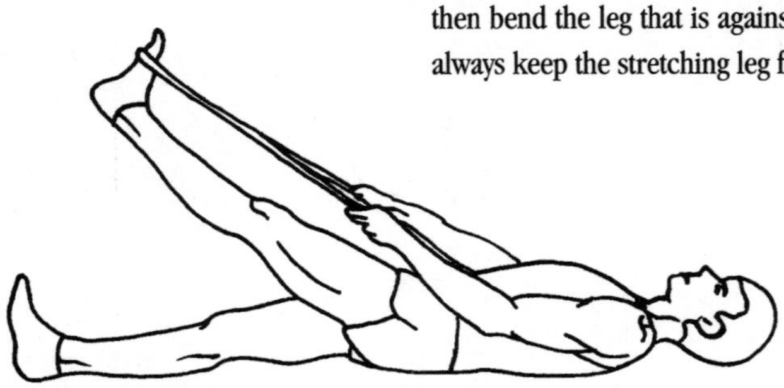

Figure E.2

◆ Place your left ankle across your right knee and gently push your bent leg away. Push and relax eight times.
◆ Place your ankle across your knee (as above) and clasp your hands behind your thigh. Pull your knee straight back to your chest (Figure E.3). To increase the stretch, clasp your hands on your shin just below your knee.

Figure E.3

◆ Place a belt or band around your foot, bend your leg, and pull your knee down toward the ground. Lower leg should remain perpendicular to the ground (Figure E.4). To increase the stretch, grab your foot with your hand.

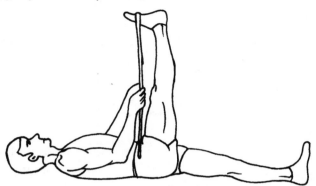

Figure E.4

◆ Draw your left leg up toward your chest, support your left knee with your left arm, and use your right arm to bring your lower left leg across your body line. Draw your left knee up and slightly across your body line. Increase the range of motion of the stretch by making semicircles with your left knee, moving your left leg back and forth across your body.

◆ Lie on your side with your bottom arm extended to support your head. Your pelvis should be forward, and one knee should be on top of the other. Clasp your top ankle with your hand and bend your knee, pressing your heel toward your buttocks (Figure E.5). Be careful not to overextend your knee. Stop if you feel any pain.

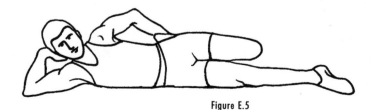

Figure E.5

◆ On your back in a half-lotus position, lift and press down your bent knee (Figure E.6). When you are lifting your bent knee, use your lower abdominal muscles to press the small of your back against the ground. You will find that the movement assists with the opening of this stretch. You are likely to need a belt to support the ankle of your bent leg. Complete fifteen to thirty cycles.

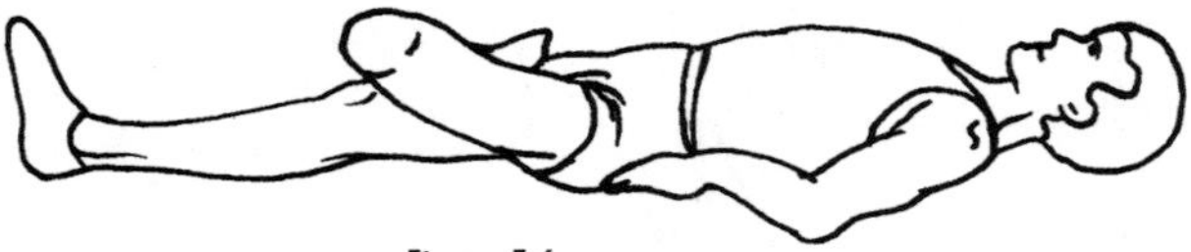

Figure E.6

◆ On your back, place a belt or band under the ball of your foot and repeat the straight-leg hamstring stretch. This time, slowly make circles with your straightened leg, alternating small to big to small in both directions.

◆ Cross your left ankle over your right knee again. This time make circles with your knee (instead of drawing straight back). This stretch should give you feedback as to whether you have been successful in opening your hips (a little).

Be patient with your body. Most athletes find that it takes six to eight weeks before they notice a material range-of-movement improvement. The progression outlined here, if done three times per week, will enable you to achieve a better aero position in twelve to sixteen weeks.

Index

About the Authors

Joe Friel has trained endurance athletes since 1980. His clients have included amateur and professional road cyclists, mountain bikers, triathletes, duathletes, swimmers, and runners. They have been from all corners of the globe and included American and foreign national champions, world championship competitors, and an Olympian.

Friel is the author of *Cycling Past 50*, *Precision Heart Rate Training* (co-author), *The Cyclist's Training Bible*, *The Triathlete's Training Bible*, and *The Mountain Biker's Training Bible*. He holds a master's degree in exercise science and is a USA Triathlon and USA Cycling certified coach. He is a featured columnist for *Inside Triathlon* and *VeloNews* magazines, and writes feature stories for other international publications and Web sites.

Friel speaks at seminars and camps around the world on training and racing for endurance athletes, and provides consulting services for corporations in the fitness industry. Every year he selects a group of the brightest coaches with the greatest potential and closely oversees their progress as they advance into the ranks of elite-level coaches.

For more information on personal coaching, seminars, camps, developmental coach mentoring, certification of coaches in the Training Bible methodology, coaching symposia, and consulting go on-line to www.Ultrafit.com. There you will also find e-Tips, a free newsletter that provides monthly updates to the Training Bible methodology. For all of the tools necessary for effective self-coaching using the concepts of this book, including a "virtual coach," go to www.TrainingBible.com.

Gordon (Gordo) Byrn is an elite long course triathlete and coach. He is a certified coach with USA Triathlon, Triathlon Australia, and the American Swim Coaches Association. In 2000, he qualified for, and raced in, Ironman® Hawaii as an age group athlete. In 2001, he raced professionally with his best performance being a Top Ten placing at Ironman® Canada. Byrn ended his 2002 season by winning Ultraman Hawaii, a three-day ultra-endurance triathlon that covers over 500 kilometers. In addition to his racing and coaching, Byrn is a columnist for XTri.Com.